INCOGNITA
The Invention and Discovery of Terra Australis

Allen Mawer has written extensively on maritime affairs and Australian history. He searched with notable success for Jack Doolan of Castlemaine, the original Wild Colonial Boy, as recorded in the *Australian Dictionary of Biography*. Ahab's Trade, his history of South Sea whaling, was shortlisted for both the New South Wales and Queensland Premiers' History prizes. *Canberry Tales*, his seventh book, was shortlisted in 2013 for the New South Wales Premier's Community & Regional History Prize.

INCOGNITA
The Invention and Discovery of Terra Australis

G.A. Mawer

AUSTRALIAN SCHOLARLY

First published 2013, reprinted 2019, by Australian Scholarly Publishing Pty Ltd
7 Lt Lothian St Nth, North Melbourne, Vic 3051 TEL: 03 9329 6963
EMAIL: enquiry@scholarly.info WEB: scholarly.info

ISBN 978-1-925984-45-3

Cover illustration: Globe by Jacques de Vaulx 1583

Design and typesetting Art Rowlands
This book is typeset in Minion Pro 10.5

For Ben and Jasmine
whose flights of fancy and voyages of discovery are just beginning

Contents

List of Images

Plates

In text

Acknowledgements

This book had its genesis in preparations for the 400th anniversary of the first European sighting of Australia. The volunteers of *Australia on the Map*, of whom I was one, prompted, organised and rounded up funding for a year of events to commemorate the voyages of Jansz and Torres to the Cape York peninsula in 1606. As a non-Netherlander I found myself outnumbered by Rupert Gerritsen and Peter Reynders in some vigorous and enlightening debates about the relative contribution of various navigators, in which I was happy to uphold the claims of the Spanish but not, for reasons that will become apparent, the Portuguese.

Courtesy of the Australian Hydrographic Service, I was able to spend a fortnight on HMAS *Benalla* as she surveyed in Torres Strait, which enabled me to sea-truth my reconstruction of Torres' route. Lieutenant Richard Mortimer and his crew went out of their way to make me welcome and enthusiastically assisted with observations and photography. It was Commander Paul Hornsby, then President of the International Federation of Hydrographic Societies and a keen supporter of *Australia on the Map*, who had persuaded the RAN to take me on board.

Back on dry land, I benefitted from the minute researches of Dr Robert King, who has traced the origins of a goodly number of obscure place names from the Age of Discovery. I am also grateful to Dr Martin Woods, curator of maps at the National Library of Australia, for casting a critical eye over the manuscript. His valued comments do not, of course, absolve me of responsibility for the final product. The skeleton maps of *Incognita* are the work of Dr Brendan Whyte, editor of the *Journal of the Australian and New Zealand Map Society*, who showed more patience with my cartographic limitations than I had any right to expect.

More generally, I have benefited greatly from the privileges extended to me by the National Library as one of its Petherick Readers. It is hardly going too far to say, of that assistance, *sine qua non*. Finally, I have much appreciated the support of my publisher, Nick Walker, a self-confessed maps tragic who here continues to swim against the tide by challenging the Australian reading public with unconventional history. In this he is ably seconded by his assistant, Terryn Whiteoak, who has a talent for calming troubled waters and disturbing unwarranted calms.

Introduction

As Ferdinand Magellan stared into the gathering gloom he was uncertain. This strait was leading him west around the southern flank of the New World, but he had not expected it to be so narrow a channel. Was that far shore an island or something more? Could it be the headland of yet another continent? Whatever it might be, as night fell he could tell that he was not its discoverer. Pinpricks of light disclosed the presence of humans. He called their home Tierra del Fuego, the Land of Fire.

A century later Europeans were not much the wiser. On honest maps the southern hemisphere was mainly blank; on less scrupulous ones it was a dumping ground for every geographical theory and construct imaginable. Africa and South America were present in outline but together they occupied less than one-tenth of the whole. It was inconceivable that there were not austral worlds still to be discovered and conceiving them was a common enthusiasm. In 1605 Sir Francis Bacon, Jacobean statesman and philosopher, summed up the prevailing outlook when he condemned as 'ill discoverers' those who 'think there is no land when they can see nothing but sea'. In that same year Dutch seamen found what they took to be a southerly extension of New Guinea. It was in fact Australia, the first of the larger portions of *terra australis incognita* to claim a place on the world map. For the Dutch more than most other Europeans the sea was a highway to new places with new commercial possibilities. In Baconian terms they were good discoverers for whom *Incognita*, the blank, was a challenge to find land that was almost universally assumed to exist.

That assumption had begun as a generic – *terra australis,* southern land. By degrees it became capitalised as a brand – The Southland – and because it was what Donald Rumsfeld, the former US Secretary of Defense, would have categorised as a 'known unknown', it was also tagged *incognita*. In fact it had much in common with Iraq's weapons of mass destruction, which were likewise wishful thinking rather than a presence established by evidence. Even as Francis Bacon was pontificating, an English satirist was querying the logic of the situation. Why was the Southland called *Terra Australis Incognita*? If people knew that there was a Southland it could not be Unknown; if Unknown, it could not be said to exist. It was a point lost on the cartographers. Unwilling to be left behind, many had allowed their imaginations to give form to the thought and filled the blank on their maps accordingly.

It was a time-honoured practice: in the course of the previous hundred thousand years *homo sapiens* had occupied most of the globe without being aware of the process or conscious of the achievement. As a result, European navigators of the so-called Age of Discovery were met on the beaches by long-lost relatives. Many of these native communities had elaborate myths about how they had come to be there, but none spoke of trekking out of Africa. In the absence of much, if any, recorded history, they had called on imagination to make a time and a place for themselves in the great scheme of things. Modestly, they credited their creation to supernatural forces. The Europeans would have scoffed at the notion that this did not differ much from their own cosmology, but they too carried a lot of mental lumber, including a story about expulsion from a place they called Eden. The difference, the visitors would have protested, was that they had history and they had science. In fact, they had rather more of the one and not nearly as much of the other as they supposed. Reference to what they thought they knew of geography frequently betrayed them.

Deference to ancient authority was a common failing. Enigmatic classical and biblical texts were cited in support of geographical theories, and without a good reference a would-be explorer had little chance of getting a commission. The Unknown South Land, a counterpoise to the Known Northern World, was one such. So respectable was the pedigree of this notion that new sightings of land in the southern hemisphere were usually hailed as evidence that the navigator had found, at last, the headland of a great continent. Tiny islands in vast expanses of ocean were represented as gateways to impressive and fabulously wealthy civilisations like those of India, China, Mexico and Peru. Here might be gold, spice and elephants, or a society exotic beyond all experience because, above all, this was space to dream. Some dreamed of exploitation, others of finding a society in which exploitation, among other vices, would be unknown. All found ancient authorities to draw on.

To sophisticates of the twenty-first century, alive to sub-texts and confident of their ability to detect imposture, the idea that the southern hemisphere might be four parts land and only one part water is ludicrous. Nonetheless, that is how the geographically literate of the fifteenth century imagined it and imaged it. Rather than smile, it might be better to recall that satellite photographs, the most direct evidence most of us have today, are also nothing more than images, representations of reality conceived in the imagination and given form by science and technology. In the last half-century a few humans have been able to see what our ancestors could only imagine and model; astronauts have directly observed Earth in the majesty of its three dimensions. Not being so privileged, the Flat-Earth Society is still sceptical.

It took nearly four centuries of European voyaging to whittle away, little by little, the unknown portions of the globe in which one or more southern continents might still be hiding. The process was inexorable but not linear, a work in progress in which a promontory might be added here even while a peninsula was being demolished elsewhere. From the sidelines, the philosophers and geographers – some earnest, some playful and some plain dotty – continued to theorise, but with ever less room to manoeuvre. The dream of a warm, fertile and inhabited continent in the south had eventually to be abandoned, though not without a prolonged struggle. An expectation, once raised, takes on a life of its own and the flimsiest of evidence will satisfy those who have been conditioned to believe. This book tells the story of the inventors who sent the dream abroad and of the navigators who brought the reality home, sometimes in spite of themselves.

The legend of Atlantis

Everything that deceives may be said to enchant. – Plato
Plato is dear to me, but dearer still is truth. – Aristotle

Two and a half thousand years ago the Pythagoreans, intoxicated by numbers, suggested that the earth was round. As the circle and the sphere were the most perfect of shapes, both one and infinite, it seemed to them that the universe, and the motion of the heavenly bodies, and the form of the earth itself would all share that perfection. But for them, as for all Greeks of the classical age, the known world ended at the Pillars of Hercules – the straits of Gibraltar – traditionally inscribed with the warning 'No Further'. Beyond was the inscrutable Ocean, said to be unnavigable because of treacherous shoals.

Plato gave the notion literary form in the Dialogues. Socrates, he tells us, disappointed at being unable to convince himself that his ideal society – eventually to flower into Plato's Republic – could work, called on his companions to provide historical examples. Critias had one. Long ago, on an island far, far away – Atlantis. Nine thousand years before their day the Atlantic shoals had been a great island, larger than Asia (Minor) and (North) Africa together. This island was home to a mighty civilisation, whose ambition it was to master the Mediterranean. Athens alone resisted. Then in one cataclysmic day and night the island and its dreams of empire were devastated by earthquake and tidal wave. Athens too suffered grievously. And, Critias added, Atlantis was not the only land beyond ocean. Around the rim of this circular, disc-shaped world was a continent that encircled ocean even as ocean girdled the known world and Atlantis.

This was neither history nor geography. Echoing through Plato's tale, making it credible for his audience, were folk memories of the subjection of Athens to Minoan Crete – the source of the Theseus legend – and the destruction by volcanic explosion of the Aegean island of Thera. The latter had occurred some 1,250 years before Plato's time. In this context, the continent beyond was Africa, specifically Libya. For Plato, the extremities of the inhabited earth in the distant past were a stage on which a speculative philosopher could theorise without interference from inconvenient facts, but to this day there are those who believe that Atlantis once existed and that traces of it might yet be found. Indeed, when cable-laying ships detected the mid-Atlantic ridge in the nineteenth century Jules Verne sent Captain Nemo on a visit to the lost city.

In the same vein, Plato's 'continent beyond' has been cited as evidence that Critias knew of America. If so, he should also have known of Australia, which similarly lies beyond the Afro-Eurasian landmass.[1] The problem with immense authority like Plato's is that it legitimises indiscriminately, deforming as well as informing the thinking of succeeding ages. With Atlantis, Plato doomed literal-minded readers to millennia of frustration. On average, a new book on the subject has appeared every 14 months since his time (albeit most of them in the last century). The writers have wandered into Plato's academy while looking for Aristotle's lyceum, mistaking allegory for natural history. In the lyceum, the emphasis was as much on man in nature as on the nature of man. Observation and analysis of the natural world allowed general laws to be derived from particular instances. Astronomy, geography and the other disciplines of natural philosophy or natural history were given form and method. Many a traditional explanation, including that of a sunken civilisation in the Atlantic, would be tested and found wanting. Others, including the existence of continents beyond, would fare rather better.

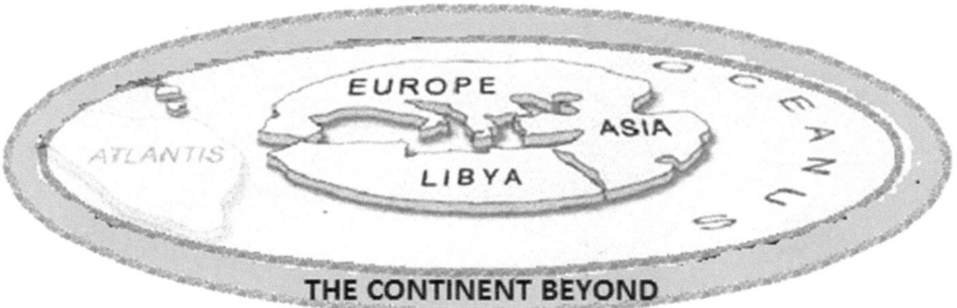

Plato creates a sunken home for his Republic and tells of an all-encompassing continent beyond

1

An Earthly Paradise

Plato's most famous pupil was Aristotle, who remade the Western mind; Aristotle's most famous pupil was Alexander the Great, who remade the Western world. The conquests of the Macedonian demonstrated that the inhabited world extended far beyond the Mediterranean. Even the conqueror's southernmost city, Patala[1] at the mouth of the Indus, was not the end of it – further still was an island called Taprobana [Sri Lanka]

Aristotle had even more astounding news for them. He pointed out that the earth cast a curved shadow across the face of the moon during an eclipse. It must be a sphere, not a disc, which was why Europeans could see the constellation Arctos, the northern pivot of the axis around which the celestial sphere revolved, but not its theoretical southern opposite, Antarctos, which was always hidden by the curvature of the earth. Moreover, the terrestrial sphere seemed to be of no great size in the heavenly scheme of things – some stars seen in Egypt could not be seen in more northerly regions. The fact that elephants were found in India as well as Africa suggested 'continuity' between the two. It might be possible to reach India westward from the Pillars of Hercules.[2] Only sea prevented habitation around the entire northern hemisphere and, although the equatorial regions were observably too hot to live in, beyond them there had to be a temperate zone in the southern hemisphere that corresponded to the inhabited one in the northern. Importantly, Aristotle did not say that men lived under Antarctos or even that there was land there.

Another of Aristotle's pupils, Dicearchus of Messana, sought to plot the shape of the northern inhabited world. He noted that the number of hours of sunlight on midsummer day were the same at the Pillars of Hercules and at Rhodes. The two places must therefore be equidistant from the equator and a line drawn between them would be parallel to it. The distance between parallels could be expressed in terms of hours of sunlight at midsummer. Unfortunately, Dicearchus lacked reliable observations that would have enabled him to locate places relative to each other north-south on his parallels but Eratosthenes of Cyrene was ideally placed to build on his insight. He too had studied in Athens and, as librarian of the great collection at Alexandria, had at hand the accumulated knowledge of the classical world. Furthermore he was knowledgeable in many fields, so many that to contemporaries he was beta-man, second best at everything or – more positively – pentathlos, the all-rounder. He would accept the challenge of reforming the map of the world, but to do that he had first to establish how large that world was.

Far to the south of Alexandria lay Syene, today's Aswan. There, it was reported, the noonday sun on one day in the year shone back from the water at the bottom of a deep well. There was no shadow. Eratosthenes seized upon the observation; the well must be on the Tropic of Cancer and the day in question must be the first of summer. Assuming that the sun's rays struck the Earth in parallel, at the next summer solstice he carefully observed how far from the zenith the noonday sun was at Alexandria. He measured the shadow cast by the gnomon in his sun-bowl as one-fiftieth of a circle.[3] The distance to Syene, which he assumed was due south of Alexandria, must therefore be one-fiftieth of the circle that is the circumference of the earth.

The 5,000 stades to Syene from Alexandria? Eratosthenes appears to have overestimated, but Syene lies at the northern edge of a belt where the noonday sun is vertical at the solstice so he may have made allowance. According to the most commonly accepted value of the stade, his experiment indicated a circumference of 39,375 kilometres, short just 625 kilometres at the equator, an error of less than two per cent. As luck would have it, the shortcomings of his data and his false assumption largely cancelled out, leaving his method deservedly triumphant.[4]

Eratosthenes now had an essential tool for his reform of the map. He extended his prime meridian, the Alexandria-Syene line, to intersect Dicearchus' line at Rhodes. Like Syene, Rhodes is not exactly on Alexandria's meridian, but by assuming that it was, Eratosthenes could draw two axes that passed through Rhodes at right angles. In theory,

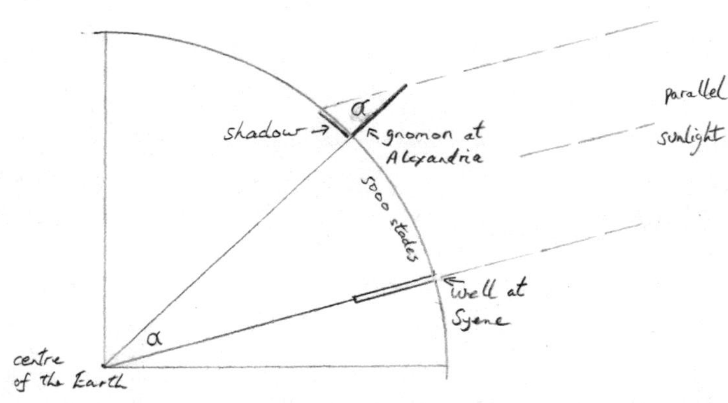

α = one-fiftieth of a circle. Alexandria to Syene = 5,000 stades, therefore the Earth's circumference is 250,000 stades

it was now possible to describe any place on the face of the globe in terms of how far north/south and east/west of Rhodes it was.[5] He tried to construct a grid of parallels and meridians, but the further from the Mediterranean the less reliable was the information on which they were based. The most intractable problem was longitude. The best data to hand were sailors' estimates of distance, based on sailing times between places on the same parallel in the Mediterranean. For the lands east of the Mediterranean Eratosthenes had some distances recorded by the pacers who accompanied Alexander's army but more often than not he had to rely on travellers' itineraries.

The result was a quite credible map of the Mediterranean but in delineating Asia he went much too far. Although his inhabited earth, the *oikoumene*, ended at the Ganges, according to him that was fully a third of the way around the globe on the Rhodes parallel. Beyond the Ganges, as beyond the Pillars of Hercules, there was Ocean. Eratosthenes did not deny the possible existence of land beyond the Pillars but, like possible land in the southern temperate zone, it was purely speculative and therefore not amenable to realistic representation on his map. As a mapmaker he ignored them but *pentathlos* was also a poet, and as a poet he could assume that the temperate zone south of the equator was inhabited like its northern equivalent.[6] Aspiring globe makers faced a bigger challenge; in order to make space for all the detail available about the habitable earth one needed a very large sphere, of which only a small fraction would have anything on it.

The feet beneath

When Crates of Mallos, the royal librarian at Pergamum, designed such a globe in the second century BC, the temptation was too much for an orderly and systematic Greek mind; he filled in the blanks. Homer, he said, tells us that Menelaus went home from the Trojan War by sailing south around Africa. That grouped Europe, Asia and Africa, with their surrounding ocean, to fill one quarter of a globe. The other three quadrants should likewise be occupied, and not just by land. Aristotle had taught that nature did nothing in vain, so in the northern hemisphere beyond the sunken Atlantis would live Plato's *perioikoi*, the dwellers around. On the other side of the equator, south of Afro-Eurasia, would be the *antioikoi*, dwellers opposite. These would be Ethiopians who, according to Homer, had been sundered from their northern brethren to become 'the furthermost of men'. The remaining quadrant, also in the southern hemisphere, would be home to the *antipodes*, who walked with their feet opposed to those of the Greeks. Greek popular opinion derided such notions, not because it was sceptical about how Crates had come by this information, which has been described as 'more accurate ignorance',[7] but because the *antioikoi* and *antipodes* would fall off.

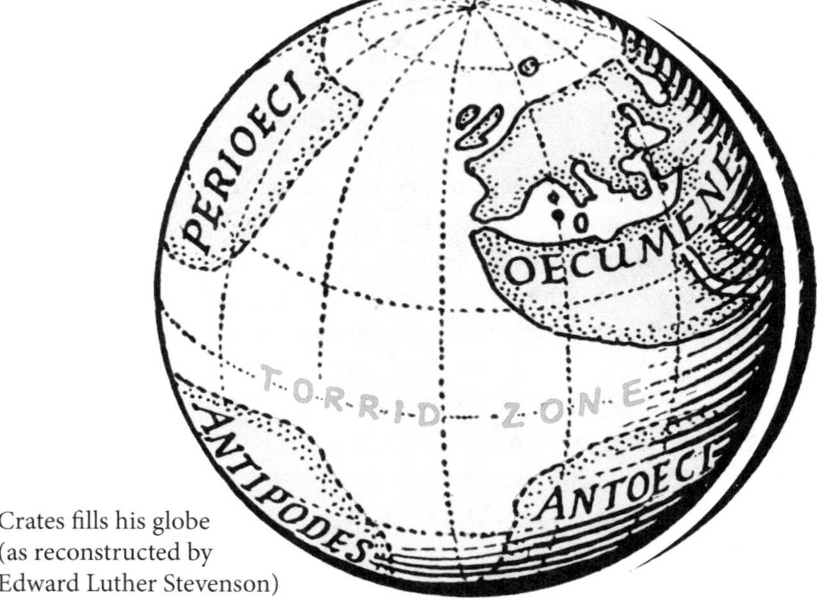

Crates fills his globe (as reconstructed by Edward Luther Stevenson)

Posidonius of Rhodes tried to refine Eratosthenes' measurement of the earth by using elevation of the star Canopus as his reference point. Unfortunately, his observations gave a figure of one forty-eighth of a circle, about fourteen per cent short of the reality. Worse, the value he used for the distance between Alexandria and Rhodes was an underestimate. The result was an earth circumference about a quarter less than it should have been. As we shall see, his error would reverberate for centuries, misleading geographers and navigators up to and including Columbus.

The unknown land of the Ethiopian Fish-eaters

At the beginning of the Christian era Strabo, a Romanised Greek, drew together and critiqued the collective geographical wisdom of his predecessors. His work concentrated on the known world but at the margins he tried to make sense of the alleged circumnavigations of Africa by Meneleus and others, and to account for Homer's sundered Ethiopians. He read Homer to mean that Ethiopians were to be found along the entire northern seaboard of the Indian Ocean, but divided by the Red Sea.[8]

Thanks to Strabo, by the second century AD Claudius Ptolemy of Alexandria had hundreds of years of theory, experiment and data from which to compile a guide to map-making. He painstakingly recorded the location of every place that came to his notice, listing its latitude and longitude and cross-checking where he could, but he was still hostage to his predecessors. Just one misreported eclipse led him to overestimate the distance between Babylon and Carthage as one-eighth of the globe instead of one-twelfth. Ironically, the predecessor of whom he was most critical, Marinus of Tyre, had made a much better estimate of how far the Ganges was to the east. Ptolemy's globe, following Posidonius, was much too small.

Whether Ptolemy's *Geography* in its original form included maps is still a subject for debate, but his instructions for making them were clear enough and by the time Byzantine manuscript copies of his book resurfaced in medieval Europe they included a full suite of regional maps and an overview, the latter usually attributed to Agathodaimon of Alexandria. Because Ptolemy wrote of 'unknown land' east of China, Agathodaimon showed land extending to the right margin of his map. At the bottom, 'unknown land' also runs along the Tropic of Capricorn, making the Indian Ocean an enclosed sea like the Mediterranean. This is the most egregious misconception in the *Geography* and it arose

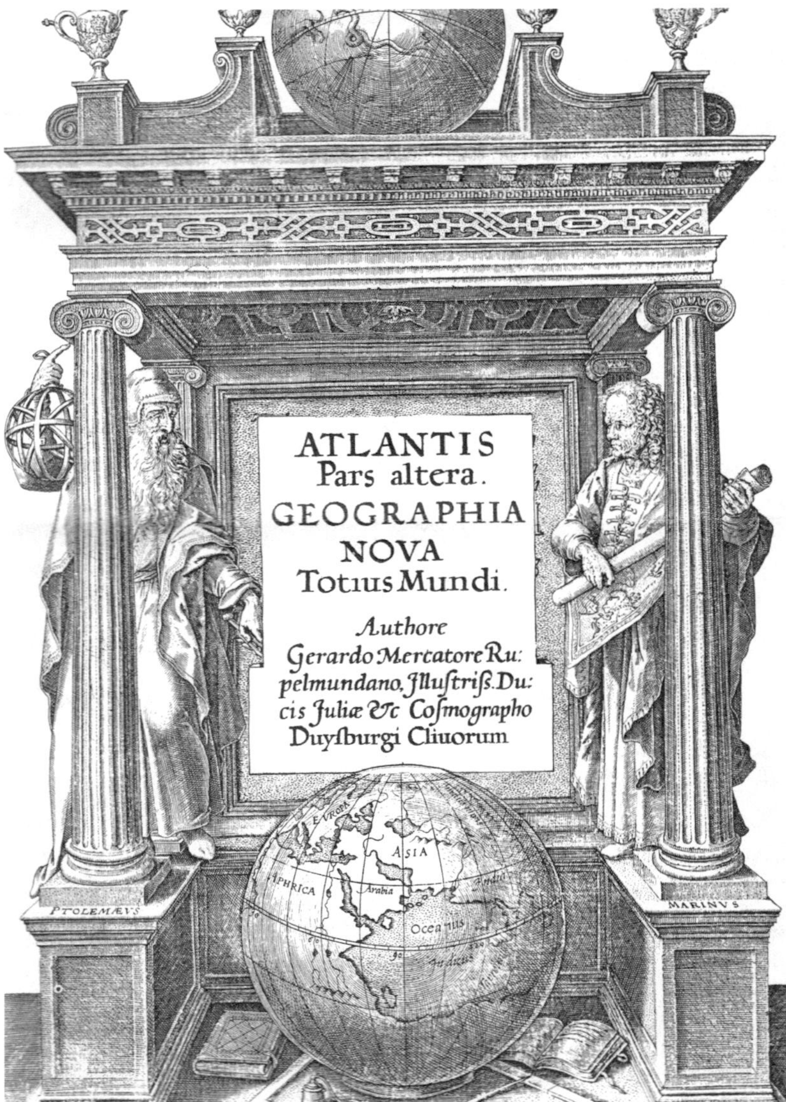

Mercator imagines Ptolemy and Marinus of Tyre debating the respective merits of spherical and plane representations of the Earth (and the length of its circumference)

because Ptolemy in this instance had relied on ancient rather than contemporary sources. Following Homer, as read by Strabo, Ptolemy obediently placed Ethiopian Fish-eaters on the west coast of Africa with a second group of them as far away as was possible, beyond the Ganges.[9] He also cited unnamed ancient sources as authority for an inhabited earth which, so far from being surrounded by Ocean, was almost everywhere land-locked. Thus there could be two east-west land-links between the ichthyophagic homelands: 'Asia is joined to Africa by … Arabia … and by the unknown land which is washed by the Indian sea.'[10] Ptolemy's Asiatic Ethiopians are neighbours of the Chinese, living near Cattigara Sina in the south-eastern corner of the Indian Ocean. Nearby is Iabadiu[11], the Barley Island, rich in gold.

Agathodaimon's map did not indicate how much further south the unknown land might extend, but such was its suggestive power that many of those who saw it assumed that land must fill the southern hemisphere. It was a reasonable interpretation given Ptolemy's Delphic utterance that he was uncertain how far the south pole was from the inhabited regions of Africa.[12] The theologians of the Middle Ages were divided. Some argued that as the known world was mainly land, the unknown parts must be much the same. Otherwise the world would be unbalanced, a state of affairs reflecting badly on its Creator, and in the Middle Ages the Creator's reputation mattered. St Augustine was more concerned about the implications for the Church's mission. Christ had charged the apostles with carrying the gospels to all peoples. Was it being suggested that they had missed some? And how could anyone have crossed Ocean to get to the south? The descendants of Noah had all disembarked at Mount Ararat.

With the triumph of barbarism and Christianity – as Gibbon characterised the decline and fall of the Roman Empire – much geographical knowledge was lost. The remnants, preserved mainly in the monasteries, were refracted through the prism of holy writ. The Scriptures supplemented Plato as texts for geographical interpretation. The 'mainly land' school of clerical scholars was particularly impressed by 2 Esdras 6:42, which declared that on the third day of Creation the waters were gathered into the seventh part of the earth, leaving six parts land. This gloss on Genesis, numerically relating the presence of Ocean to God's decision to rest on the seventh day, was accorded the status of revealed truth. Importantly, it could be more or less squared with classical theory. If each of Crates' four quadrants contained a continental complex the size of Afro-Eurasia, which filled most of the *oikoumene* quadrant, they would indeed occupy six-sevenths of the globe.[13]

In the late medieval period these theoretical constructs were complicated by the testimony of travellers, some authentic, some dubious. The reasonably reliable accounts of Marco Polo and the more popular but highly questionable travels of the elusive Sir John Mandeville (published 1357), expanded the horizons of European readers. Polo, returning from China by sea via the Persian Gulf, disproved the notion of a landlocked Indian Ocean. There had to be a strait somewhere near Ptolemy's Cattigara. He reported that 1,500 miles to the south-south-east of Champa (central Vietnam) lay the largest island in the world, called Java.[14] Unfortunately for later cartographers, he or his editor then went on to say that south of Java were the islands of Sondur and Condur, with Locac further on and Petam further south still. In reality, the only land between Java and Antarctica is Christmas Island and the Cocos group, but the passage makes more sense if Polo's second reference to Java is a misprint for Champa, because he also says that 90 miles beyond Petam lies the kingdom of Malaiur, which has been identified with the Sumatran city of Palembang or an adjacent kingdom. Furthermore, Polo places Petam close to Java the Less, which he describes as 2,000 miles in compass. This is Sumatra, 2,300 miles in circuit, which was Jawah to the Arabs.[15]

Geographical confusion apart, Polo's matter-of-fact accounts of what he personally observed or was told, exaggerated and fantastic though they seemed to his countrymen (who called him *Il Milione* and were sceptical about things like dog-headed men), anticipated the rationality of the Renaissance. Mandeville, on the other hand, was a curious mixture of medieval and modern, interspersing genuine geographical information with religious and other wonders such as his near approach to the Garden of Eden. From it flowed, he assured his readers, the Tigris and the Euphrates, the Nile and the Ganges. He had found this Terrestrial Paradise, he wrote, at 'the end of the East', but could say no more. Its mysteries were not for mortal eyes.

Dante Alighieri was more forthcoming. He had visited Venice after Polo's return and may have met the traveller. To locate Purgatory, he wrote, one had to turn one's mind to the southern pole, where there were four stars hidden from northern eyes.[16] In the *Inferno* he gives directions; the Mountain of Purgatory lies south-west and atop it is the Garden of Eden, antipodal to Jerusalem. Poetic licence allows Dante to commission Homer's Ulysses for a last voyage to seek it. Sailing through the Pillars of Hercules, the Greek hero steers for the southern horizon until Arctos is lost to sight and the stars that light the night are 'of the other pole'.[17] This Garden of Eden is in the Pacific, south of Capricorn, not far from Tahiti; to the first European visitors three centuries later, Paradise twice over. The Mountain is the only land in a watery southern hemisphere, contradicting 2 Esdras. The 'new' geography – that of Ptolemy and the travellers – was beginning to challenge that of the Church.

7. Mandeville's world, with the four rivers emerging from Paradise in the east and the Nile making its way to Africa south of the Indian Ocean (anonymous map of c. 1500)

The Polo and Mandeville accounts first circulated in manuscript. The introduction of printing made such travellers' tales accessible to a much wider audience, but the explosion of secular learning in Europe during the fifteenth century was largely based on wholesale recycling and reinterpretation of classical knowledge. Among the authors so revived were Pomponius Mela and Macrobius. Mela, writing at the start of the Christian era, had taken Eratosthenes at face value. He had declared that the temperate zone beyond Ocean was inhabited by the *antichthones* ('people of the hemisphere opposite'). In the fifth century Macrobius had restated, in a text that was to be influential throughout the Middle Ages, the notion of four inhabitable quarters of the globe. By the twelfth century, editors had elaborated his original illustrative diagram into a map that showed Afro-Eurasia filling the northern half of the eastern hemisphere. Below the equator, separated by ocean, was a larger landmass, confidently labelled 'Antipodum' but qualified as 'known but undetected'. Variants of the same map were used to illustrate Mela. When the Portuguese reached the East Indies via the Cape of Good Hope, confirming that Polo could have sailed from China to the Middle East, they had not disproved the Southland as such; they had simply decoupled it from Afro-Eurasia, bringing Ptolemy into line with Mela and Macrobius. One should not lightly discard the wisdom of two millennia.

Macrobius' illustrators speculate that the Southland is as large as the Known World

The Garden of Eden

When others looked west they saw only a setting sun; Christopher Columbus saw a rising star – his own. If he appeared less certain about what else might be found in that direction, it was because in seeking patronage for his project he tailored the story to the audience. To João

II of Portugal he promised a shorter and better trade route to the Orient than would be found by trying to sail around Africa. To Isabella and Ferdinand of Spain he spoke sometimes of reaching the Indies by a route different to that sought by the Portuguese, at other times of finding unknown lands.

The lack of clarity perplexed the Spanish savants who assessed his proposal; they recommended rejection. As reported by one of Columbus' earliest champions, Las Casas – 'the Apostle of the Indies' – their reasons were a mixture of obscurantism and scepticism.[18] They were more inclined to credit the notion of limitless Ocean than Crates' continents. First, how could Columbus know of something unknown for thousands of years, even to Ptolemy? Second, the world is infinitely large, and many years of navigation to the west would not bring one to the end of the East. Third, most of the terrestrial sphere is ocean and can only be navigated coastwise, as the Portuguese do. Fourth, Columbus would not be able to return because, if the world is round, west is downhill, and ships cannot sail uphill. Fifth, St Augustine doubts that there are Antipodes. Sixth, three of the five zones of the earth (the two frigid zones and the torrid) are uninhabitable.

By Antipodes, both Columbus and the savants were referring loosely to the unknown regions of ocean between Asia and Europe where Crates had placed the land of the *perioikoi*, the dwellers, around. Strictly speaking, the *antipodes* would be found south of them, on the other side of the Equator. The savants believed in neither. They had every reason to expect that St Augustine would clinch the argument, but Columbus had another card to play. This seeker after fortune and position was also a profoundly religious man who fervently desired to see the Holy Land returned to Christendom. Jerusalem had been in Muslim hands ever since the failure of the Crusades, and in Columbus' own infancy Constantinople, the eastern bastion of Christian faith, had fallen to the Ottoman Turks. At the same time, the Moorish state of Granada still stubbornly clung to southern Spain. Islam, in its religious and political manifestations, was both a spiritual affront and a strategic threat to the Christian states of the Mediterranean.

Columbus believed that it was part of his mission in life to make possible another crusade, one that would free Jerusalem and secure the future of Christian Europe. He saw his role as that of facilitator, providing access to the wealth that the monarchs of Europe would need for the purpose. This lay in the East, where fabulous kingdoms were known to be open to trade. God willing, they might also be open to conquest by the Cross if a route could be found that was not subject to interdiction by the Turk. It was an idea that particularly appealed to the devout Isabella, but the struggle with Granada was approaching its climax. This was no time for expensive distractions. Columbus' proposal was dismissed.

A great deal of analysis has been devoted to the development of Columbus' obsession, much of it speculative in the absence of reliable information about his early life. It is almost certain that he was largely self-educated and it is not uncommon for a welcome concept first met through untutored reading to become an *idée fixe*. Certainly Columbus argued his westerly thesis for more than a decade in the face of almost all informed opinion of the day. The seemingly final Spanish rejection of his scheme, his withdrawal from court and the amazing about-face in his favour by Isabella and Ferdinand following the fall of Granada in 1492 are rightly the stuff of legend, and Columbus was deeply impressed as well as grateful for what he interpreted as divine intercession. It seemed to him that, with Spain secured, God had moved the Spanish monarchs immediately to begin the next phase of the Columbian crusade.

If Columbus' account of the monarchs' motivation can be believed, they were deeply impressed by his story of the Great Khan who lived in India and who, in bygone times, had unsuccessfully appealed to Rome for learned men to instruct him in Christianity. Isabel and Ferdinand commissioned Columbus to reconnoitre the princes, peoples and lands of the East with a view to conversion. He would be Admiral and Viceroy and perpetual Governor of 'all the islands and lands that I might discover and gain and from now on might be discovered and gained in the Ocean Sea.'[19]

Columbus carried letters of fraternal greeting from the monarchs to the Khan, and an interpreter to translate the Arabic he might speak, but the holds of the Spanish ships were piled with cheap truck like mirrors, beads and hawks' bells. As these would have been a gross insult to any eastern potentate, they can only have been intended for the unsophisticated natives of the islands and lands that Columbus expected to discover on his way west. He hoped that his chosen course would take him to Antillia, said to have been settled by the Portuguese in ages past, and he even briefly diverted to search for it. He had to press on, because sacred duty could not be subordinated to personal gain, but perhaps Antillia was not the only island in this Ocean. He might yet come across the legendary Brazil[20] or maybe St Brendan's Isle, allegedly discovered by four Irish monks paddling a hide-covered coracle.

The tangle of thought that led Columbus to his theory of a westward route is still debated, although its strands are well known. He had read Polo and Mandeville and knew many of the classical authorities, although mainly second-hand through works like the *Imago Mundi* of Pierre d'Ailly. He had it on the authority of Sylvanus Piccolomini (subsequently Pope Pius II) that all of Ocean was navigable, that all climates were habitable, and that there were Antipodes. He preferred Posidonius and Marinus of Tyre to Ptolemy because their Afro-Eurasia was wider, which brought the Orient, if sought westwards, more or less within the sailing endurance of ships of the day. Columbus improved the odds by shrinking the problem. He seized on d'Ailly's report of a calculation by the ninth-century Arab astronomer, Al-Farghani, that a degree of longitude at the equator was 56 ⅔ miles. What Columbus failed to realise, or deliberately ignored, was that Al-Farghani's mile was half as long again as the Italian mile. Correspondence with the Florentine cosmographer Toscanelli allowed Columbus to convince himself that Cipangu (Japan) was little more than 4,000 Italian miles west of the Azores, and that between the two was the lost island of Antillia. These were navigable distances.

Cipangu was in fact 14,600 Italian miles distant from Columbus' starting point in the Canary Islands. Could he have reached Japan if America had not been in the way? It seems highly unlikely, given that even before the ships reached the Bahamas, after only five weeks at sea, his crews were nervous about how far they had come and their chances of returning safely. Without this 'Antillian' landfall, or one shortly thereafter, mutiny would have been inevitable. Despite the absence of civilised Orientals and great cities, Columbus was emphatic that he had found what he was looking for almost exactly where he had said he would find it. Hispaniola (Santo Domingo), where the expedition found quantities of gold, was Cipangu, Polo's land of golden roofs. After his second voyage, Columbus told the monarchs that Hispaniola was also Solomon's Ophir. He declared that Cuba was the Chinese province of Mangi, even though, according to Polo, it should have been 1,500 miles beyond Cipangu. He went so far as to have his men take an oath that Cuba was a peninsula, so that he could continue to maintain that it was part of China.

His claim to have reached Asia was treated with scepticism in Spain. Peter Martyr, a humanist scholar who became a member of Spain's

Council of the Indies, wrote to his ecclesiastical patrons that Columbus had in fact discovered the 'western antipodes'. Martyr believed that this was a 'New World', unknown to the ancients, but Columbus continued to deny it. If he had not reached the Indies, as contracted, then his entitlement to the promised rewards was problematic, a point quickly seized upon by some at court, like Bishop Fonseca, who were alarmed at what now appeared to be the excessive generosity of the monarchs.

From this time on, Columbus increasingly scoured classical and biblical texts for passages that would validate his discoveries as the Indies. Posterity would see it as a self-defeating exercise, because the more he could demonstrate ancient knowledge of his discoveries the more he diminished his own achievement. He was convinced that he had fulfilled the prophecies of Isaiah 60:9 – that Tarshish (Spain) had taken the lead in bringing slaves, silver and gold from far away – and 41:4-5 – 'I, the lord, are the first and the last. The islands saw it, and feared: the ends of the earth were astonished: they drew near, and came'. Convinced that he had found 'the end of the Orient', Columbus named the eastern point of Cuba the Cape of Alpha and Omega.

On his third voyage, in 1498, he chose the Cape Verde Islands as his departure point for the crossing. He was chasing a rumour. In 1494 João II of Portugal had renegotiated the Papal demarcation that divided the unexplored world between his kingdom and that of Spain. The Treaty of Tordesillas had pushed the line further out into the Atlantic. Now it was said that the Portuguese had a chart showing a continent south of the islands discovered by Columbus. Spain, and Columbus, needed to know whether such a place existed and, if so, on which side of the revised line it was. He crossed the Atlantic this time in about 8° north, was delayed by the Doldrums, and was then prevented by unfavourable winds from making further south.

Landfall was at a big island that he named for the Holy Trinity, but more interesting was the immense surge of water that forced its way out between this Trinidad and what appeared to be mainland. It was fresh. Columbus had found the delta of the Orinoco River. Further exploration of the Gulf of Paria confirmed that large rivers were pouring such unimaginable quantities of fresh water into this arm of the sea that it was drinkable almost everywhere. Here was a challenge to Columbus' Indies theory that temporarily threatened it even in his own mind. On 13 August 1498, off the island of Margarita, he admitted to his diary that this was 'a very large continent which till now has remained unknown.'[21] How could this be squared with its position at 'the end of the East'?

Columbus retreated into an idiosyncratic mixture of mistaken observation and religious inspiration. He fancied himself as a scientific navigator but his mastery of the more advanced instruments of his day was far from perfect. While using the quadrant for celestial observation during the passage he had found that the pole star was not keeping the position it should have been if the world was a sphere. It was typical of his self-confidence that, rather than suspect observational error or inadequate theory, he concluded that the world's shape was irregular – which it is – but he was not thinking in terms of a slight bulge at the equator.

> … it is the shape of a pear which is everywhere very round except where the stalk is, for there it is very prominent, or that it is like a very round ball, and on one part of it is placed something like a woman's nipple, and that this part, where this protuberance is found, is the highest and nearest to the sky, and it is beneath the equinoctial line …[22]

He believed that his ships had risen gently towards the sky, which accounted for the milder climate he noted in the western Atlantic. So ships *could* sail uphill. To his mind, the mildness also caused the increasing westward shift in compass variation. Where had this ascent taken him? Four mighty rivers flowed thence. This must be the source of the Tigris and Euphrates, the Nile and the Ganges. And where did those rivers have their origin? In the Terrestrial Paradise, the Garden of Eden, the part of earth closest to heaven. It was the Dantean vision, and in the direction that the poet had indicated. For one as devout as Columbus, it might be supposed that such a revelation would be succeeded by an irresistible urge to reach this 'New Heaven and New Earth', but he heeded Mandeville's warning: Paradise was not for mortals.

The Antarctic coast

As Columbus fretted in Seville in February 1505, sick, prematurely aged and resentfully petitioning to obtain the rewards he had been promised, he was glad to receive a sympathetic visitor. Amerigo Vespucci was a Florentine merchant who had been so impressed by Columbus' first voyage that he had been inspired, in middle age, to 'abandon the business career and to devote all my efforts to worthier and more enduring ends'.[23] He was now on his way to the Spanish Court to set out his own case for preferment, based on western voyages he had made in the service of Spain and Portugal. He offered to do whatever he could in Columbus' cause while he was there. The Admiral was pleased and recommended Vespucci to his son Diego, who was already at court: 'He always showed a desire to please me, and is a very respectable man. Fortune has been adverse to him, as to many others.'[24] The remark reveals two things about Vespucci. He was very plausible and he was convinced that he had not received his due. Had he been less respectable, Columbus might not have accepted the Florentine at his own estimate.

Throughout much of his working life Vespucci had been attached to the house of Medici, latterly in their Spanish enterprises. Even his mid-life crisis was managed as a business opportunity. No running away to sea for him; instead, even as he started investing in Indies voyages, he educated himself in navigation and cosmography. Two years before the Seville interview Vespucci had written to his patron, Lorenzo di Pierfrancesco de Medici, about a voyage that he had made to the Indies in 1501–02. Except Vespucci had not called them the Indies: 'It is proper to call it *a new world*, because none of these countries were known to our ancestors.'

And it was as *Mundus Novus* that the letter was published in August 1504. Columbus would not have been concerned: the discoveries it claimed were well to the south of his own and made some years later. But what Columbus surely cannot have known, in recommending Vespucci to Diego, was that in September 1504, five months before their meeting, another Vespucci letter had been published. This one was to Soderini, the Gonfaloniere of Florence, and purported to describe four voyages, on the first of which Vespucci claimed he had discovered the mainland of the New World in 1497, a year before Columbus had found the Garden of Eden. And it was along the same stretch of coast. This was larceny on a continental scale, but the identity of the thief remains unknown because most scholars today dismiss both of the letters as forgeries.

Remarkably, the internal dating has Vespucci embarking on his second voyage before returning from the first. Even more remarkably, the paradox probably contains an element of truth, because the first voyage is almost entirely made up of incidents lifted from the second, as is evident from other accounts of this, the expedition of Alonso de Hojeda. It was not a royal expedition but one authorised by Bishop Fonseca, who had persuaded his sovereigns that it was necessary to limit the extent of the privileges they had so imprudently given to Columbus.

The expedition's specific objective, which totally disregarded Columbus' exclusive rights, was to seek the pearl fishery that the Admiral had found off the mainland in 1498. Hojeda later confirmed that Vespucci had accompanied his fleet in 1499. Vespucci's ship may have separated from the others and explored as far south as the Amazon River and Cabo Sao Roque, looking for the Cape of Cattigara that had allowed Marco Polo to enter the Indian Ocean, but there is no corroboration for an earlier voyage in 1497. Vespucci returned to Spain in September 1500.

More reliable are three other Vespucci letters to Lorenzo, unpublished in his day and unearthed far later, but even these, although written by a man who liked to contrast his precision as a navigator with the limitations of mere pilots, are infuriatingly self-serving and vague. He does not mention the commanders of the two expeditions he describes (the second and third of the Soderini letter), leaving the distinct impression that he was the principal figure in them. Like the published letters, they are replete with descriptions of exotic encounter but casual about the where and the when of it. Common to them all, published and unpublished alike, are accounts of native customs and social arrangements. It was these, 'more inclined to be Epicurean than Stoic', which would provoke almost as much learned discussion in Europe as the New World thesis. These strange people placed no value on gold or silver or precious gems. Furthermore,

> Having no laws and no religious faith, they live according to nature. They understand nothing of the immortality of the soul. There is no possession of private property among them, for everything is in common. They have no boundaries of kingdom and province. They have no king, nor do they obey anyone. Each is his own master. There is no administration of justice, which is unnecessary to them, because in their code no one rules. They live in communal dwellings, built in the fashion of very large cabins.[25]

After participation in the Hojeda expedition, Vespucci hoped that he would be sent to discover Ptolemy's Taprobana, 'which is between the Indian Ocean and the Gulf or Sea of the Ganges', but Spanish plans came to nothing. He was easily tempted when a summons came from Portugal. The Portuguese were testing possibilities in the west, beyond the Spanish discoveries, even as they exploited the Orient. In 1500 a ship of the fleet sent to follow up Vasco da Gama's breakthrough to India unexpectedly returned to Lisbon. The expedition's commander, Cabral, had sent it back to report a rediscovery.

Sweeping far into the Atlantic west of the Cape Verde Islands, the expedition had found an extensive coast. Cabral advised his king to look in the treasury for an old map by Pedro Vaz Bisagudo, which would show its location. It appeared to be on the Portuguese side of the Tordesillas line. And now there were rumours that the Spanish had found another coast to the north-west. Who better to send to establish the line of demarcation than a man who could find longitude, for as Vespucci told Lorenzo, it was a difficult thing, requiring much night work to observe the conjunctions of the moon with the planets. It had cost him much sleep and shortened his life by ten years.

In May 1501 Vespucci sailed south in the fleet of Gonçalo Coelho. At Cape Verde they came across two vessels of the returning Cabral fleet, and Vespucci interrogated a man called Guaspare 'who has been working on ships between Cairo and a distant region which is called Molecca and is situated on the shore of the Indian Ocean.'[26] Guaspare had not heard of Taprobana, but Vespucci concluded that it could be identified with Ziban (Sri Lanka) or Stamatara (Sumatra). On the strength of Guaspare's information, Vespucci hoped that on his present voyage, although bound to the west, he would be able to run through a large part of those regions.

Coelho's fleet reached the New World mainland at Cabo Sao Roque. It then coasted to about 32°S. Here, the Soderini letter claims, the ships' captains were instructed to do whatever Vespucci commanded for further conduct of the voyage. He directed them to take on wood and water for six months, and the fleet then left the coast and sailed south. In 49 or 50°S they encountered a wild uninhabited coast which they sailed along for 20 leagues until 'the commander of the fleet and I' decided that deteriorating weather was one misery too many. They turned north for milder climes and home.

The wild coast has been variously identified as Tierra del Fuego (which was inhabited) or more plausibly the Falkland Islands (uninhabited, but too far south) or South Georgia (uninhabited and further south still), but it seemed sufficiently important to Matthias Ringmann of Lorraine, when preparing a translation of *Mundus Novus* in 1505, to entitle his book 'Of the Antarctic Coast'.[27] The reason that Vespucci gave for leaving the mainland was that they had been ten months there without finding gold. Against this, the relevant unpublished letter says that the voyage was entirely one of discovery. Vespucci's excursion was probably intended to short-circuit a slow and dangerous coastal navigation, hoping that further south there would be open sea to the west.

There is another possibility: Vespucci may have been trying to sail, until he encountered the wild coast, the arc of a great circle from 32°S on the South American coast to 33°S in the Indian Ocean west of the longitude of Calicut, where he believed Malacca would be found. If so, it was a breathtakingly audacious attempt to shorten the voyage, based entirely on Vespucci's confidence that he could accurately find longitude. Longitude was essential for great circle sailing. Without it Vespucci would not have known when to adjust his course northwards towards the desired landfall. 'Pilots' would simply have followed the compass needle east, accepting the distance penalty such latitude sailing entailed. But even had he succeeded in reaching the general vicinity of his goal, Vespucci would have found nothing there except tiny Amsterdam Island – if he had been exceptionally lucky.

There is slight indirect evidence in favour of this theory and of South Georgia as his landfall but, like the landfall itself, it is from the doubtful Soderini letter. In it, Vespucci claims that his next, fourth, voyage will be in search of the route to Malacca, not yet reached by the Portuguese but reputed to be the chief entrepot for the trade of the 'Indian and Gangetic seas'. He believed that it could be reached 'along the eastern side following the wind-route called Africus'. Africus was the south-south-westerly wind believed to prevail below Capricorn. 'Wind-route' might refer to the direction from which the wind blew, but more likely Vespucci meant the direction in which a ship could sail with the wind – east.[28]

Be that as it may, the problematical Antarctic coast was his southernmost 'discovery' and, as it was the furthest south till then claimed by any navigator, he was at pains to highlight its significance. From Lisbon to 50°S, he wrote, was a quarter of the earth's circumference. A person at one of these places would be standing at right angles to a person at the other. To illustrate the point he instanced an orthagonal triangle.[29] Its horizontal line (*illi*, them) is longer than its vertical (*nos*, us), implying that the earth is wider at the Antarctic coast than at Lisbon.

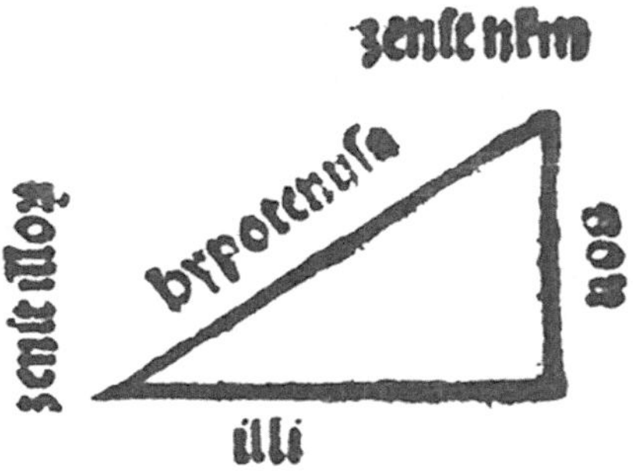

He reinforced the point by denying that the southern hemisphere was 'completely' or 'properly' hemispherical but his explanation of the phenomenon is so obscure as to give rise to suspicion that this too was something found in Columbus' pocket. Vespucci speculates that 'if the terrestrial paradise is in some part of this land, it cannot be very far from the coast we visited'[30] and so situated that it could not be improved. The inhabitants, although cannibals, live in a state of nature, as naked as Adam before the fall. Nowhere is Columbus' pear-shaped world acknowledged but, should it prove to be so, to Vespucci would go the credit for a 'scientific' observation in place of speculation about ascending towards heaven.

The published Vespucci letters are a mixed bag out of which, at this distance in time, it is all but impossible to winnow the grain from the chaff. Although he claimed to have sailed to 50°S, and the maker of Cracow's Jagellonian globe (c.1510) placed the 'discovery' near Madagascar as *America noviter reperta*,[31] many historians have doubted that he went further than Brazil's Cape Frio. Against this, he tells us that for eleven days he sailed entirely by southern stars because the north polar constellations, the Greater and Lesser Bear, were not visible. This he could have predicted by astronomy alone, without observation, but he also tells us that twice he saw 'a white rainbow' towards the middle of the night. It was most likely a fogbow but might have been the southern aurora.[32] Vespucci could not have been sure that the light display would occur in the south even had he been familiar with its northern equivalent, and his tentative description indicates that he was not.

More problematical still is his account of the Southern Cross. He wished to be the first author to identify 'the firmament of the other Pole' but could not find a prominent star within ten degrees of it. He had read Dante and noted the poet's vision of four stars 'which may turn out to be true', because Vespucci too had seen four stars. But these four moved little (whereas the Cross, being 30 degrees distant from the celestial pole, moves through 60 degrees in the course of a year) and were in the shape of an almond. Vespucci then vows that he will not return from his next voyage 'without discerning the Pole'!

On his fourth voyage, again under the Portuguese flag, Vespucci fell out with Coelho, again his commander. Coelho had wrecked the flagship near Cabo Sao Roque and continued south along the mainland coast in another, contriving to leave Vespucci behind to look after the shipwrecked crew. Vespucci landed these 24 men at Cape Frio, built a fort for them, and sailed back to Portugal. His masters were unimpressed, and so it was that when Vespucci visited Columbus, on his way to ingratiate himself with the court of Spain, he was feeling hard done by. Better fortune was at hand. Various other projected voyages came to nothing but he was naturalised and in 1508 became Pilot Major of Spain. His value lay in his claimed ability to calculate longitude by observing the moon's apparent distance from the planets. The Spanish wanted him to teach the difficult technique to other navigators. It was an impressive appointment for someone with so little to his personal credit as an explorer, but his real achievements were by now of less importance than the exaggerated published accounts. He had become famous.

The Soderini letter had been widely published. Matthias Ringmann copied it for his patron René, Duke of Lorraine. With an associate, Martin Waldseemüller, Ringmann then translated it into Latin. Publishing as Hylocomylus – Waldseemüller's surname in approximate Greek – in 1507 they included the translation in *Cosmographiae Introductio*, the book that accompanied Waldseemüller's map and globe of the world. They had been impressed with Vespucci's declaration that he had found a new world. Columbus, who had died the year before, had made no such claim. It seemed appropriate to Ringmann and Waldseemüller to name this 'fourth part of the earth' after the man who claimed to be its discoverer. As Europe and Asia had been named for women, they feminised Amerigo, and America was presented to the world.

So emphatically did the court of public opinion endorse it that in 1516, when better knowledge of Columbus' voyages led Waldseemüller to replace Vespucci's name with Terra Nova and Brazil, Land of Parrots, it was too late. The damage had been done. Las Casas was disgusted.

> This fraud or mistake [Vespucci's first voyage], whichever it might have been, and the power of writing and narrating well and in a good style, as well as Americo's silence respecting the name of his captain … and his care to mention none but himself, and his [ie. Ringmann's] dedication to … René, these things have led foreign writers to name our mainland America …[33]

Las Casas thought that in justice the mainland should be Columba or Columbo, but from popular judgement there was no appeal. The formula for success was simple, then as now: write for impact, use only the vertical pronoun, and find a good publicist. It seems to have impressed the Spanish court.

Las Casas' inability to decide between fraud or mistake has long given comfort to Vespucci apologists. They assert that the inconsistencies and errors in the published letters can be attributed to changes by an unnamed Florentine anxious to claim for his city the credit that would otherwise go to a Genoese, Columbus. But if the letters were forgeries, why did Vespucci not repudiate them? Furthermore, in both published and unpublished letters Vespucci refers to a book entitled *Four Voyages*, where he says that all details of his discoveries will be found. The book has some of the characteristics of the voyages: in one place he writes as if he has finished it; in another he intends to write it; in a third he is waiting for the Portuguese to return some of his materials. If completed it was never published and no manuscript has yet been found. Vespucci lived until 1512, but seems to have been content to let forgeries stand as the definitive record of his explorations. And why not, given their general acceptance by contemporaries?

Waldseemüller knew that Vespucci's interpretation of the western discoveries was controversial and urged his readers not to imitate the proverbial myopia of the rhinoceros but, even so, he still stopped short of full endorsement. His plane projection 'followed Ptolemy as regards the new lands … while on the globe … we have followed the description of Amerigo.' This, however, confronted him with Crates' dilemma about empty space: if Amerigo had found a continent to the west which was not the Indies, and in the furthest east Cipangu was an island, there must be ocean between the two. And so a south sea, mildly surmised, was shown on his globe six years before Balboa gazed from that peak in Darien. Waldseemüller clearly had reservations about Vespucci's wild coast; his New World mainland goes no further south than 42°, and the South Atlantic is empty apart from the imaginary islands of St Brendan in 30°S.

Waldseemüller baptised America but he missed a second opportunity. Had he repeated in the waters west of America the label he affixed to the other side of the Pacific, the whole might be still be known as the Eastern Ocean.

For all the subsequent controversy surrounding his claims, Vespucci's influence on the cartographers was almost wholly positive. He forced them to look at the western discoveries without the baggage of theories about the Indies. Against this, his tacit acceptance of the published letters exposes him as someone unwilling or unable to distinguish between ambition and achievement. As he wrote when excusing his brief exploration of the Amazon estuary, he would 'take the will for

Naming rights: the Vespucci vignette at the top of Waldseemuller's map (the label America appears on the map proper)

the deed'.[34] If his concepts were right – and he was sure that they were – those who disagreed or put obstacles in his way deserved no better than to be ignored. And yet he would appeal to experience if it served his purpose, as when he denied the ancient notion of the inhabitability of the tropics: 'rationally, let it be said in a whisper, experience is certainly worth more than theory'.[35] It is equally rational to blur the line between theory and experience when you are sure that the second will merely confirm the first. To Vespucci's way of thinking, entitlement to the honour of discovery should not depend on such trifling distinctions.

Vespucci had returned from his third voyage in September 1502. He wrote of it to Lorenzo before the end of the year. In June 1503 a vessel named the *Espoir* sailed from Honfleur for the Indies. The Pope's division of the world notwithstanding, the Spanish and Portuguese were not the only European countries keen to trade with the east. This French expedition was commanded by Paulmier de Gonneville. It sailed far into the Atlantic, where the ship encountered a ferocious storm that carried it to an island, position unrecorded. There the natives were so impressed by the wonders of French civilisation that the son of the chief accompanied Gonneville on the three-month return voyage, married his daughter and settled down as a respected resident of Honfleur. The descendants of Essomericq, or Binot Paulmier de Gonneville as he became known, prospered. In the absence of reliable information, speculation about his mysterious place of origin rippled outwards as time went by. Did he come from beyond the Cape of Good Hope? Was his *terre australe* an unknown continent?

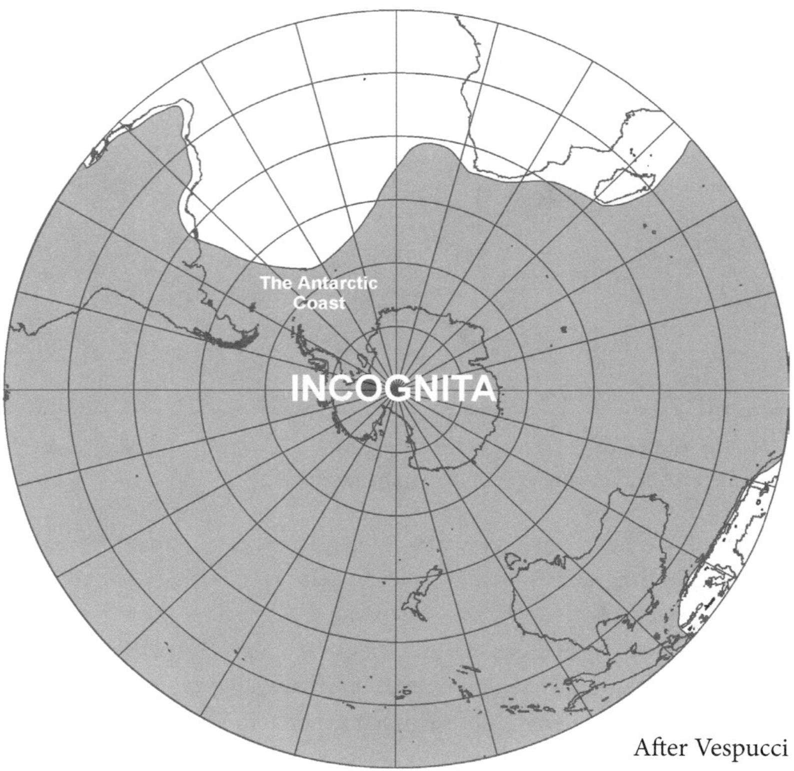

After Vespucci

The nonsense of Utopia

Avoid impious soothsayers, especially when
they tell the truth. – St Augustine

Sir Thomas More, we should remember, was as famous for his wit as for his learning and piety. Even when he wrote in Latin a very English sense of humour gleamed through the dust. He was among the best-read men of his day and he had read Hylocomylus. The *Introductio* prompted him to write a little book of his own. It took the form of an elaborate hoax, but the joke masked a serious purpose.

More tells us that while he was visiting Antwerp in 1515 his friend Peter Gilles, the city's recorder, introduced him to one Raphael Hythlodaeus, a sailor of philosophical bent. Hythlodaeus claimed to be one of the mariners left by Vespucci at Cape Frio. By giving him a Greek name, More was taking advantage of those who might just have been able to read his book but, like Shakespeare, had little Latin and less Greek. They were not to know that Hythlodaeus translated as 'dispenser of nonsense', or that Utopia, the title of More's book, meant 'not place'. And even those with Greek would have got only half of the joke unless they had also been familiar with the Ringmann/Waldseemüller book.

Hythlodaeus told More that he had gone exploring beyond Cape Frio with the aid of carts and rafts supplied by a friendly Brazilian chief. He and his companions had travelled south, beyond the wastes of the uninhabitable tropics, until they reached temperate regions where the locals sailed in sensible European-style ships. There they found, separated from the mainland by a narrow strait, the island of Utopia, where the chamberpots were made of gold. Everything else was likewise inverted, as the ancients had predicted. That part of the world 'is diametrically opposed to ours, no less in a social and moral sense than in a geographical sense'.[36]

More's Utopia is not so much an ideal society as one constructed on principles different to those then prevalent in Europe. He is exploring the social arrangements of Vespucci's children of nature to test their possibilities for more civilised communities. His method is to contrast Utopian communism, religious tolerance and egalitarianism with the very different ethos of Europe. By employing Hythlodaeus as a narrator he can make such contrasts, often unflattering to the great and powerful of Europe, without exposing himself to criticism or worse. Speech was not free in More's day; authors sometimes paid dearly.

More was frank about his inspiration. 'Like Plato's Republic, only better', Peter Gilles enthuses, and so it is, because More has devised an imaginary voyage to get to his imaginary polity. This creation of an entire literary genre was lost on his contemporaries; fiction pretending to be fact was a lie but Sir Thomas would not lie so Utopia must be a real place. After all, Peter Gilles was a well-known and respected official. In deference to the conventions of exploration, More had even provided a view-cum-map.

Hythlodaeus points out the sights of Utopia to Sir Thomas More but Peter Gilles is too far away to hear where it is. Ambrosius Holbein's woodcut from the 1518 edition.

Where was this place? Sir Thomas cannot say. Regrettably, just as latitude and longitude were being disclosed, he had been distracted by a servant whispering in his ear. He had since conferred with his friend Peter but unfortunately, although Gilles had been straining to hear, someone had happened to cough at the critical moment. Nevertheless, Peter is fully apprised of the importance of the matter and has undertaken to pin down Hythlodaeus the very next time he sees him. It could be some time off, however, as Peter suspects that Hythlodaeus might have departed on another voyage. Or returned to Utopia. Or died. This is pure Pythonism: More was a great scholar, but his humour is sometimes distinctly undergraduate.

The hoax seems to have achieved at least one of its objects. Three years later More's publisher referred to 'a certain fathead' who could not understand why More was so famous for Utopia when all he had done was take down Hythlodaeus' story. But how had Hythlodaeus been able to return to Europe to tell it? Well, after sailing hither and thither in the south temperate zone for some time, 'by an amazing stroke of luck' he had reached Taprobana. From there he had made his way to Calicut where he found some Portuguese ships and, 'quite unexpectedly', was able to take passage home.[37]

We can assume that More had tried to make his imaginary geography as credible as possible, the better to impose on some of his readers about the existence of Utopia. It must therefore represent a snapshot of what a relatively well-informed person could accept about the geography of the southern temperate zone after the third voyage of Vespucci and before Magellan's circumnavigation. The land is mainly inhabited, with offshore islands. It might not be continuous from Brazil to Taprobana, but it is very extensive. It could be Macrobius' Temperate Antipodes or, more likely, Vespucci's Antarctic Coast.[38]

More's Taprobana has been identified with Sri Lanka, but it seems unlikely that he would single out for separate mention a place so close to Calicut. It is more probable that he means Vespucci's Stamatara, because in 1511 a Portuguese fleet under Affonso d'Albuquerque had attacked and taken Malacca, thus commanding the narrow strait that separates Sumatra from the Malayan peninsula.

2

Magellanica

Among Viceroy Albuquerque's soldiers at the capture of Malacca was Fernão de Magalhães, better known to English-speakers as Ferdinand Magellan. Portugal was now in a position to dominate the trade between the Indian and China seas. Within the year the Viceroy had sent ships further east to find the source of the cloves, nutmeg and mace, that fetched such extravagant prices in European markets. Magellan's friend Francisco Serrão commanded one of them. Nobody could be sure that the Spice Islands were within Portugal's Tordesillas treaty area, but it was equally certain that no Portuguese administrator would try to answer the question before he had to. From Albuquerque's viewpoint therefore, Serrão would have been committing an indiscretion when he wrote to Magellan from the Moluccas with an exaggerated account of how very far to the east of Malacca the islands were.

Magellan was by then in Europe. He had fought for Portugal in Morocco, where he was accused of trading with the Moors. After that there was no future for him in Portuguese service, but it occurred to him that Serrão might have sent him something saleable elsewhere. He took himself to the Spanish court at Valladolid and sought an interview with Bishop Fonseca, still the monarch's most influential adviser on the Indies. Magellan told the prelate that by rights the Spice Islands belonged to Spain. These Moluccas probably lay in the half of the globe allotted by the Pope to Spain. The longitude of the Tordesillas anti-meridian was uncertain, but Magellan could confirm it if the king would commission him to form an expedition.

His audience was receptive but cautious. How could he get there without being intercepted? Was there a route that respected Portuguese rights in the east? There is, said Magellan, and produced a neatly painted globe. Las Casas, the disappointed champion of Columbus, was present. According to him, the globe left much to the imagination. South of the River Plate it was blank. In that space, said Magellan, is a strait to the west. He had seen a map of it in the treasury of the King of Portugal. Why then, he was asked, did it not appear on his globe? Surely that was obvious: it was a valuable secret. Las Casas then asked Magellan what he would do if he failed to find the strait. Magellan coolly replied that he would then have to take the Portuguese route. Fonseca and his colleagues could not lightly violate the Tordesillas treaty, however keen they might have been to circumvent it; they would have called for the padrón real.

This was part of Vespucci's legacy, his master chart that recorded on a cumulative basis all discoveries that came to Spanish notice. It has not survived in the form in which he left it but, if true to purpose, it should have included the Chief Pilot's own widely-advertised discoveries, including the Antarctic coast in 50°S. Omission of it would have been tantamount to admission that his reputation was built on a fraud.[1] Since Vespucci's death the estuary of the River Plate had been discovered, explored and dismissed as a possible passage to the South Seas, but between it and the latitude of the Antarctic coast there was still a sixteen degree blank which *might* be a strait. Who was the author of this map that Magellan claimed to have seen? An excellent man called Martin of Bohemia, replied the would-be explorer. The advisers were impressed, but puzzled. This was the cosmographer whose globe, made in 1492, showed that anyone sailing west from Spain would soon reach Cipangu, and so anticipated Columbus' first voyage. But Martin Behaim of Nuremburg, as he was also known, had died in 1507. Any map of his would be more than ten years out of date.

Behaim's 'map of the strait', which figures prominently in gentleman-volunteer Antonio Pigafetta's first-hand account of the voyage, has not survived. The sources of the map, indeed its very existence, have been debated for centuries. The most recent attribution is to the medieval Chinese voyages of Zheng He.[2] If that seems a bit far-fetched, it is reassuring to know that there were two possible sources closer to home. The first was a globe made in 1515. On it, a strait in 45°S separates America from a large southern landmass labelled Brazilie Regio. Its maker clearly did not know how to relate Brazil to the Spanish discoveries. The globe is unsigned but an inscription indicates that it was made in Nuremberg.[3] Magellan might have just assumed that it was the work of Nuremburg's Behaim. It was most likely the work of Johannes Schöner.

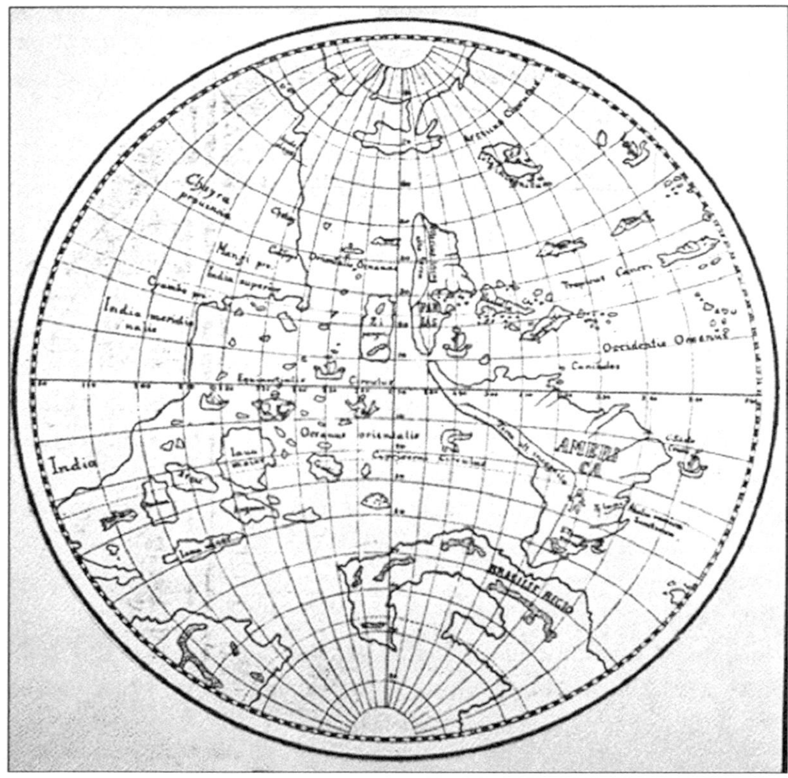

Schöner's manuscript globe of 1515

Another possibility is that there was a Behaim map that, like Waldseemüller's book, relied on the Soderini letter. It is ironic to think that in this matter Vespucci might deserve some credit.

Magellan was heartened by his interview with Bishop Fonseca. He wrote to Serrão in the Moluccas that he might be joining his friend by way of Spain rather than Portugal, but that in any event Serrão should wait for him. Carlos I, the teenaged grandson of Ferdinand and Isabella – soon to become the Holy Roman Emperor Charles V – had to be convinced, but it was not difficult. Magellan's globe or map showed the Moluccas to be 2½° on Spain's side of the line.[4] That was enough for any Hapsburg, but the instructions he gave to Magellan were careful to observe the niceties, warning him against doing anything to the prejudice of 'the most serene King of Portugal, my very dear and well-beloved uncle and brother'.[5]

Magellan's five ships put to sea from San Lucar on 20 September 1519. His officers were mainly Spaniards, who resented serving under a Portuguese captain-general. Relations were tense but manageable until they reached 49½°S on the South American mainland. They had reached the latitude of Vespucci's Antarctic coast, the end of the blank. Where was the promised strait? The mutiny that broke out was repressed by Magellan with great severity. It might be imagined that he would then feel a need to reassure the loyal men that he knew what he was doing. Not he. If we fail to find the strait, he told them, we sail on to 75°S, where there will be no night.[6] So much for dependence on the map.

On 21 October 1520, the Feast of the Eleven Thousand Virgins, the ships reached a headland that Magellan named accordingly. Its latitude was 52°S. The bay beyond appeared to be closed, but Magellan sent two ships to reconnoitre. At the head of the bay was another small cape; the onshore wind required them to round it if they were to rejoin the other ships. They failed to double the cape and were in grave danger of running aground until they saw a small opening that appeared to be a sharp turn. 'Like desperate men they hauled into it, and thus they discovered the strait by chance', wrote Pigafetta, the chronicler of the voyage. Beyond it was a bay, and then another strait and another bay.[7] They had found a way west.

The land of fire

The good news did not dissuade one of the crews from deserting, taking their ship with them. They hurried home with complaints against their Portuguese captain-general of arrogance, mismanagement and treachery. Magellan by then was beyond recall, even had his masters attempted it. First they would have had to find the strait. At the Atlantic end it was only three kilometres wide. Beyond the entrance a tortuous channel meandered westwards. It meandered more than 500 kilometres to another cape, also in 52°, on another ocean. Like the Panama isthmus, it might delimit Vespucci's continent from another. By night, native fires burned along the south side of the strait. Tierra del Fuego, Magellan called that side, but he suspected that it might be islands rather than mainland, as they occasionally thought that they could hear surf pounding the other side. Pigafetta believed that there was now no obstacle to sailing directly west.

Had Magellan attempted it he would have been disappointed. The wind is usually contrary and sometimes downright hostile to ships sailing west in those latitudes. Magellan's plan was different, and better suited to the winds he found. He was seeking a landfall north of the Moluccas, and he sailed with the westerlies abeam until he reached the zone of the South-East Trades, which bore him gently north of west through this Pacific Ocean. Through waters littered with archipelagoes, Magellan found only two desert islands. He called them collectively the Unfortunate Islands, although they were 1,200 kilometres apart.

Pigafetta nonetheless believed that there were others: before they crossed the equator he recorded that they had passed south of Cipangu. Another island, Sumbdit Pradit,[8] was thought to be closer, but that was not where they were bound. They were navigating towards 12°N 'or thereabouts', where Magellan believed he would find Gaticara because 'that cape (with the pardon of cosmographers, for they have not seen it) is not found where it is imagined to be ...'[9] Such was Magellan's cover story, but it was something short of the entire truth, because in one of the documents with which he had planned the voyage he had substituted 'Ofir' and 'Tarsis' for a reference to the Ryukyu Islands. The Emperor had sent him for King Manuel's spice, but he and Serrão were more interested in King Solomon's gold.

His ambitions came at a price for his crew. For three months and twenty days they sailed an apparently endless ocean without opportunity to refresh.

> They ate ship's biscuit, and when there was no more of that they ate powder of biscuit swarming with worms. It stank of rats' urine. They drank yellow water, putrid for many days. They ate the hides used to prevent chafing of the rigging. Sun, rain and wind had made them exceedingly hard, so they left them in the sea for four or five days, and then placed them in a pot on the fire, and so ate them; and much sawdust. Rats were sold for half a ducat apiece, or even a ducat.[10]

Pigafetta recorded that swelling of the gums and consequent inability to eat (classic symptoms of scurvy) killed 21 men and incapacitated another 25–30. He believed that only good weather had prevented them all from starving to death, and that the voyage would never be made again.

The ships made landfall at Guam, then sailed west to Samar in the Philippines. From there Magellan coasted south, looking for the cape that would allow him to find Ophir and Tarshish. At Cebu the natives knew of the Moluccas. As Magellan believed that he was only 164° west of the line of demarcation it seemed likely that the Moluccas would indeed be found in Spanish waters, but he was in no hurry to get there. He was every bit as much a conquistador as Cortés or Pizarro. There was gold in these islands and he was determined to exploit it for himself under his agreement with the Spanish king, but he miscalculated when he intervened in a dispute between local rulers. Even as Cortés was conducting the great siege of Mexico City that would destroy the Aztec Empire, Magellan was killed in petty skirmish on a Philippine beach, his body riddled with bamboo spears. Eight of his men also fell in that fight, and another 24 died as a result of subsequent treachery.

But his plan lived on. After destroying one of the ships because it could no longer be manned, the expedition sailed west instead of making south to the Moluccas. Brunei, in Borneo, was judged to be only about a degree short of the line of demarcation but there was little chance of over-awing the powerful local rulers with two ships. It was time to attend to the business of King Carlos. If the Moluccas were anywhere to the east of this place, they would belong to Spain. The ships backtracked, and with the aid of local pilots arrived at Tidore in November 1521. There they were told that Magellan's friend Serrão, who had been based on the adjacent island of Ternate, was dead. The ruler of Tidore had poisoned him. Although nominally a Portuguese agent, Serrão had treated the Moluccas as a personal fiefdom and his death had created a power vacuum that was hard to fill. The current Portuguese representative, however, told the Spanish that they had been expected: Portuguese fleets had been sent east and west from Europe to intercept them.

A captain in one of these interception fleets, Cristóvão de Mendoça, has been put forward as the unacknowledged European discoverer of Australia. The claim is based on his cruise in search of Magellan, of which no record survives. The speculation rests on the instruction given to Mendoça to look for Magellan in 'the Isles of Gold' reported in 1518 by Diogo Pacheco. Pacheco said that he had found the isles south-west of Sumatra, which is where Ptolemy had located Iabadiu (Java), but the Portuguese would not have equated Ptolemy's Java with Magellan's 'Ofir and Tarsis', which were in the Ryukyu Islands. To intercept him, Mendoça would have had to sail north, not east. In the absence of such information he might have searched south-east and found the real Java, but neither course would have taken him to the east coast of Australia, as alleged.[11]

Undisturbed by Portuguese fleets looking for them in the wrong places, the Spanish quickly secured a cargo of cloves. They were also given a beautiful natural curiosity, said by the islanders to come from the terrestrial paradise. Even in death, the long and lustrous plumage of this Bird of God was incomparable. A live specimen would have been a gift fit for an emperor but, alas, it was native only to a big island further east, in the lands of a ruler 'exceedingly rich in gold' who, the Spanish were told, was called Raya [Raja] Papua.[12]

The expedition prepared to leave for home, but the *Trinidad* was found to need extensive repairs. It was agreed that the *Victoria*, now commanded by Juan Sebastián del Cano, could not afford to miss the northern monsoon that would carry her across the Indian Ocean. The plan was to have the *Trinidad* repaired by the time the south-west monsoon came around and then to sail her east to Panama, a base from which Spain could exploit these new possessions free of Portuguese interference and without having to use Magellan's inconvenient strait. The *Victoria*, with Moluccan pilots, sailed past Ambon into the Banda Sea. In Timor they found sandalwood, but by then all Cano really cared about was finding Gaticara, the way out. They had been in this enormous archipelago for nearly a year, with each island only leading to another.

At Timor they interrogated their Moluccan pilots. Westwards from here, the oldest said, there is a chain of islands – Ende (Flores), Tana, Butun, Creuo, Chile, Bimacore, Aranaran, Mani, Zumbaua (Sumbawa), Lomboch, Chorum, Java Major – that reaches as far as the cape of Malacca. And to the south? South of Java Major, he had heard, there was an island called Acoloro.[13] It was populated by women who were made pregnant by the wind and killed their male offspring, likewise any man who happened that way. The Spaniards did not credit the story but were satisfied: Timor was in 8°S, where Ptolemy's atlas located the Cape of Gaticara. This must be it.[14] From here they could sail south-west to the Cape of Good Hope without fear of interception from Malacca.

Five weeks into her long haul across the Indian Ocean, the *Victoria* made a landfall. The bold, high island was south of India, not Java, and there were no women, fierce or otherwise. This was desolate Amsterdam Island which had nothing to recommend it to seekers of gold, spice or even Amazons. Its isolation led Pigafetta to doubt that there was anything substantial to be discovered in the southern hemisphere north of the 52nd parallel. He believed that from Magellan's strait it would be possible to circumnavigate in that latitude without finding other land until one came again to the cape of the Eleven Thousand Virgins in the

New World.[15] They sailed deep into the Indian and Atlantic Oceans in an effort to avoid detection. Seven months later, after losing half the crew to Portuguese detention at Cape Verde, the *Victoria* dropped anchor off San Lucar. There were just eighteen survivors of the more than 240 men who had sailed three years earlier.

The *Trinidad* did not reach Panama, mainly because she was first taken north looking for Magellan's golden islands. Eventually the poor condition of the ship forced her back to the Moluccas, where she was captured and the crew became Portuguese prisoners. Few of them ever saw Spain again. Cano reported to Seville that the Philippines and Moluccas, and perhaps even Malacca, were rightfully Spain's. The logbook of his pilot, Francisco Albo, showed that only 106½° of longitude separated the Strait of Magellan from Guam. Longitude seldom featured in Albo's daily record, which leaves a suspicion that he mainly relied on dead reckoning, a daily estimate of distance sailed. If so, it did not serve him well. His Strait-to-Guam distance is 33½° short, leaving an unaccounted-for space on the globe large enough to swallow the entire East Indies, from Sumatra to the Moluccas. But right or wrong, the information was of immense propaganda value. Charles V commissioned Peter Martyr to write a definitive account.

As Europe absorbed the import of Magellan's achievement, one of the points of debate was the nature of Tierra del Fuego. There were two schools of thought. A few writers took it at face value: here was a long coastline, the southern side of which was unknown. Some believed that it was more, a foothold on the fabled southern continent. On his woodcut map of about 1527, Franciscus Monachus of Antwerp represented Tierra del Fuego as the most southerly coastline of a continent that extended everywhere to the pole. The land bore the inscription 'this part of the world detected but not yet discovered by our navigators'. Like Schöner's globe before it, it was a persuasive and enduring image.

So enduring was it that half a century later Mercator and Ortelius were still mapping Tierra del Fuego as part of a circumpolar continent. But Abraham Ortelius also kept a foot in the other camp. The frontispiece of his *Theatrum Orbis Terrarum*, the first modern atlas, is an allegory of the continents. Asia and Africa, bearing gifts, defer to sovereign Europa, at whose feet sprawls America, naked and magnificent. Beside America is another figure, half-realised, a bust emblazoned with a flame. This Land of Fire might yet prove to be a fifth part of the world, but it is still only detected, not discovered.

DE ORBIS

SITV AC DESCRIPTIONE. AD REuerendiss. D. archiepiscopum Panormitanum, Francisci, Monachi ordinis Fraciscani, epistola sanè quã luculenta. In qua Ptolemæi, cæterorumq; superiorũ geographorum hallucinatio refellitur, aliaq; præterea de recens inuentis terris, mari, insulis. De ditione Papæ Ioannis. De situ Paradisi, & dimensione miliarium ad proportionẽ graduum cœli, præclara & memoratu digna recensentur.

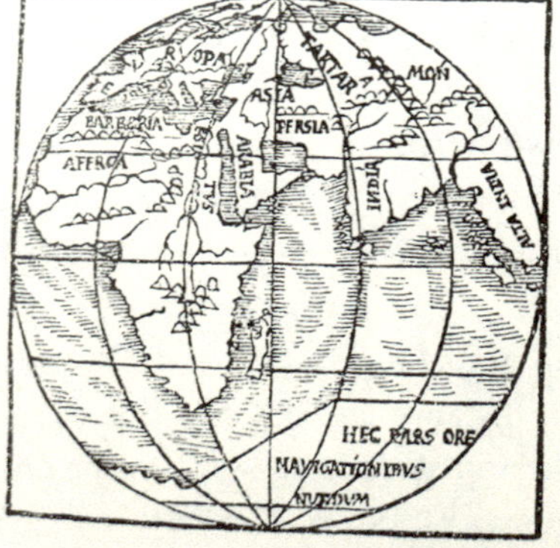

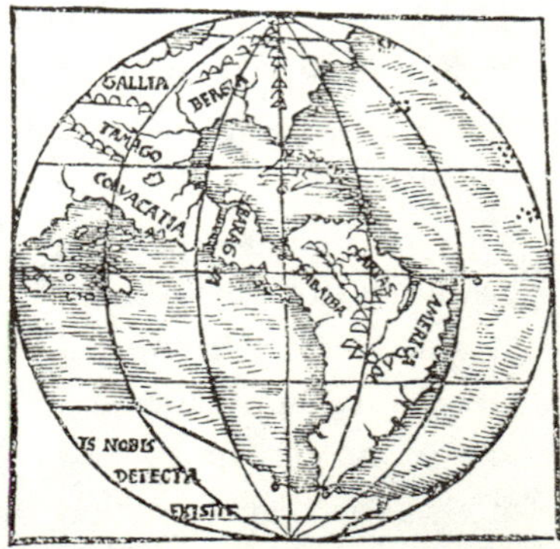

CVM PRIVILEGIO INVICTISSImi Romanorum imperatoris Caroli quinti, ad quinquenniũ, ne quis uel typis excudat, uel excudendos curet hos codices geographicos, una cũ globis, sub mulcta amittendorum exemplariũ, aliáq; pœna Principis seueritate inferenda.

A 2

Franciscus Monachus blocks in a detected but undiscovered Southland

Abraham Ortelius half-acknowledges a Southern Continent, Magellan's Land of Fire

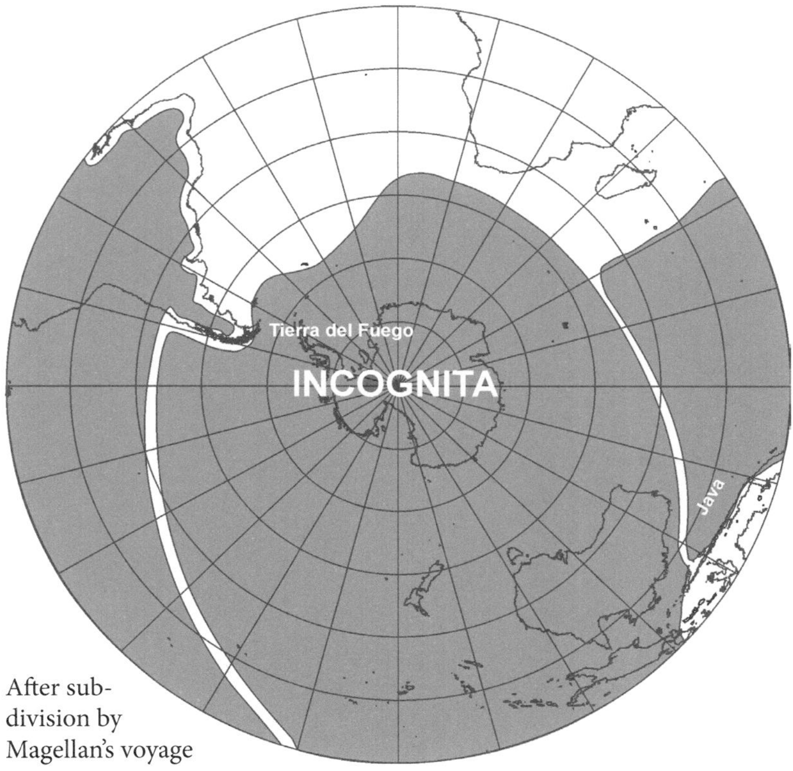

After sub-division by Magellan's voyage

Os Papuas

Charles V wanted recognition of his claim to the Moluccas. He sent his experts to confer with representatives of King Manuel's successor, João III. The junta came together in March 1524, on the border bridge at Caya, and then met alternately in Badajoz and Elvas. The Spanish delegation, which included Cano, Sebastian Cabot and heirs of both Columbus and Vespucci, produced a claim allegedly based on information from the Magellan voyage. It will be recalled that Albo, Magellan's navigator, had logged Brunei as being little more than a degree east of the line of demarcation, but this did not inhibit Juan Vespucci from placing the line west of Malacca, a good 13° from Brunei. The Portuguese were no slouches at exaggeration either. The discrepancy between the two estimates of distance eastwards to the Moluccas was fully 46° of longitude. A sketch map that Juan Vespucci submitted in evidence showed the American coast as far south as the latitude of Magellan's Strait without showing the Strait itself.[16] Neither side was giving anything away.

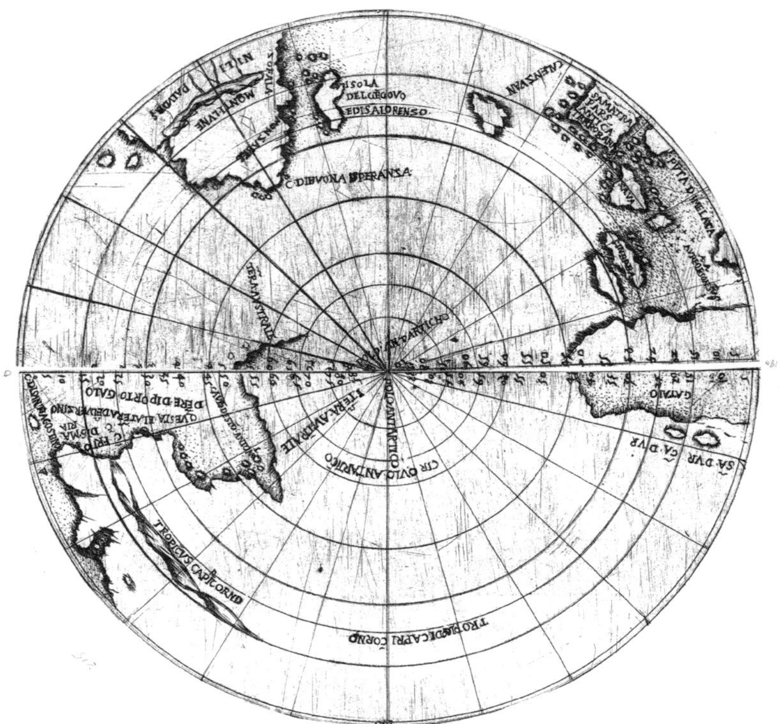

Juan Vespucci charts his uncle's Antarctic Coast as Terra Australe but hides Magellan's strait. His reverse line of demarcation passes between Sumatra and the Malay pensinsula. In this composite of Vespucci's southern hemisphere, the land mass to the right is Gataio (Cattigara/ Cathay) with Polo's Sondur and Condur offshore.

The negotiators had been asked to decide what fell on one side or the other of a notional line on the other side of the world; it is hardly surprising that they could not agree. A cheeky urchin hailed them as they left one futile meeting and offered to show them where the line was. He pulled up the tail of his shirt and displayed a neatly divided posterior. Or at least that is what he thought he was doing because he, and they, could only imagine what their backsides really looked like.

With nothing resolved, Charles decided to assert his claims to the Moluccas by sending them a governor, and so began a struggle for a part of the world where the Spaniards found it difficult to deploy ships and, indeed, to extract them. Neither the governor, García Jofre de Loaisa, nor his his second in command, Cano, survived the Pacific crossing. A few survivors, including one Andrés de Urdaneta, made it to the Moluccas but were stranded there with the *Trinidad*'s men. Three of Loaisa's ships had been lost in Magellan's strait alone. The route was clearly too difficult, but Spain was now established on the Atlantic and Pacific coasts of Mexico and one of Loaisa's vessels, separated at the Strait, took news of the expedition's alarming state to Cortés. Seeing an opportunity to tap the riches of the spice trade, he sent his cousin, Alvaro de Saavedra Cerón, to the rescue.

Saavedra lost two of his three ships in the crossing. When he reached the Moluccas in February 1528 he was nearly as much in need of help as able to give it, but he ransomed some of Loaisa's men, fought off the Portuguese, loaded with cloves, and attempted to re-cross the Pacific. He was looking for a direct route to the Isthmus of Panama, across which his cargo could be carted and floated down to the Atlantic. Two years earlier the Portuguese governor of the Moluccas, Meneses, had been carried east and forced to winter on a coast populated by black people whom his Moluccans called *os Papuas*. So began European contact with the second largest island in the world, much larger than Java but untouched by civilisation, cursed with a dangerous navigation and of uncertain value.

In his search for a route, Saavedra followed up Meneses' discovery but adverse winds detained him on the coast for a month. After naming one large island *Isla del Oro*, the Isle of Gold – probably Biak – he returned to the Moluccas. He tried the southern route again in 1529, but the sources disagree about whether he was any more successful. By Saavedra's reckoning he had sailed 383 leagues from Tidore when he came across an island. His most intriguing claim is that from 2°S he followed its coastline for upwards of 500 leagues, to 4–5°S.[17] Five hundred leagues is about the length of the north coasts of New Guinea and New Britain combined. The strait between the two islands is easy to miss if one is simply trying to find an east-west passage, as subsequent navigators were to demonstrate. Significantly, the northern tip of New Britain lies in 4°S. This was a large landmass, with a northern shore four and a half times the length of Tierra del Fuego; large enough to be a headland of the southern continent.

What did the Spaniard make of it? He had a surveyor's eye – having pointed out several routes by which a canal might be cut across Central America – but we cannot even be sure why he named the discovery as he did. It may hark back to Pigafetta's mention of the gold-rich Raja Papua. Be that as it may, Saavedra was finally thwarted by contrary winds. He turned north, seeking a west wind and an open ocean. He was still seeking that favourable wind when he died, far from anywhere. Once again his ship returned to the Moluccas. By then, Charles V had cut adrift the faithful subjects who had been trying to enforce his claims. The Emperor, perennially short of ready money for his European wars, had negotiated the Treaty of Saragossa. For a consideration of 350,000 ducats (700,000 Magellanic rats) he had agreed to fix the anti-meridian at 145°E, effectively mortgaging his claim to the Moluccas. Some Spanish grumbled at this sacrifice of national interest to dynastic ambition but Charles had soldiers to pay and a wedding bill to meet, for he had just married the sister of João III.

The payment bought a few years of peace for the Portuguese but in 1537 one of Cortés' subordinates mounted another expedition from Mexico via Peru. What Hernando de Grijalva thought he was about, given the Emperor's treaty with the Portuguese, remains obscure, but his men were under the impression that this was to be a smash-and-grab raid on the Moluccas, and when their captain tried to turn back they murdered him and continued the voyage. Sailing west almost along the equator, they sighted several small islands in the Gilbert group and passed north of New Ireland, but ran aground on the north-west coast of New Guinea. News of their arrival eventually filtered back to Ternate.

The captain of the Portuguese in the Moluccas at the time was Antonio Galvão, a vigorous and far-sighted young man who was consolidating his hold on the islands and extending his country's reach. Even so, he did not see the Grijalva survivors until Portuguese missionaries brought them in two years later. They were able to add considerably to his knowledge of the big island to the east, including a description of the cassowary, 'a bird as big as a crane, that flies not, nor has any wings to flee with'.[18] It should be noted that anyone who could record the cassowary probably also knew of the tree kangaroo, which might account for the pouched (but tailless and earless) camel-like creature on the frontispiece of the de Jode atlas of 1597, which has been claimed as evidence of a forgotten discovery of Australia in the sixteenth century. It more likely records a hazy description of the opossum, chosen by de Jode to represent American fauna.

In the absence of substantial force – the Portuguese had only about 100 soldiers in the islands – Galvão's missionaries were as much an instrument of state as of church, and with them he not only pacified the Moluccas but extended Portuguese influence far into the Philippines. The known direction of the Philippines, north from the Moluccas, placed them in the Portuguese hemisphere but this had not been made

Representing the four known continents: the horse of Europe, the lion of Africa, the camel of Asia and the opossum of the Americas. No Australian fauna here

explicit at Saragossa. Furthermore, by 1537 the Emperor knew that the treaty was a very bad bargain. In 1529 the Portuguese had told him that they were making little profit from the paltry 800 quintals of cloves, nutmeg and mace landed each year at Lisbon. It turned out that the sting was in those last two words. When Urdaneta, survivor of the Loaisa expedition, made his way back to Spain after eleven years of dour struggle with the Portuguese in the islands, he reported that twenty times the Lisbon traffic, an additional 600,000 ducats' worth, was going into the Middle East market annually through the Portuguese trading post at Hormuz on the Persian Gulf. The Emperor had been flim-flammed, and Grijalva's voyage may have been one way of intimating to the in-laws that he knew it.

Galvão's term of appointment ended in 1540, when he was 37 years old, but in spite of his achievements he was neither rewarded nor further employed. Indeed, having spent his own fortune in his country's interest in the Moluccas, he was reduced to penury. He devoted his last years to writing a history of discovery, including the account of Saavedra's last voyage as outlined above, and concluded that by the year 1555 'all is discovered and sailed from the east unto the west almost even as the sun compasseth it'. Looking south, however, he found the case to be very different. Most of the southern hemisphere was 'undiscovered' but, unlike Monachus, Galvão did not seem to think that there was anything very substantial still to be found in the temperate latitudes. He must have concluded that even a north coast as long as that of Os Papuas indicated no more than another large island in an archipelago of large islands, probably comparable in size to Sumatra, Java, and Borneo. In his geography there was no southern continent but his views were of no account against those of Ptolemy, especially as the latter had Gerard Mercator, the foremost cartographer of the day, for his advocate.

The earliest depictions of New Guinea on world maps showed it as either a headland of Terra Australis or a chain of small islands. In 1569 Mercator published his great world map, the first to use the navigation-friendly projection that bears his name. He showed New Guinea as a single large island, separated by a narrow strait from Terra Australis. This was an innovation and in later centuries it was cited as evidence that Mercator had somehow learned of Torres Strait and, by implication, Australia. In fact, his inscription reveals that this is old conjecture, not new knowledge: 'Perchance [New Guinea] is the Isle of Labadiu (Iabadiu) of Ptolemy if it really be an isle, for it is not yet known whether it be an isle or a part of the southern continent.' Mercator assumes that Ptolemy's southern continent exists. What remains to be discovered is whether New Guinea is part of it; if not, perhaps this Isle of Gold is the one described by Ptolemy (and sought by Pacheco).

Galvão had inadvertently provided some support for this thesis. In his account of the Magellan voyage, he wrote that beyond Timor the Spanish had discovered certain islands 'under the Tropic of Capricorn', all inhabited. This was a misreading of Pigafetta (who had not visited the islands he reported west of Timor) and perhaps of Maximilianus Transylvanus, a student of Peter Martyr, who had used the phrase 'beyond the Tropic of Capricorn' to locate the Cape of Good Hope.[19] Galvão was aware of the limitations of his sources. Indeed, he complained that he had found the Magellan voyage 'not exactly written'.[20] So where was the definitive account that Charles V had commissioned from Peter Martyr?

Martyr had begun by diligently interviewing survivors of the circumnavigation. He had then taken it on himself to find explanations for their more outlandish stories, such as the extra day they had somehow gained in following the sun around the earth. His book took five years to complete and was to be published to a standard worthy of the greatest voyage of all time, made by command of the greatest monarch since Charlemagne. It could have been printed to the highest contemporary standards in the Netherlands, safely within the boundaries of the Emperor's dominions, but only the cachet of Italian printing was good enough. The manuscript went to Rome. It was lost when an army invaded and sacked the city in 1527. The army was that of Charles V. It was protesting about not being paid. Thomas More could not have done better.

Although it became a general practice among cartographers, whether or not they showed Mercator's strait, to label the New Guinea/Terra Australis connection as 'uncertain', their engravers were less inhibited. The vignette that illustrates Magellanica on the bottom Petrus Plancius' world map of 1594 shows it as a land of spice, birds of paradise, elephants, white cockatoos and off-white bears, a continent that stretches from the Equator to the South Pole.

The inflation of Java

Java, according to the reports of some well-informed navigators, is the largest island in the world.
– Marco Polo

When the northern European cartographers sought to add Magellan's track and other discoveries in the Indies to their maps, the materials were far from satisfactory. Their own navigators were not yet making voyages to those regions and the secrecy inspired by Iberian rivalry was vexing. They could read about the voyages of Portuguese and Spanish explorers as these were printed, but access to the charts was more limited. They amended their own as best they could from what they could glean. So what could they make of Polo's largest island, said to be more than 3,000 miles in circuit?

The earliest first-hand account of a European visit to Java is by Ludovico di Varthema, a native of Bologna. In 1502 he began an overland voyage to the east that he said took him as far as Banda and the Moluccas, although his geographical descriptions of those islands are suspect. While in the Indies, however, he did gather the first reliable information about the sources of spice. In Borneo he and his companions chartered a vessel to take them south to Java and while at sea they pumped the captain for information. The north star was no longer visible, so how did he steer? The captain pointed to the Southern Cross and also told them that on the other side of Giava, towards the south, there were other races who navigated by those stars. Moreover, beyond Giava the day did not last more than four hours, and in that region it was colder than in any other part of the world.[21]

The captain did not say that there was land in those cold parts, but it was implicit that the Southern Cross navigators had sailed there. The passage is ambiguous in several ways. The 'other races' would have to be Javanese because no other navigators live further south, but why are they 'other'? It is possible that Giava is Madura off Java's north coast. We have it on Pigafetta's authority that among local pilots 'Java Minor' was another name for Madura: the old Moluccan who had briefed Cano referred to Madura by that other name and told him that it was only half a league from Java Major, which it is.[22]

Other explanations were possible. Gerard Mercator concluded from Varthema's description that beyond Java Major there was another inhabited landmass that extended as far as 63°S.[23] This he equated with Polo's Locach. But if Varthema did mean Java Major and not Madura, and it went that far south, how could his account be reconciled with Pigafetta's? The *Victoria* had sailed south of Java Major and we can be sure what Pigafetta meant by that name because the Moluccan pilot had told him that its towns included Magepaher (Majapahit), Sunda and Cirubaia (Surabaya).

Here was a puzzle. It was left to an anonymous Nuremburg gore-maker to suggest a solution. In about 1535 he made gores for a globe that showed Magellan's track. South of Borneo is an unlabelled island of a shape and size compatible with modern Java. Immediately to its south, separated by a channel through which Magellan's track passes, lies a landmass that extends to 13°S. It is not the largest island on the globe but it is many times the size of Borneo; it is labelled Java.

The gore-maker had no first-hand knowledge. Nor, until the late 1520s, did his French counterparts. Even then, the Parmentier brothers of Dieppe got only as far as Sumatra, where both died of typhoid. Jean Fonteneau,[24] a native of Saintonge, may have served on their expedition but this is uncertain. In his *Cosmographie*, dated 1545, Fonteneau claimed to have made a voyage to *La Grande Jave* and *Jave Mynore*, but feared that much of what he had to tell would not be believed. For example, some had said that the two Javas were islands, but from what Fonteneau had seen Big Java was mainland, reaching from 15–16°S to the Antarctic pole. His manuscript chart, which shows only the north of these islands, is nonetheless unambiguous: Big Java is modern Java, with Madura offshore, and his Little Java is Sumbawa.[25]

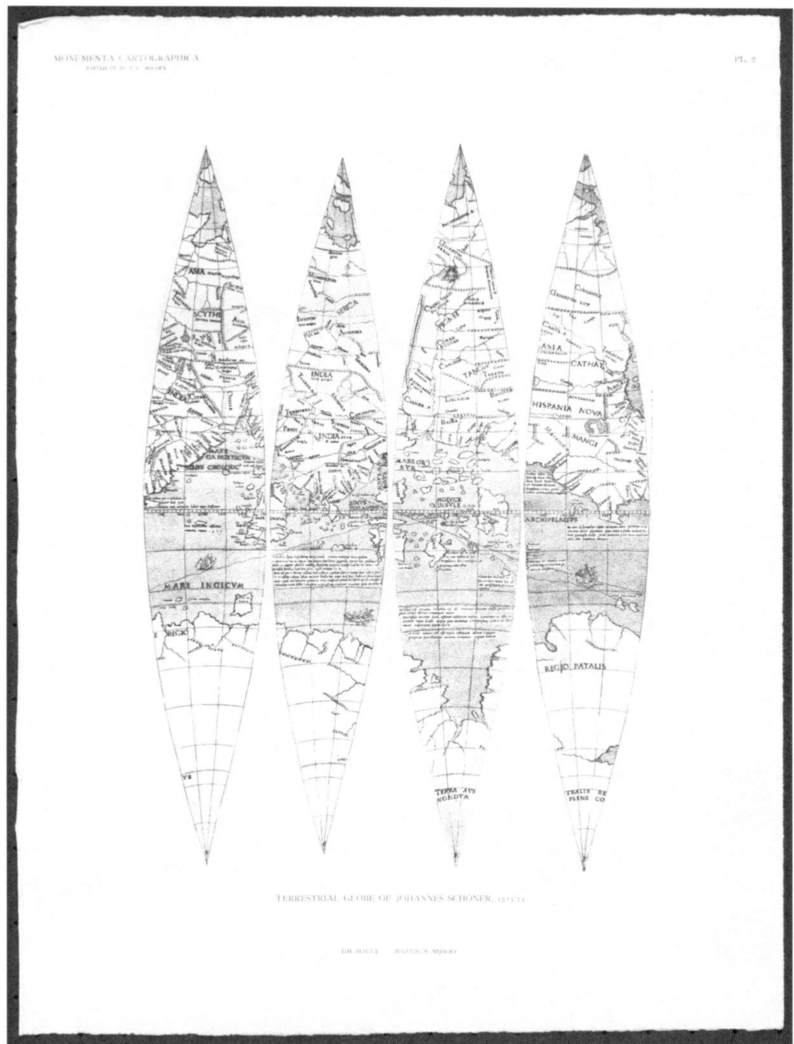

The Nuremberg gore-maker divides Java to let the *Victoria* through

Fonteneau makes it difficult to separate what he saw from what he only heard, particularly when he tries to reassure his readers by personal testimony. He has only heard that Big Java extends to the pole, but he has been in a place *there* where the day lasted three months reckoned by the revolution of the sun, and did not wish to stay longer for fear that night would overtake him. *There* could be Antarctica, but it is just as likely to be the seas around Newfoundland, where Fonteneau voyaged in 1542 with the Roberval expedition. As for the extent of the mainland of Java, 'in the west it is held to *terre*

Australle, and from … the east to the land of Magellan Strait.'[26] Is this independent evidence or an elaboration of Varthema's information, which Fonteneau endorses? Furthermore, Varthema and Fonteneau are only compatible with Pigafetta's transit south of Java if the Nuremburg globemakers's strait is available.

It was a solution that appealed to Dieppe cartographer Jean Rotz. He too may have been in eastern waters about the same time as the Parmentiers, but the Portuguese had continued hostile to other Europeans and in 1531 the Admiral of France had prohibited further voyages. Looking for employment, in 1542 Rotz presented a manuscript *Boke of Idrography* to Henry VIII as a job application. What was Java Major to Pigafetta appears on Rotz's maps as Lytil Java, with Madura clearly identified just off its north coast. South of Lytil Java, separated by a channel conveniently oriented ENE-WSW and just wide enough to let the *Victoria* through (Pigafetta's half league), is Fonteneau's *La Grande Jave*, to which Sumbawa has been joined as a northern headland. East of these, clearly labelled, are the islands of Flores and Timor.

The Londe of Java, as Rotz called *La Grande Jave* on his map of the eastern hemisphere, stretches from the longitude of Calcutta to that of Christchurch, and from 8°S nearly to the Antarctic circle on its eastern side. Its coastal features are detailed, as though surveyed by a navigator, but apart from the Sumbawa coast few of them are labelled, even on his large-scale regional map. Other Dieppe maps, notably those in the Vallard atlas, are more generous with names but no more familiar with reality. Rotz was uncertain about what was further south and left his eastern and western coastlines incomplete. In shape and position, his Londe is a much larger version of the Nuremburg globemaker's island south of Java. This was attempted reconciliation on a grand scale, from Polo to Pigafetta. It was the product of Varthema's reportage, the globemaker's inspiration, Fonteneau's enthusiasm and Rotz's exaggeration.

Fonteneau seems to have worried that he would not be taken seriously. He concluded the account of his *Voyages avantureux* with an appeal to the reader not to marvel, 'for it is written as I have seen it and made the voyages, and those who have made them or read it in books will know if it is true'.[27] He need not have been concerned; he was taken at his word by his countrymen. Big Java became an ever more elaborate feature on French maps. By 1543 Guillaume Brouscon of Le Conquet had extended the land to the South Pole. It reached fullest expression in the work of Desliens and Desceliers, who filled its northern parts with idolaters, palm trees, elephants and even camels – Java writ very large indeed. Desceliers enlivened his work with a touch of humour. He shows two men at work on the Nuremberg gore-maker's channel. They might be digging it out, keeping it open or filling it in.

There are some who have seen in Big Java the evidence of an early European visit to the Australian continent, possibly by the Portuguese or the French. Their documentary evidence is the maps of the Dieppe school and the writings of Fonteneau. As we have seen, both could have been mistakenly derived from earlier known sources. No 'lost' voyages are necessary to account for them. The discovery of a continent south of Java was a feat of imagination, not of navigation, and was admitted to be such by Guillaume Le Testu, himself one of the Dieppe mapmakers. Although he was responsible for one of the most beautiful of all Big Java maps, his planisphere of 1566 displays a confession. 'This part of the same land of the south called Australie which has not yet been discovered because there is no record that anyone has searched it out and because it is only drawn from imagination.'[28] Cartographers elsewhere in Europe agreed. Although shameless copiers from each other, none of them ventured down the Dieppe path. Their southlands remained variants of Polo's Beach, well separated from Java by large expanses of unexplored ocean.

3

Gold, Spice and Elephants

The Imperial administration in Mexico was undeterred by the failure of Grijalva's venture to the Spice Islands. In 1542 the Viceroy tried to persuade Urdaneta to undertake another cross-Pacific voyage, this time in command, but the veteran excused himself on the grounds that he had recently taken holy orders. The Viceroy then turned to a relative by marriage. Ruy López de Villalobos was sent with a six-ship fleet to dislodge the Portuguese from the Moluccas. The fleet reached the Philippines in February 1543 and Villalobos detached a vessel to report to Mexico. The *San Juan*, under Bernardo de la Torre, started across the North Pacific but got no further than the Bonin Islands before being driven back.

In the following year Villalobos attacked the Portuguese strong points in the Moluccas. The campaign did not go well and in 1545 he again detached the *San Juan*, this time under Ynigo Ortiz de Retes, for return to Mexico. Retes, heedful of the failure of Torre but oblivious to the earlier experience of Saavedra, tried to find a southerly route and likewise failed. Making the best of a bad job, he named the coast he found New Guinea – for the perceived similarity of its black inhabitants to those of the African coast – and claimed it for Spain. Having sailed far along it, Retes reported that so extensive a coast must be part of a continent.[1] Villalobos, hanging on by his fingertips in the Indies, was in no position to enquire further. In the end the Spanish force had to surrender and Villalobos died at Ambon in 1546. Twenty years would pass before a Viceroy of Mexico again sent a fleet west, and then its mission would be to establish a trading colony in the Philippines rather than search for a supposed continent.

Not that the spirit of conquest and pillage was dead in Spanish America; it had simply migrated to the Viceroyalty of Peru. A generation after Pizarro had plundered the country, adventurers were still flocking there in hopes of making a quick fortune. One of them was Pedro Sarmiento de Gamboa, only in his twenties but already a veteran soldier. He believed that the New World was a part of Atlantis that had escaped destruction. Further, he had observed that the Mexicans resembled Greeks and speculated, following Dante, that they were the descendants of Ulysses. As all of the obvious gold appeared to have been liberated in Peru, Sarmiento made himself useful to the administration by enquiring into Inca history. This, he thought, would be useful in pacification and might unearth more booty.

Sarmiento's native informants told him the story of a voyage to the west in the previous century by the great Inca, Tupac Yupanqui. There the Inca had found the islands of Avachumbi and Ninachumbi, from which he brought back much gold, black people, a brass chair and the skin and jawbone of a horse.[2] Sarmiento judged that these islands must be outliers of the southern continent that extended, according to writers like Monarchus, north-west from Tierra del Fuego. The islands later appeared on Mercator's 1569 world map, vaguely inscribed as 'somewhere about here' on the parallel of Arica on the South American coast, and about which there was common report of gold. The continent itself, 'the unknown land of the south', Sarmiento identified with Cattigara.

Peru in the 1560s was still a dangerous place. Inca insurgents controlled the remoter parts and, as usual, the Spanish squabbled endlessly amongst themselves. In 1564 the Viceroy was murdered and Lope Garcia de Castro assumed the government. At about this time the local Inquisition began to take an interest in some of Sarmiento's activities. He had made rings and engraved them with strange writing. That smacked of necromancy and he was sentenced to penitence and permanent banishment. Intervention by Castro kept him in Peru but this second dose of Church discipline – he had also come under notice in Mexico – led him to think that he might not be as lucky a third time.

He told Castro of the Inca stories and of his own geographical researches; 700 to 1,000 leagues west of Peru, he said, in 15°S there is a continent.[3] One of Pizarro's conquistadors, Alonso de Montemayor, claimed he had visited an island in 15°S, 600–700 leagues from Peru.[4] Also, Sarmiento appears to have read or heard of the *San Juan*'s voyage

Sarmiento's Islands of Gold as placed by Mercator, west of South America but a long way short of the Solomon Islands. Vespucci's Antarctic Coast has become the Gulf of San Sebastian.

to New Guinea but wrongly attributed it to Torre rather than Retes. It was a mistake that would later be used to question his credibility. In Sarmiento's version, the *San Juan* had sailed along the coast of New Guinea for 500 leagues, from 1°S to 8°S, as far as a Cabo de la Cruz.[5]

King Solomon's mines

Castro was receptive. He had already told the King that he was interested in sending an expedition to discover 'some islands, called Solomon, which lie over opposite to Chile and in the region of the Spice Islands'.[6] Threatened with continuing social unrest by disappointed adventurers, he saw in Solomon's gold a lure to rid Peru of some of them. Also, the continent might be a golden opportunity for his young nephew, Alvaro de Mendaña de Neira. Sarmiento, who could hardly be denied some role, was given command of the *capitana* (flagship) and perhaps told that he could advise in the vague capacity of *jefe de ruta*.

On 19 November 1567 the expedition sailed from Callao to look for 'many islands and continents'.[7] The promise of gold, as expected, had attracted many adventurers. Some imagined that they were on a get-rich-quick cruise, but the instructions given to Mendaña were to form a settlement, convert the natives and send a ship back for reinforcements (that is, more malcontents). Castro hoped that he was issuing one-way tickets to informal exile.

Sarmiento was disgruntled. He had a ship and believed that he had been given the right to direct the navigation, but he was not even chief pilot. That role had been allotted to an experienced seaman, Hernando Gallego, and Gallego was not about to be told his business by a landsman. Sarmiento indicated that the course should be WSW until they reached about 23ºS. When Gallego kept well to the north, Sarmiento complained to Mendaña that they 'would miss the discovery and be lost'.[8] He anxiously scanned the southern horizon each day and once saw Tupac's islands in a cloud bank, 200 leagues west of Peru, but Gallego held resolutely west. Castro had told Gallego that the islands were 600 leagues from Peru in 15ºS, and that was where they were going to look. Once they had passed Castro's mark, Gallego 'determined not to follow this latitude further, for I saw no signs which could promise me that there was land about that region.'[9]

He steered an easier, more northerly course, the ships running free before the wind, and gradually lost latitude towards the equator. On 12 January 1568 he was asked how much further west was the land. 'Three hundred leagues', he replied. If it was New Guinea that he had in mind, as seems likely, his estimate was about 200 leagues short. Three days later a small island was sighted. According to Gallego they were then 1,450 leagues west of Peru.[10] Mendaña named this find the Isle of Jesus. It was Nukufetau in the Ellice group. Sarmiento was convinced that they had found the volcanoes that formed high islands off the coast of New Guinea. It was pointed out to him that this was a low island in a different latitude. Mendaña was more impressed by the void they had just crossed. He even gave it a name: the Gulf of Conception was 'the largest gulf navigated, nor was any larger seen in the whole discovery'.[11] And much wider than his uncle's 600 leagues.

Sarmiento urged Mendaña to take possession of the island and then proceed south in search of the continent that he had promised to discover, as this must be an outlier of it. Gallego, nervously eying the reefs, was reluctant to approach them, and by the time Mendaña got around to giving a direct order the ships had been carried to leeward and could not regain the island. Sarmiento told some of the soldiers that they 'had left a kingdom behind' and complained that Mendaña would not do as he advised.[12] They continued west and on the eve of Candlemas sighted another small island, which they called Candelaria.

A week later, on 7 February 1568, it seemed that Mendaña had made the correct decision: land was sighted, 'so large and high we thought that it must be a continent.'[13] He named it Ysabel, after the saint on whose feast day they had sailed. It was also the name of his betrothed, waiting for him in Lima. Inland reconnaissance by Sarmiento and others, in the face of native hostility, revealed it to be no more than a large island.

Some of the pilots announced that these islands were 1,700 leagues from Lima. The crew were frankly disbelieving: that would put them near the longitude of the Philippines, so why were there no signs of wealth here, or people more civilised than the savages they had so far seen? [14] Mendaña exploited his men's disappointment at not finding nuggets on the beach. They assembled the brigantine brought in frame, planked it with local timber, and set out from Santa Ysabel to explore the neighbourhood. They found that the island group comprised parallel chains separated by a sound littered with smaller islands. Of the main islands, the pilots explored the coasts of Guadalcanal, San Cristobal and Malaita.

Strangely, given the expectation that a mainland was nearby, they did not visit the far coasts of the western chain, although Gallego said that at the point where they left Guadalcanal the coast ran westward as far as they could see. Stranger still, Gallego implied that Guadacanal was an island of near continental dimensions, asserting that it would take him six months to circumnavigate it, although he had sailed the length of its eastern coast in a matter of days. The explanation is probably that Gallego conceived of Guadalcanal as the headland of a very large New Guinea rather than of the separate continent that Sarmiento had promised.

While the pilots were charting and speculating about the coasts of Mendaña's new empire, the men were looking for gold. Some thought they could detect grains in the sand of streams or solid gold in the ironstone clubs of the natives. There was also enthusiasm for inland exploration, at least until the natives made their displeasure plain at these strangers greedy for food as well as information. Somehow, the Spaniards found, the gold was always over the next ridge or on the next island, anywhere except in the village where the questions were being asked.

Ten Spaniards who were careless ashore were massacred. Reprisals followed, which only made it all the more difficult for the Spanish to supplement their rations with food from the natives. Although Mendaña was only 26 years of age, he led his motley followers with considerable maturity. He consulted widely among his friars, his pilots, his seamen and his soldiers, but this does not seem to have been interpreted as weakness. He tried very hard to avoid violence against the natives, and it is to his credit that, although he failed, there was no unauthorised savagery of the kind that disfigured so many Spanish expeditions. He could see potential in the islands, but he could also see growing unrest among his men. Where was the gold?

In three voyages the brigantine explored the islands to their southern limit. By then it was August and the remaining stores were only sufficient for five more months. Mendaña consulted his men. His preference, he said, was to sail to 20 or 22°S, where he understood that land would be found. If that was not agreed, should they settle in the islands, as originally intended? That proposition attracted just one speaker in support. It was Sarmiento, who said that they should obey Castro's instruction. Juan Moreno, a Lombard who had mined for gold, and Martin Alonso Pinzón believed that there was gold where they were, but they could not convince their fellows. Gallego and the other pilots favoured going north, saying that the ships would have to tack into the wind to 30°S before they could expect to find a fair wind and current for Peru.[15]

Another speaker said that they could be no more than 600 leagues from New Guinea and it would be more sensible to go there. Mendaña wryly noted that there was no talking the pilots around; 'the landsman reasons and the seaman navigates', they told him. Nonetheless, when the captain-general announced that there was a majority in favour of heading for Chile via Sarmiento's southern continent, the pilots merely shrugged. It would be plain soon enough that the only courses a helmsman can steer are those that the wind will allow.

For three weeks the ships fought against the south-east trades, but they could make no southing and, despite Mendaña's assurances that the wind would change at the equinox, concern grew as supplies dwindled.[16] On 4 September 1568 Gallego consulted the other pilots and they petitioned Mendaña. Having sailed from Peru in 15°S before going on to a more northerly course, they said, there was no point in trying to go back in the same latitude expecting to find land. Mendaña wanted to continue but accepted their advice. He ordered them to sail according to the wind – north.

Even Sarmiento seemed chastened. He advocated sailing northwards for the nearest land (presumably California) 'because of the danger to the people and ship'.[17] The search for Sarmiento's continent seemed to be over and he was not the only one disappointed. As they crossed their outward track near the Isle of Jesus, Gallego ruminated about what might have been had they kept on.

> They would not let me go on a voyage of discovery ahead, whither I wanted to go; and I consider it certain that, if they had let me go on ahead, we should have found a land very prosperous and rich … And we were not very far from it, and of its goodness I did not wish to speak at this time, because all, being despondent, desired to return to Peru.[18]

Gallego seems to be saying that he wanted to continue west, so perhaps he did think of Guadalcanal as a mainland that he was prevented from exploring. Or was it New Guinea that he had in mind?

Two weeks later, near the equator, much timber and other flotsam were seen near the ships. Gallego believed that it came from New Guinea 'and Inigo Ortez de Retes discovered it, and no one else: for Bernardo de la Torre did not see it; nor is there a Cabo de Cruz, as he says'.[19] So that for you, Sarmiento de Gamboa! I, Hernando Gallego, Chief Pilot of this expedition, know who has found what in this man's ocean, and I don't need any book-worm, who believes every tale he's been told by Indians, braggarts and chair-bound mapmakers, to teach me how to navigate'. That neither of these Spanish gamecocks was right is poignant evidence that Galvão had failed in his attempt to set the record straight, 'for the memory of Saavedra as then was almost lost, as all things else do fall into oblivion, which are not recorded, and illustrated by writing'.[20]

For reasons that are obscure but might have something to do with the illness of the *almiranta*'s commander, Sarmentio was transferred to that ship from the *capitana*. Almost immediately thereafter, in what Gallego interpreted as a deliberate act, the *almiranta* parted from the flagship. The separated ships were struck by storms and the men had to cut away the mainmasts. Gallego, 45 years at sea and 30 as a pilot, had never seen such heavy weather. The course was now east, but progress was painfully slow in half-crippled vessels and the provisions began to give out. Some of the *capitana*'s men, despairing of reaching California, wanted Mendaña to turn around and steer for the Philippines, a course that would certainly have meant the end of them all. The Captain-General stood firm, and on 20 December they reached Baja California.

To the amazement of all, the ships met up again at the port of Colima, three months after parting. Between them they had lost more than 30 men on the return voyage, one in five of those who had sailed from Peru. Their presence having been reported to Mexico City, the Alguacil-Mayor of that town arrived to enquire who they were. His report, eventually sent on to the King, was less than enthusiastic. The two ships had come from 'the Western Islands, the Solomon Islands and New Guinea', which seemed of little importance 'although they say that they had heard of better lands'. Apart from slaves, the only possibility for profit would be to found a settlement and discover the mainland, 'where it is reported that there is gold and silver, and that the people are clothed'.[21]

Sarmiento was also disappointed. He made it clear that he intended to complain to the King about Mendaña's conduct of the expedition and tried to sail the *almiranta* independently for Peru. Mendaña overtook him at Acajutla and relieved him of his responsibilities. Sarmiento then left the expedition. In his brief account of the voyage to the Western Islands, 'commonly called the Isles of Solomon', he complained that Mendaña did not wish to examine them, nor take possession. 'The good land for trading for gold may be gathered from this account as being on the left hand towards the south, opposite Chile'.[22]

Many years later a Portuguese captain, quizzed by English captors, gave it as his opinion that the Solomon Islands were so named by Mendaña, 'to the end that the Spaniards, supposing them to be those isles from whence Solomon fetched gold to adorn the temple at Jerusalem, might be more desirous to go and inhabit the same'.[23] The attribution was wrong but the motivation was right. Mendaña did not coin the name, but it suited his purposes. What Castro had initiated, his nephew encouraged. Without the lure of gold, it was difficult to see how Mendaña could persuade anyone of the need for a royal expedition to reassert his personal rights. Sarmiento too wanted to return, offering to 'discover and populate' the Solomons.[24] When, many years later, the authorities finally gave him his own expedition, he found that he was directed to less salubrious islands and for a very different purpose.

The Aforesaid Coast

Francis Drake was a pirate, but he was Elizabeth's pirate. The Queen and the commoner shared more than red hair and avarice; they were both risk-takers on an heroic scale. Drake knew that he was expendable but he also knew that in all but the last extremity he could rely on her because, at heart, she too was a pirate. The proposal for an English expedition to the Pacific originated with a circle of court figures, servants of the crown and sea dogs. It quickly found its way to the ear of the

Queen, who became a silent partner and co-conspirator in the efforts to hide the enterprise from William Cecil, her chief counsellor, who was trying to mend fences with Spain. The object of the expedition was to find lands where English goods could be traded and English shipping employed. Where these lands were to be sought is recorded only in a fire-damaged draft plan of the voyage that was located in the British Museum by Professor Eva Taylor. It is an enigmatic fragment.

> an
> the powlle &
> the sowthe sea then
> far to the northwards as
> alonge the saied coaste a
> as of the other to fynde owt pl
> to have trafick for the vent
> of thies her Ma[jes]ties realmes, wh
> they ar not under the obediens of
> prynce, so is ther great hoepe of
> spieces, druges, cochynille, and
> Speciall comodites, suche as maye
> her highness domynyons, and also
> shippinge awoork greatly and
> gotten up as afore saied in to xxx d
> the sowthe sea (yf hit shalbe thowght
> by the fore named fraunces Draek to proc
> far) then he is to return the same way
> whome wards, as he went owt, w[hi]ch viage
> by godes favor is to be performed in xiii month.[25]

The plan appears to direct Drake to two Pacific coasts, one of which stretches northwards from Magellan's Strait as far as 30°S. Neither is acknowledged to be subject to the King of Spain. Such places did not exist, as the Spanish crown claimed every coast east of the line of demarcation. Perhaps the key word was 'obedience', implying the presence of Spanish subjects, and certainly there were few enough of those along west coast of South America as far the latitude specified. There could be, of course, none at all on the 'other' coast if this refers to the southern continent, which on Mercator's map extended from Tierra del Fuego north-west across the Pacific.

Drake's personal aim may have been no more complicated than to get into the Pacific and there do to the Spanish what he did to them in the Atlantic, but there is a whiff of the draft plan in the account penned by the chaplain, Francis Fletcher, about what happened to the fleet after it emerged from Magellan's Strait in September 1578. The cold was intense, and Drake determined to go north to improve the health of his crew 'and not to sail any farther towards the pole Antarctic' which, it is implied, was his original intention.[26] Drake's only reason for deliberately going south would have been to coast Tierra del Fuego until it turned, as expected, west and north to become the coast of the southern continent. If he had been looking for an alternative west-east route south of Magellan's Strait he would surely have sought it before entering the Strait.

The weather ignored Drake's wishes and put the draft plan into effect. South they went, driven deeper into what Fletcher called Mare Furiosum. There was no relief until they had reached 57⅓°S, beyond which there was neither mainland nor island to be seen to the southwards, but where the Atlantic and the Pacific met unconfined. Unable to weather the southernmost island seen, Drake brought the *Golden Hind* to anchor under its lee and went ashore. Leaving his boat crew, he took a compass and climbed to the southernmost cliff edge, where he lay down and stretched his hands over the void. On return, he told his people that this was the furthest known land in the south of the world, and he had been further south on it than any of them or, indeed, any man. He had not disproved the existence of a southern continent, but he had demonstrated that Tierra del Fuego was not its headland, at least on this western side. Fletcher put the discovery into perspective.

> It hath been a dream through many ages that these islands have been a main[land], and that it hath been terra incognita, wherein many strange monsters lived. Indeed, it might truly before this time be called incognita, for howsoever the maps and general descriptions of cosmographers, either upon the deceivable reports of other men, or the deceitful imaginations of themselves (supposing never herein to be corrected), have set it down, yet it is true, that before this time, it was never discovered of certainly known by any traveller that we have heard of.[27]

Fletcher made a sketchy, south-oriented chart of these parts. His label on Tierra del Fuego describes it as 'terra australis bene cognita' (well known). And very small, he could have added. When the wind became more amenable, Drake turned for the coast of Peru and plundered his way northwards. He entered Callao, the port of Lima, unopposed and cut adrift the shipping he found there. The Viceroy, Toledo, sent two ships in pursuit, and aboard one of them was none other than Sarmiento de Gamboa. As usual, he was subordinate to a commander of better birth and higher rank who, in spite of these attributes, was happy enough to see the *Golden Hind* disappear over the horizon, not least because nearly all of his hastily-embarked soldiers were seasick. To Sarmiento's chagrin the Spanish ships returned to Lima.

The Viceroy remained determined and fitted them out for a more sustained effort, this time under the command of his relative, Luis de Toledo. Sarmiento was made *sargento major*, the fourth-ranking officer of the flotilla, but again his influence was slight. Drake had a fortnight's lead, so Sarmiento strongly urged that they should cut across the Gulf of Panama to intercept him on the coast of Nicaragua. It was a sound strategy and, as Drake was indeed hugging the coast, one with a fair chance of success, but the younger Toledo simply trailed in the Englishman's wake. At Panama the Spanish learned that in passing Drake had captured another treasure ship, taken its 400,000 pesos, and vanished to the northwards. Toledo prudently disembarked and left Sarmiento and the other commanders to take the bad news back to the Viceroy.

With the entire west coast of Spanish America on the alert for the *Golden Hind*, Magellan's strait was not a promising return route. After a half-hearted attempt to find the Pacific entrance to the North-West Passage, Drake made for the Moluccas, where he loaded with cloves. Storms drove him east of Banda but he found the north coast of Timor and followed it west. The Sunda Islands led west to the south coast of Java, where for a fortnight Drake enjoyed the hospitality of the rajas of the island. There was no land in sight to the south, nor was any seen between Java and the Cape of Good Hope. What expectations of southern land did Drake have in this part of the voyage? He had a copy of Mercator's 1569 map, but he also had more immediate information.

In 1573 Drake had teamed up with the French navigator and mapmaker Guillaume Le Testu to plunder a Spanish silver convoy as it crossed the Isthmus of Panama. Unless we choose to believe that the matter was never discussed between them, Le Testu would have told Drake that he could ignore any map, including the Frenchman's own, that showed a continent just south of Java. Their partnership was short-lived. Le Testu, badly wounded in the attack on the convoy, had to be left behind. The vengeful Spanish executed him out of hand and displayed his severed head as a warning to other trespassers.

When Sarmiento brought the news to Lima that Drake had eluded his pursuers, the Viceroy's first concern was to secure Magellan's strait against the pirate's return. In October 1579 Sarmiento was appointed Captain-Superior of a two-ship flotilla. He was instructed to kill or capture El Draque should the Englishman appear, although just how he was to do it with far fewer guns than were mounted in the *Golden Hind* was not explained. His *capitana* was the *Nuestra Señora de la Esperanza*. The *almiranta*, *San Francisco*, was commanded by Juan de Villalobos and carried Hernando Lamero as Chief Pilot.

Lamero had been one of Gallego's party in opposition to Sarmiento on the Mendaña expedition and it can safely be assumed that there was no love lost between them, but it played out in a strange way. As the ships made their way south, Sarmiento found himself on the other side of an old argument. Lamero wished to press on, beyond the entrance to the Strait, 'to a land that was undiscovered'. Sarmiento revealed his own belief that there was such a place even as he insisted that the Viceroy's orders had to be followed: Lamero's plan would have them make 'landfall in too high a latitude for the service they had to perform'.[28]

The weather intervened, separating the ships and driving the *San Francisco* far to the south. The English were later told that the ship had been blown to 58°S but we, knowing Lamero's wishes, might be forgiven for thinking that the passage was voluntary. If so, it was a disappointment, for there was no land. Villalobos made a half-hearted attempt to rejoin Sarmiento but had to yield to the demands of his crew. The *San Francisco* returned to Callao. Sarmiento pressed on, meticulously charting the Strait. He then claimed it for his sovereign,

> … that it may be notorious to all, and that no nation, barbarous or civilized, Catholic or not Catholic, faithful or infidel, may pretend ignorance … nor shall have the audacity … to enter, settle, or establish themselves in the regions and lands of this Strait … in the belief that they are unoccupied lands having no Lord or King to whom they properly belong …[29]

The words refute those of Drake's draft plan. They also implicitly acknowledge that appeals to Papal bulls and lines of demarcation carry no weight with Protestant heretics. They herald the emergence of a new international order, one in which overseas territorial claims will have to be made good by occupation.

His survey completed, Sarmiento sailed for Spain as Toledo had instructed. At the Cape Verde Islands he learned that Drake had returned to England in triumph, laden with plunder, and that many were planning to follow in his wake. This alarming intelligence added weight to his recommendation that the Strait be fortified. Philip II, as ignorant as Sarmiento of the outflanking open sea that Drake and Villalobos had found further south, accepted the advice, appointing Sarmiento Governor-Designate and Captain-General. Sarmiento also sought and was granted a licence to settle there, at his own expense, colonists who could create for him the kind of fiefdom that Mendaña had aspired to in the Solomons. Thirty personal servants would maintain the dignity of his office.

What he was not given was command of the fleet that would convey the fort-builders and settlers to the Strait. That honour fell to Diego Flores de Valdés, later notorious for self-indulgence and failure to follow orders when commanding a squadron of the Spanish Armada. The expedition to the Strait was an ignored warning of his talent for disaster. The 23-ship fleet sailed in September 1581.

It was February 1584 before Sarmiento and what was left of his colony was put ashore at the Strait. Diego Flores had already sailed for home after more than two years of muddle, timidity, disease, shipwreck and negligence. Less than half of the people, stores and materials intended for the Strait had reached their destination and the colony was soon in desperate circumstances. In May Sarmiento was using his last ship to communicate between the settlements that he had established when a gale blew him from the Strait. Unable to regain them, he sailed north to seek assistance.

For two years he attempted to organise relief, but to no avail. Finally, in mid-1586 he resolved to put the matter before the King in person. His ship was captured near the Azores by vessels belonging to Walter Raleigh, which carried him to England as a prisoner. There he was treated as a person of consequence. Raleigh lodged him at Windsor Castle. He was taken to London to see the Queen, with whom he conversed in Latin. He was of course pumped for information, but his relationship with Raleigh was cordial, even jovial. One day when they were poring over the charts Raleigh, whose passion for colonisation was not limited to Virginia, asked Sarmiento about the suitability for fortification of a particular island in the Strait. 'That is the Painter's Wife's Island', said Sarmiento. Raleigh looked puzzled. The Spaniard explained that when the mapmaker was drawing in the islands his wife said that she would like to have one of her own; so he drew another, just for her. Raleigh was vastly amused.[30] But if mapmakers could make up islands, might they not also have invented continents west of Peru and south of Tierra del Fuego?

By August 1587, when Sarmiento arrived in England, another English trespasser was already on his way to the Strait. It was choice, not necessity, which took Thomas Cavendish there, for he had heard of another route in a higher southern latitude that cut across to the middle of the Strait, avoiding the fortifications. This was almost certainly information from Drake's voyage. In Cavendish's judgment the route was too risky because of the number of islands likely to be encountered.[31] In the Strait he found no fortifications and only fifteen men and three women, the starving survivors of Sarmiento's colony, which three years earlier had numbered over 300 persons.

Sarmiento never saw his colony again, but he did not forget it. He died in 1592, when corpses were all that remained on the shores of the Strait, still memorializing his sovereign 'to call to mind' those abandoned subjects who were 'trusting … that you would visit and succour them'.[32] Philip initially had some excuse for neglect. Failure of his Enterprise of England involved losses that took years to make good, but no relief was sent even after Spanish sea power had been restored.

The Discoverer's Wife's Island

One of the first things Mendaña had done on return to civilisation was to marry his Ysabel. For her part, Doña Ysabel de Barreto saw in the islands the promise of family fortune, and not exclusively for the family she had married into. Mendaña found that along with a wife he had acquired a clutch of relatives. With his uncle Castro at his side he pressed his claims at court and in 1574 was granted the Solomon Islands by Letters Patent. In the following year the King instructed him to observe lunar eclipses, expected in September 1575 and 1578, to determine the longitude of the islands.

It seemed that he would soon be on his way, but in the Spanish empire even the King's instructions lost much of their force by the time they reached remote viceroys and governors. Mendaña was briefly arrested on a minor matter in Panama and was fearful that Toledo would similarly interfere when he reached Peru. He was almost ready to sail when Drake burst into the Pacific and induced paralysis in the colony. Toledo forbade Mendaña to sail and even imprisoned him. He wanted no colonies in the islands that El Draque or other English pirates might be able to raid for replenishment or, worse, seize. Even though the King further instructed Mendaña to observe a lunar eclipse in the Solomons in July 1581, and addressed him as Adelantado (Governor), the Viceroy was unmoved.

Not until Toledo was replaced by García Hurtado de Mendoza in 1590 were preparations allowed to go forward. Even then, progress was glacial until the King made a proposal that appealed to the Viceroy; in 1594 Philip revived Castro's policy of seeking new discoveries as a potential depository for idlers. Mendoza had more than enough of those to spare. In a year the expedition was ready to sail. By then Mendaña was middle-aged, setting out to claim lands that he had not seen for more than a quarter of a century.

The fleet, two ships attended by a galeot and a frigate, sailed from Callao on 9 April 1595. The *capitana*, *San Jeronimo*, was commanded by Lorenzo de Barreto, Ysabel's brother, and among the members of the expedition were two other brothers and a sister. The *almiranta* had been purchased by Mendaña out of his wife's dowry. The Chief Pilot was the Portuguese Pedro Fernández de Quiros, a veteran navigator of Philippine and American waters.

Mendaña had instructed Quiros to prepare charts that would show only the coast of Peru and two points, in 7° and 12°S, 1,500 leagues west of Lima. The islands they were looking for, he told Quiros, were closer than that, but he was allowing 50 leagues for error. No other islands were to be shown as they might encourage diversion or desertion. There can be little doubt that the point in 7°S was the Isle of Jesus. Quiros identified the other, in 12°S, as San Cristobal in the Solomons, although its true latitude is 10½°S. Gallego had stated that the Isle of Jesus was part of the same archipelago. It had been shown as such, and in the same longitude as San Cristobal, in a map published by López de Velasco twenty years earlier.[33] By definition then, the two would be equidistant from Peru. Another possibility is that Mendaña meant it for the 'kingdom left behind' that Sarmiento had been so sure lay to the south of the Isle of Jesus.

For someone who had definite ideas about his destination and was alert to the dangers of diversion, Mendaña was easily deceived. When the fleet came to a group of islands in 10°50'S, he convinced himself that they were the ones he sought, although according to Quiros the fleet had sailed only two-thirds of the required distance. Mendaña conceded the point, and named his new discovery the Marquesas de Mendoza, after the wife of the Viceroy. Island succeeded island on the course west, none identifiable with the Solomons, until the expedition was well beyond the longitude of the two solitary dots on the Mendaña chart.

Discontent mounted. The pilots ridiculed the chart for erasing land that had been painted in by other mapmakers, although they had to concede that if those mapmakers had been right the expedition by now would be sailing over land. When smoke was seen in the far distance on the evening of 7 September, by Quiros' reckoning they were 1,850 leagues from Peru.

When morning came there was no sign of the *almiranta, Santa Ysabel.* It was as though the sea had swallowed her and, although no disturbance was reported, the possibility that she was destroyed by a submarine volcanic event cannot be excluded. With almost half of his expedition suddenly missing, Mendaña had little choice other than to declare that they had arrived. But where? If he believed that this was one of the Solomon Islands, in spite of the fact the expedition had already come 400 leagues beyond where they were shown on his chart, he did not disclose which one it was. The smoke was from the island volcano Tinakula, in 10°40'S. Nearby there was a larger island. Mendaña may have recalled the Cabo de la Cruz of Torre and the volcanoes said to lie off New Guinea. He named the larger island Santa Cruz.

For two months Mendaña attempted to create a settlement but its purpose, if purpose it had, was unclear to the mass of expeditioners. There was talk of looking for the *almiranta* at San Cristobal, apparently the fleet's pre-appointed rendezvous, but apart from a circumnavigation of Santa Cruz and visits to nearby islands by the auxiliary vessels there was no exploration by sea. A string of islands seen extending to the south excited the curiosity of Quiros because he believed that the more inhabited islands there were, the more likely it was that they would be outliers of a continent.

On land, the expeditioners explored no further than three leagues from camp, even though the island was of no great size. The natives were docile but there was little food to be had from them, and to Spanish eyes there was nothing of value. The soldiers soon began agitating to be taken to 'a better place' or to the Solomons. Mendaña was listless, and what little direction there was came from Doña Ysabel and her clan. It seemed that the Adelantado governed in name only.

Sickness set in among the expeditioners. Mendaña was afflicted and remained aboard the *capitana*, leaving it to the Master of the Camp, a crusty old soldier named Pedro Manrique, to keep order ashore.

Mutiny was in the air and Manrique was called to account. When he visited the ship, Ysabel urged her husband to act. 'Kill him or have him killed. What more do you want? He has fallen into your hands, and if not I will kill him with this knife.'[34] Mendaña spared his Lady Macbeth the trouble. He went ashore to confront Manrique, who came to meet him unarmed. Mendaña raised his sword as a signal and his attendants stabbed the old man to death. His head was impaled on a stake to serve as a warning.

It did not stop the indiscipline, for which Manrique had not been responsible, and a friendly local chief was killed. The soldiers who committed the deed probably did it for the purpose of making the settlement untenable. Quiros was appalled, even more for the unprovoked offence than for the hazards of attack and starvation to which it exposed the expedition. Shortly afterwards, Mendaña's condition worsened. On the night of 17 October 1595, under the blood moon of a full eclipse, he made his will. The King had empowered him to determine the succession and he kept it in the family. Doña Ysabel would be the Governor and Don Lorenzo her Captain-General.

Don Lorenzo did not long outlive Mendaña. Between one and three people were dying each day, and on 2 November he joined their number. Five days later, when the death toll had reached 47, it was decided to abandon the settlement. Quiros claimed to be unsurprised, and prophesised that the devil would continue to hold the place 'until God permits others to come forward' who would be more concerned for the salvation and welfare of the natives.

Ysabel was in sole charge, and force of personality combined with inherited authority ensured that no-one would dispute it. She proposed to go to San Cristobal to find the *almiranta* and, failing that, to proceed to Manila to recruit afresh with a view to completing the discovery. Against the possibility that the Solomons were still to the west of them, Quiros set the course accordingly and they held to it for two days. Forty leagues on there was still no sign of San Cristobal and they turned north. Another day would have taken them to the longitude of the island, but they would have passed south of it.

By now Quiros was navigating in the dark. He did not know why Mendaña had pressed so far beyond where he had declared the Solomon Islands to be, but he was reasonably sure from the similar appearance of the natives of Santa Cruz that they must be nearby. Similarly, because the expedition had travelled such a distance, New Guinea could not be far, and that introduced another consideration.

The *capitana* was now so rotten and undermanned that Quiros had proposed to cannibalise the galeot and the frigate to make her more seaworthy. He was overruled, not least because the frigate was to carry the body of the Adelantado back to civilisation for proper burial. In vain Quiros protested that in Manila they could buy better replacements for as little as 200 dollars.

Rejection left him with no choice other than to adopt the course that would make fewest demands on the ship. He steered north-west, running before the wind and, as he hoped, keeping clear of New Guinea 'which was very near'. If the ship had been in better condition he would have sought the land and coasted to 'find out what it was'. He complained of Gallego's 'obscure and contradictory points' including, in connection with Guadalcanal, 'that the land he did not see was reported to be very good, but that he certainly did not see it'.

The ships ran parallel to the east coasts of the Solomons without sighting them. The weather was kind, and just as well, as by now it was hard to find any part of the rigging that was not more splicing than sound rope. One day the galeot, commanded by Felipe Corzo, quietly separated. The daily ration on the *capitana* was reduced to half a pound of flour, mixed with salt water and baked in the ashes, washed down with half a pint of water 'full of powdered cockroaches.'

But not for everyone. Doña Ysabel had an ample private store, and Quiros pleaded with her to supplement the rations of the sailors, who were now so weak that it was difficult to find enough with the strength to carry the dead on deck. Ysabel replied 'that there was more obligation to her than to the sailors who talked of her favour, and if two were hanged the rest would hold their tongues'. She relented so far as to provide two jars of oil, but when her demand for water to wash her clothes was queried, she angrily asked why she could not do as she pleased with her own property. The frigate separated, taking with it the Adelantado's body.

Surrounded by an empty sea, a debilitated crew, discontented soldiers and a governing family that seemed to have adopted the Borgias as a role model, Quiros considered his options. He decided that he had to suffer Ysabel if he was not to offend 'the name of the King's presence.' It took him two months to reach the Philippines, and at one of the first landfalls Quiros bought two baskets of rice for the common use. The price was two pairs of shoes. Ysabel also wanted two baskets of rice, for personal consumption, but was unable to agree a price. Imelda Marcos comes to mind.

When a tolerant breeze finally ushered the ship into Manila Bay, the harbour lookout who came aboard was appalled at the state of ship and people. Fifty had died on the voyage, he was told, mainly of starvation. Two pigs trotted by. Why had they not been eaten, he wanted to know. Because they belong to the Governess, he was told. He was less impressed by Ysabel's status than Quiros had been. 'What the Devil!' he said. 'Is this a time for courtesy with pigs?' One soldier, Quiros tells us, was heard to mutter sententiously, 'O cruel avarice! Which even with a gentle and pious woman turns her heart into a stone, even in a business so necessary, cheap, and clear.' Another ten expeditioners died ashore as a result of the privations they had suffered.[35]

The story of the voyage did the rounds of Manila. It was said that the ship had come from Peru to fetch the Queen of Sheba from the Isles of Solomon. Ysabel's subsequent behaviour did little to mute the scandal. With Mendaña only a few months dead, she married a local don named Fernando de Castro, cousin of the Governor. This marriage of state, which transferred her rights in the Solomons to her new husband, would have helped protect Ysabel's inheritance against challenge by her dead husband's family, but she made no particular effort to 'resume the discovery'.

Quiros strongly urged the Lieutenant-General of the Philippines, Antonio de Morga, to keep secret the expedition's discovery of the Marquesas until the King could be informed. He feared that their central position in relation to Peru, Mexico and the Philippines, if known to the English, might induce those heretics to settle them and do much mischief in the Pacific. As for himself, he would take the refitted *San Jeronimo* and the remnants of the expedition back to America.

Before they departed, news came that the galeot had reached the island of Mindanao, where Corzo had landed to kill and eat a dog seen on shore. There was also a dim report of a frigate found beached on some island, its sails flapping idly in the breeze. The hull was said to be putrid with decomposing corpses, in the midst of which was a coffin. Quiros could not bring himself to condemn Mendaña but nor could he, in all honesty, speak too well, even of the dead.

> He was a person zealous for the honour of God and the service of the King, to whom the things ill done did not appear good, nor did those well done appear evil. He was very plain-spoken, not diffuse in giving his reasons, and he himself said that he did not want arguments but deeds. It seemed that he saw clearly those matters which touched his conscience.

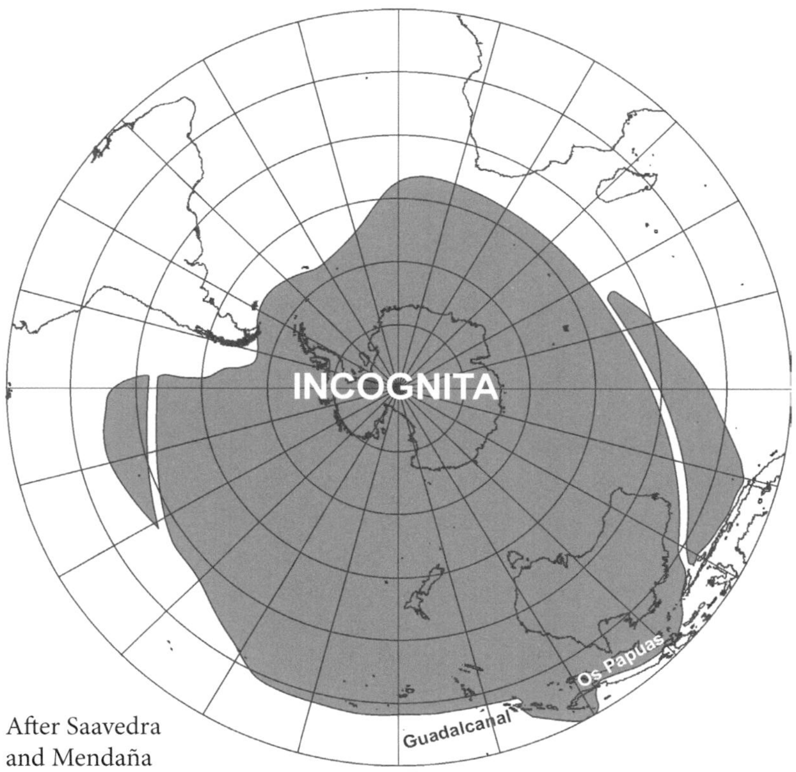

After Saavedra
and Mendaña

> It seemed to me that he might say with reason that he knew more than he performed, yet he saw nothing that passed by stealth. The Governess felt at his death, as did others, though some rejoiced at it.[36]

The wizardry of Juan Fernandez

> Tales lose nothing in the telling.
> – sixteenth-century proverb

Mendaña's voyages had given credence in Peru to the notion that there was a mainland on the far side of the Pacific, and that the Adelantado had almost reached it. More potent still, because closer to home, was a variant of the story associated with the name of the most famous of all local pilots, Juan Fernandez. His most celebrated achievement was the discovery of an easy route from Peru to Chile. In 1563 Fernandez had found that by getting well offshore from Callao it was possible to avoid the north-setting current and, having made sufficient southing, then to harness the west wind and regain the coast. The distance was greater but the voyage could be made in one month, saving two.

The feat earned him the nickname *brujo* (wizard) and the attention of the Inquisition, but rumour had it that this was not the entire story. Some subsequently claimed to have heard from the lips of Fernandez himself that on reaching a certain longitude (which Juan would disclose in good time) he had turned south ('with little deviation to the adjoining points'). 'In a latitude' (also not to be declared at this moment) he had found the coast of the southern continent. Fernandez was a long-time friend and associate of Hernando Lamero, who had sailed with Mendaña's first expedition in 1567. It is possible that one voyage has become entangled with another.

On the other hand, the rumour was true to the extent that in the early 1570s, performing just such a navigation, Fernandez had discovered the islands off Chile that today bear his name.[37] It would have been prudent to keep the location secret until they could be settled and in 1575 another voyage for that purpose was planned.[38] It apparently took place because Fernandez resided in the islands for some time until 1580, but such was the secrecy of the enterprise that it started the story on another tack: Fernandez, it was said, had sailed for a month west and south-west from Chile in 40°S (Valdivia), to where he had found 'a very fertile and agreeable continent'. Its inhabitants were white and well-proportioned, as tall as Spaniards and well-dressed. They were peaceable, gentle, hospitable and generous with the fruits of their country and of their labour. These, unspecified, were said to be 'very rich and plentiful'. Although otherwise wrong in almost every detail, including latitude, the report that the land was inhabited points vaguely in the direction of Easter Island.

Some years after the death of Fernandez in 1599, Juan Luis Arias, a Chilean cosmographer and mathematician, tried to make some sense of it all. He could not reconcile the various stories, 'but whether it happened in this or the other manner, or whether there were two different discoveries, it is a very certain fact that he did discover the coast of the southern land'. Arias was confident because he had found a witness. Pedro de Cortes, Master of the Camp, 'a man as worthy of credit as any that is known', had been employed in Chile for sixty years. He had been told of the discovery by Fernandez, who had shown him a 'description' of the coast. Cortes' statement was forwarded to the

King.[39] The old man had returned to Spain in 1614 and could have testified at court in person, but there is no evidence that he was asked to do so.

It did not prevent the continent of Fernandez, a month's sail WSW of Valdivia, becoming one of the fixtures on the charts of those whose business it was to take account of every reported sighting of land. Subsequently some came to believe that Juan Fernandez had sailed as far as New Zealand. It would indeed have been a feat of wizardry for a sixteenth century expedition to cross the Pacific in a month against the winds of the Roaring Forties, and even more remarkable for it to be greeted by peaceable Maoris.

4

Austrialia

By 1580 Portugal and Spain had been quarreling for the better part of a century over how the non-European world was to be divided between them. Then the Portuguese throne fell vacant. In the absence of a legitimate heir Philip II of Spain, a Portuguese royal on his mother's side, seized the moment and the crown. His troops marched in and the country was his, but it continued to enjoy considerable autonomy. To the extent that it suited dynastic policy to divide and administer, Hapsburg Portugal was allowed to pursue imperial interests separate from those of Hapsburg Spain. Philip, known as the Prudent, had earned the cognomen by following his father's advice not to rely on any one set of advisors, Spanish or other. He played them off against each other to keep decision-making in his own hands. Unfortunately, there were a great many decisions to be made and the King wished to make them all. Or rather, he did not want anyone else to make them, but was chronically indecisive himself.

Matters took months to get to the top of the pile, and waited there as long again. In the case of the colonies, slow communications exacerbated delay and officials often had to anticipate decisions. When these were unrealistic or out-of-date they were amended or even ignored. Mendaña had eventually got his sovereign's support for a second expedition, but it had counted for little with the Viceroy of Peru until imperial and colonial interests happened to coincide. Perhaps Philip the Tardy hoped that his Portuguese subjects would be more compliant.

India meridional

Among Philip's subjects was Manuel Godinho de Eredia, a true product of empire. His father, member of an expedition sent to convert the Macassans, had run off with a native Bugis princess. Their son, born in 1563, was given a complete Jesuit education, first in the college at Malacca and then, from age 13, at Goa. He was admitted to the Society of Jesus in 1579 but released some time later so that his talents could be employed by the State. What the State had in mind for him was mathematics and navigation, and who better fitted than an educated son of the Bugis, the most enterprising seafarers of the archipelago. In 1594, the same year that Philip proposed the establishment of new colonies from Peru, he also ordered the discovery of Meridional India to enlarge the revenues of the Portuguese crown. The king was not referring to the south of India, already well-known, but to the unknown lands of the fish-eaters said by Ptolemy to lie further south and east. It was to be Philip's second front for Iberian penetration of the southern oceans.

Characteristically, he had not allowed enough time. On his death in 1598 it was left to his successor, Philip III, to order Eredia to put aside his maps and charts and effect the discovery. To what extent Eredia actively sought the task is uncertain, but there can be no doubt that he found it congenial. He read every account he could find, from scripture and the classics to medieval travel books and shadowy native reports from the Indies. These last he was particularly keen to relate to the received wisdom of Europe. Importantly – for here we have a professional official who has access to all the records and can demand oral evidence if he wants it – his researches contain no hint of any earlier Portuguese exploration south of the Indonesian archipelago. From Marco Polo's account Eredia concluded that Meridional India comprises a continent named Lucach (Polo's Locac), Java Major (where Beach, also a corruption of Polo's Locac, is located), Java Minor (Sumatra) and minor islands such as Petan, Necuran and Agania. Beach he identifies with a mysterious land called Luca Antara that had been reported from the Indies, as had a Luca Veach (Beach/Locac), which Eredia translates as Island of Gold. He convinced himself, and conviction fired his enthusiasm.

In 1599 Eredia persuaded the Viceroy at Goa to implement the King's wishes, by which time he had a well-developed plan. An expedition would go to Timor, Flores or Sabo in January, gather intelligence, and then sail in August or September for 'the happy Island of Gold' that lay to the south.[1] In 1600 the Viceroy sent him to Malacca as Adelantado of Meridional India, promising him one-twentieth of the revenues that would accrue to the Crown from his discoveries. As *descobridor*, an administrator charged with organising discovery, Eredia was not necessarily expected to voyage himself but he responded enthusiastically to information received from an old Indies hand, Pedro de Carvalhaes.

Carvalhaes, an alderman of Malacca, had formerly been captain of the fortress of Ende on the island of Flores. He appears to be the inspirer of Eredia's original plan and in 1601 the *descobridor* took the precaution of getting his sworn testimony in writing. While on Flores, Carvalhaes wrote, he had been told by 'honourable and influential natives of the Christian community' that a small boat manned by Muslims from the port of Sabo had been blown south out of sight of land. Proceeding to the south for a little less than thirty leagues the Muslims had found an island of goats, and beyond that an island of coconuts, both uninhabited. Further still there was an island of women and beyond that Luca Veach, an island of gold. They had returned with the monsoon and brought with them all the gold subsequently in use on Sabo. As soon as he heard this, Carvalhaes had fitted out two boats for a return to Luca Veach, but …

> Just as the boats were on the point of raising anchor and setting sail, the Dominican Fathers … implored me in most earnest terms to abandon the whole voyage, on the ground that the Christians, as being unacquainted with the sea-route and having no experience of these latitudes, would undoubtedly consider that they were going to certain destruction and death in this Ocean.[2]

In addition to this anti-climactic story, Carvalhaes swore to the truth of another. Last year, he said, a boat had arrived in Java claiming to be storm-blown from a place called Luca Antara. A petty Javanese king, Chiaymasiouro, had determined to explore it and set out towards the south in an oared boat. After twelve days he had come to an island or peninsula 600 leagues in circumference, as large as Java. After being royally entertained, he had returned with the southerly monsoon. Carvalhaes himself had been present when Chiaymasiouro had told his overlord about this land of gold, spice and sandalwood.

The stories presented Eredia with a dilemma. Were Luca Veach and Luca Antara the same place? Did it/they lie south of Flores or Java, or both? He was nevertheless encouraged, but the Governor of Malacca took a different view. His territory was being attacked by Malays and the Dutch were strangling trade by holding the Bali and Solor straits.

He needed the soldiers of Eredia's expeditionary force for local defence. Eredia too was pressed into service as a fortress builder and naval commander, and although he was able to explore much of the Malaccan hinterland while undertaking those duties, his wider ambition remained unfulfilled. Bugis ancestry did not exempt him from beri-beri and he was evacuated to Goa. In 1607 he tried to return to Malacca but again his plans came to nothing when the Viceroy died and his orders ceased to have effect.

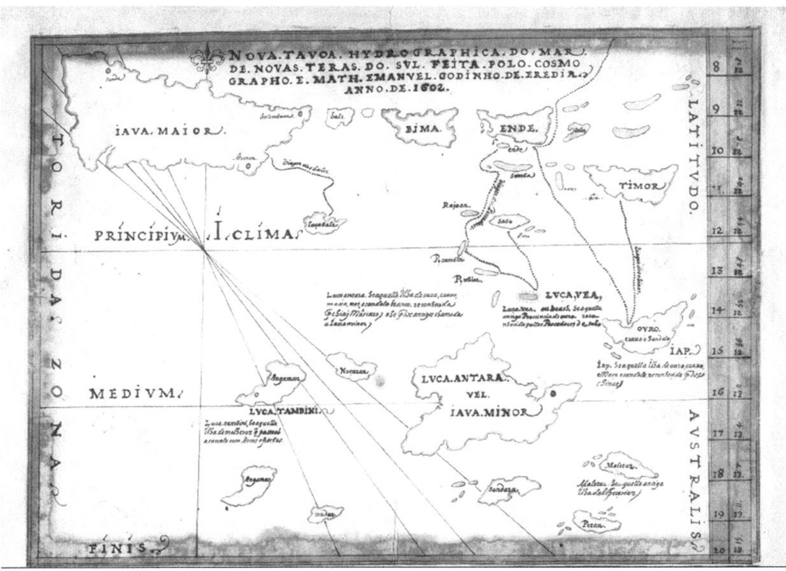

Eredia takes his informants on trust

A lesser man would have given up, but Eredia could not forget Chiaymasiouro's tale. In 1610, with his hopes for an expedition fading, he secretly instructed a servant to slip across to Dutch-dominated Java and gain more accurate information about the king's expedition. The servant did not disappoint him. From Java he wrote that at the risk of his life he had sailed with twelve fishermen to Luca Antara itself. He had, of course, found it necessary to use all of the expense money provided by Eredia, but the good news was that everything in Luca Antara was as reported by Chiaymasiouro, if not better. The people were Javanese, civilised and immensely rich.

To Eredia this was confirmation that there had formerly been an extensive trade between Java and Luca Antara, broken off by warfare 331 years earlier.[3] Further, the trade of Luca Antara was so rich that merchants from China, India and the Red Sea had sailed there in ancient times, and an attempt had even been made to extend the trade routes by cutting a canal through the isthmus of Suez. Remarkably, this information was not as totally far-fetched as it might seem. Eredia seems to have unearthed half-buried memories of monsoonal voyages across the Indian Ocean, voyaging that led to the Indonesian discovery, not of Australia, but of Madagascar. In reality, 'all the gold on Sabo' could have been brought home by Indonesians who had traded for it at Sofala on the African side of the Mozambique Channel. Further, the island of gold (Africa) does lie beyond an island of women: DNA analysis has recently revealed that the population of Madagascar could be descended from as few as thirty Indonesian women who settled on the island in the ninth century.[4]

In his *Declaration of Malacca* (1613), Eredia published maps to illustrate his discoveries. That of Luca Antara is a forlorn attempt to reconcile Polo's account with the information Eredia has received from Java and Flores. Java Minor straddles the Tropic of Capricorn, divided into the Sumatran kingdoms listed by Polo. Lucaveac, Beach and Lucac, all variants of Polo's Locac, appear here and there. Eredia, the Macassan princeling, has been confounded by European learning and misled by his Malay brethren. Luca Antara also appears on a world map in the *Declaration*, and there it bears the inscription 'Meridional India discovered in the year 1601'. This is the date of Chiaymasiouro's alleged voyage. In another document, an undated *Report on Meridional India*, Eredia claimed the discovery for himself in the year 1610, presumably on the strength of his servant's all-expenses fantasy.[5]

To confuse matters further, the maps published in the *Declaration* differ from manuscript maps by Eredia, which more closely follow the description given in the *Report*. There the mainland of Meridional India is continental Lucach. It extends southwards as far as the pole (it embraces Java la Grande), joins the Land of Parrots (Pithacoru) in the west and 'other Promontories in the South', but does not reach as far the Strait of Magellan, where there was merely 'a mass of islands'.[6] The southern continent on the manuscript maps is unoriginal, following the outline popularised by the atlas of Ortelius. The west coast, south of India, is labelled Lucantara and an inscription records that Eredia was sent to discover it by the Viceroy Saldanha in 1600 (which is not the same as saying that he discovered it).

The significance of Eredia's determined efforts to discover Meridional India lies in their failure. We should be grateful for both his scholarship and his credulity, because his enquiries and his writings reveal the gaps in Portuguese knowledge of the south at that time. If Portuguese mariners had discovered Australia at any time in the previous ninety years, their efforts had not only escaped official notice but had left no relevant trace in oral tradition. On the debit side, Eredia's reputation and cartographic skills lent credence to the travellers' tales and servant's lies that he relied on for most of his information. In the nineteenth century R. H. Major, Keeper of Maps in the British Museum, rediscovered some of Eredia's work. He was at first impressed with what he took to be the earliest documented European knowledge of Australia and then enraged at what he concluded was deliberate deceit by Eredia. He was wrong on both counts.

FIG. 5 — AUTO-RETRATO DE MANUEL GODINHO DE ERÉDIA, 1613
MANUEL GODINHO DE ERÉDIA'S SELF-PORTRAIT, 1613

With a hand on the South Pole, Eredia claims his imaginary continent south of Java

The Land of the Holy Ghost

In Quiros' relation of his voyage with Mendaña he reveals some interest in discovery and fame but much more in propagating the faith. Professional pride led him to criticise Gallego's earlier navigation, particularly his unreliable longitudes, but otherwise Quiros' concerns were chiefly humanitarian and religious. He was critical of mismanagement and abuse of the expeditioners by their leaders, and scathing of abuse and spiritual neglect of the natives by the expedition. On return from the Mendaña voyage, he asked the Viceroy of Peru, Luis de Velasco, for a ship and 40 sailors, with which he promised to discover the lands sought by Mendaña and 'many others which I suspect to exist', extending from the Cape of Good Hope eastwards to Magellan's strait and south to the Pole.

In 1600 Velasco sent him off with letters to the King and Pope to make his case. Quiros seems to have decided that in a Holy Year the Pope was the better prospect. He went to Rome where he persuaded the Spanish Ambassador, among others, that 'there could not fail to be either a continental land or a number of islands' between the Strait of Magellan and New Guinea, Java and the other islands of the great archipelago. When he reached Spain, two years later, he was armed with a sheaf of recommendations, lay and religious. The advisors of Philip III had, of course, heard it all before and urged that already discovered lands should be settled before searching for new, and that these now on offer were so distant that they would be costly to maintain even after conquest and settlement. The Council of the Indies felt that the empire was overstretched.

It was sound advice but Quiros had read his monarch correctly. Philip III was as pious as his father, Philip II, and as empire-minded as his grandfather, Charles V. It counted heavily with the King that the Pope had promised Quiros many spiritual gifts for the discovered lands. The Spanish Ambassador had recommended Quiros as 'a worker, quiet, disinterested, of decent life, zealous for the service' of God and King. The King, knowing that the Council of the Indies could worry to death any project it did not like, decided to bypass it. This expedition would proceed under the direction of the Council of State. In March 1603 the King commissioned Quiros as Captain and Commander. The post was of less status and authority than Captain-General and, in light of the fuss over Magellan's appointment, may have reflected Spanish sensitivity about so much privilege for a Portuguese.

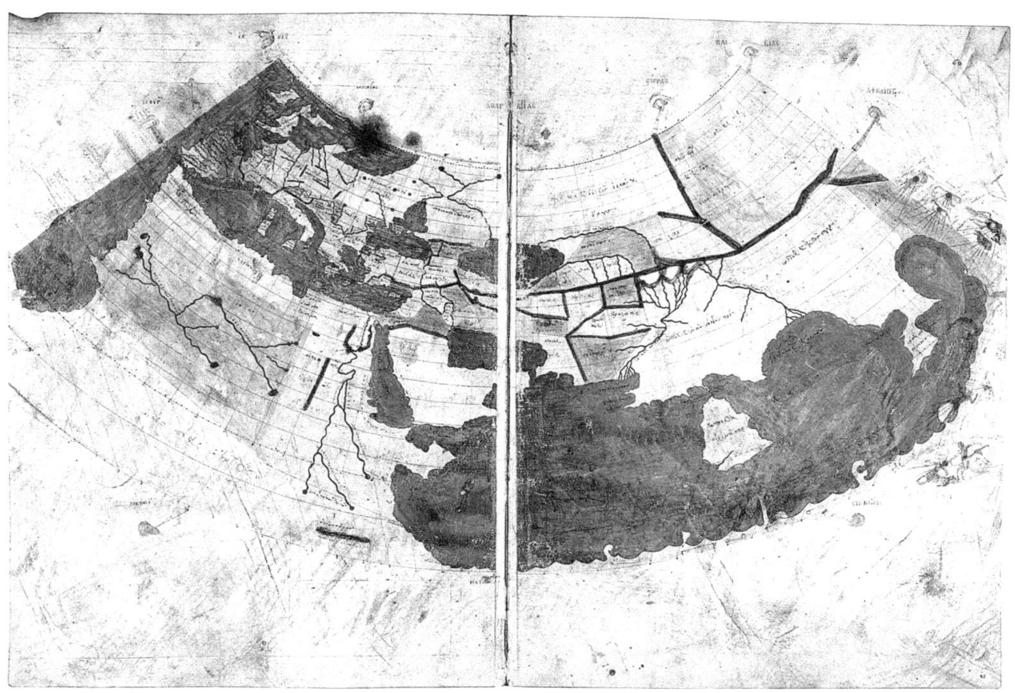

South of the Indian Ocean, the Ptolemaic map makers join the western and eastern lands of Homer's Ethiopian fish-eaters

Le Testu's Jave la Grande, east at top, drawn by him 'from imagination'

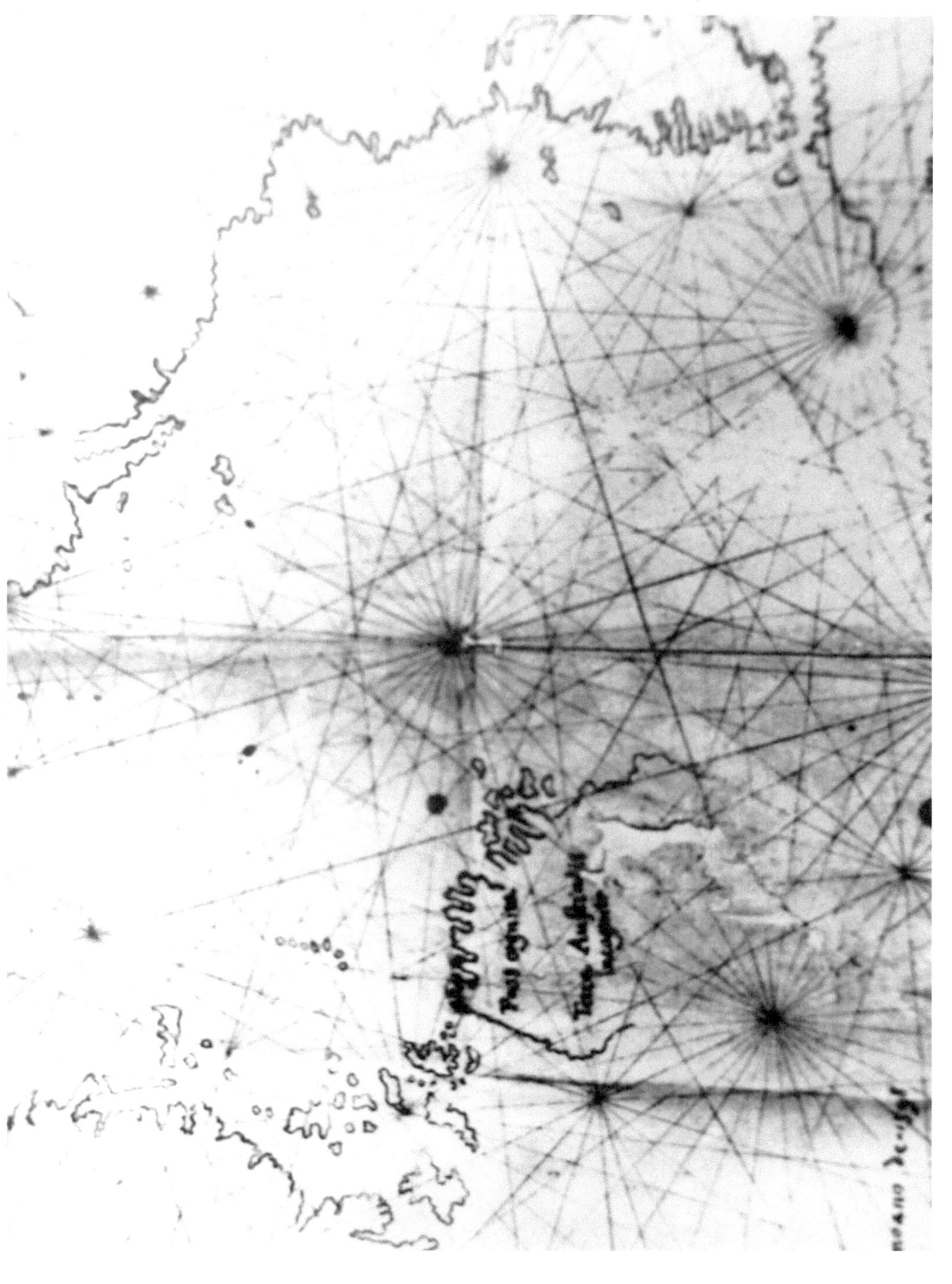

In 1598 Quiros charted New Guinea as part of Incognita but was unsure whether the nearby Solomon Islands were also connected to it

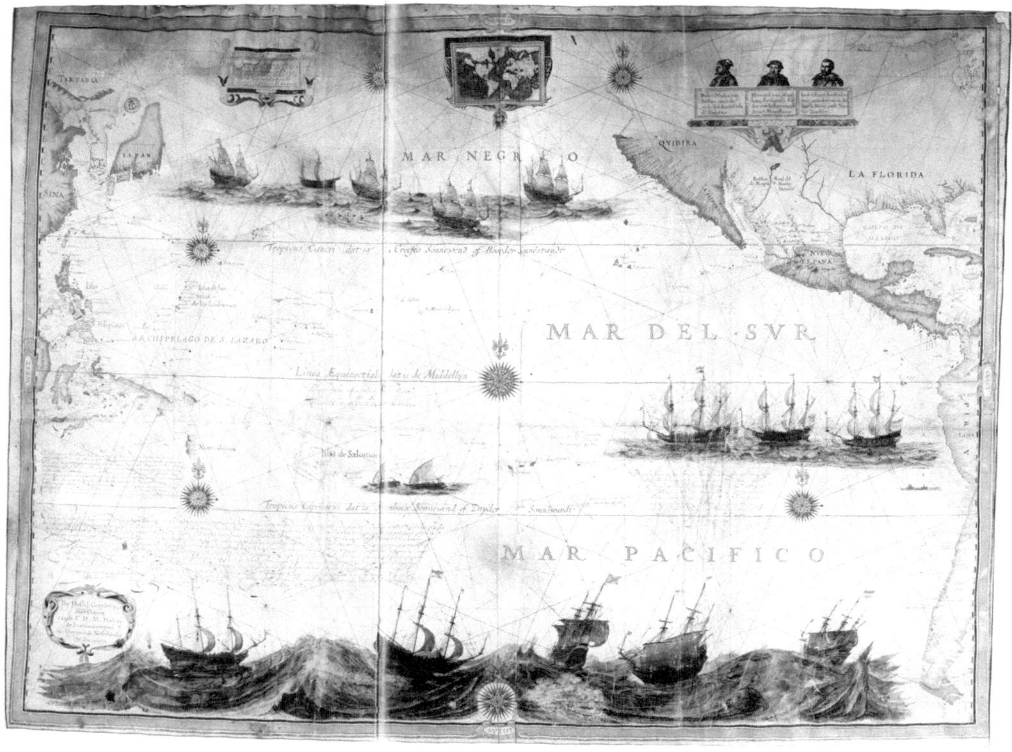

To the south-west, just above the compass rose, Gerritsz charts what he has been told is a newly-discovered extension of New Guinea. It is the north-eastern tip of Australia

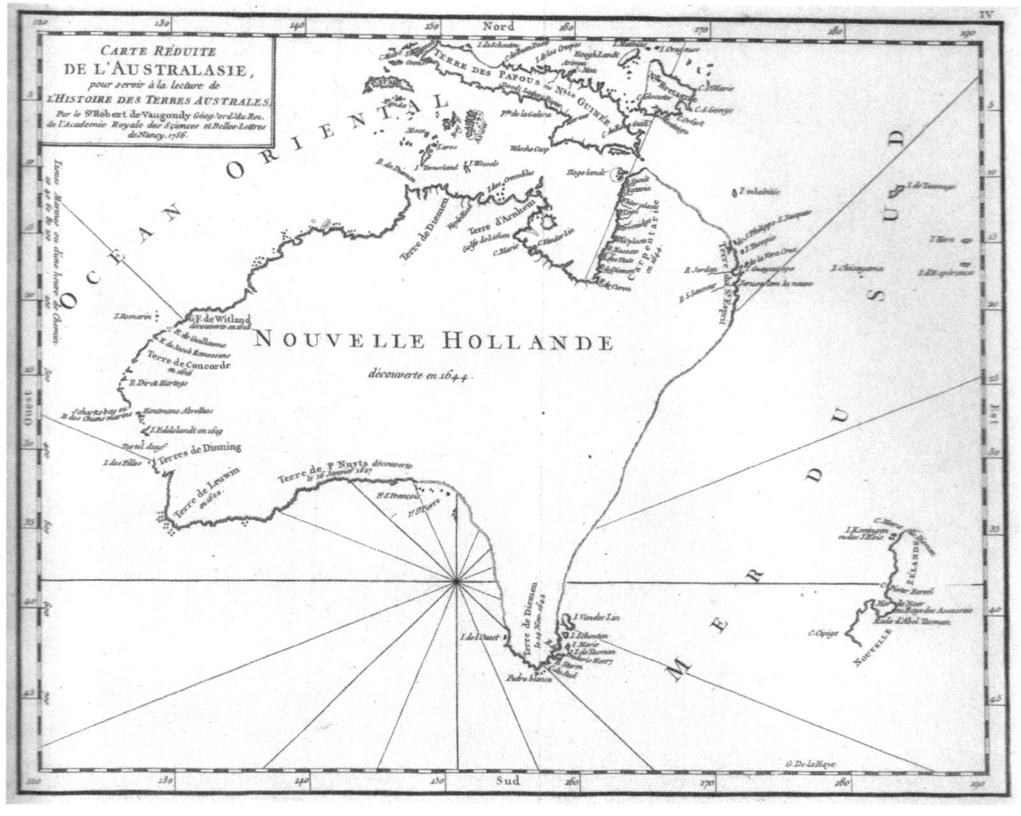

Vaugondy joins Quiros' Australia to New Holland and opens Torres Strait. But if he knew of Torres' voyage why does his New Guinea end at the longitude of Cape York?

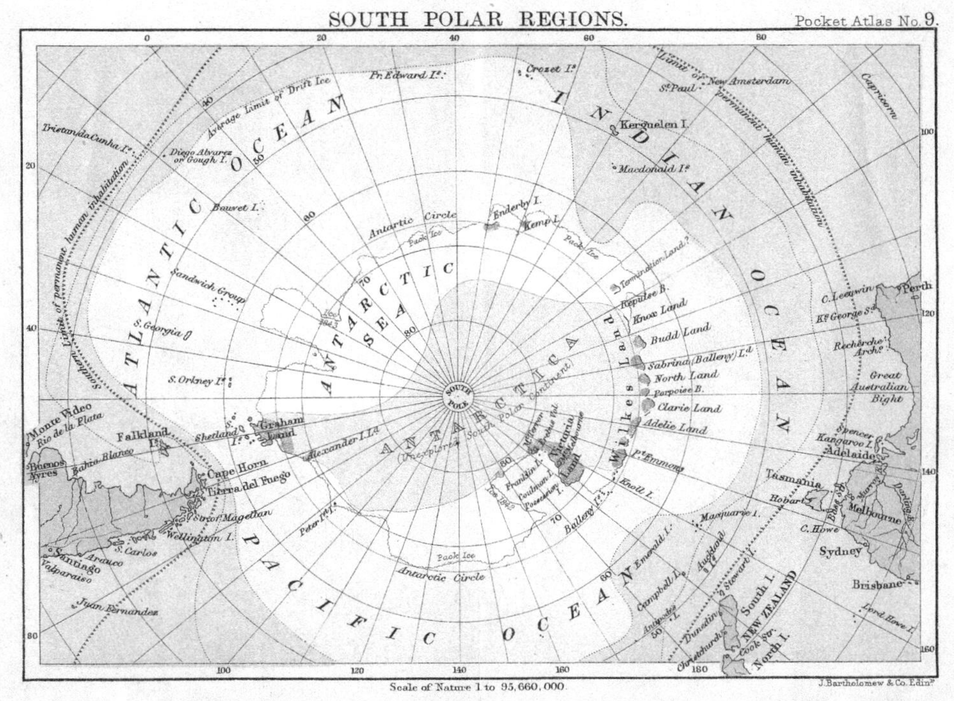

John George Bartholomew baptises a continent, 1889

Quiros was to sail from Peru 'to discover New Guinea, Java Major, and other southern lands and islands'. He would then continue west about and return to Spain, making magnetic observations as he went (because he had claimed that magnetic variation could be used as a means of determining longitude). Philip's supporting orders to the Viceroy of Peru declared that the King took 'particular inclination and pleasure' in the prospect that the discovery would bring the holy faith among those remote peoples 'for the glory of God and the public benefit'. The public that would benefit was not specified, but there can be little doubt that both Quiros and his monarch genuinely believed that Spanish rule was a material as well as a moral blessing for subject peoples.[7]

With his painful experience of Doña Ysabel in mind, Quiros sought the same rare privilege that Mendaña had been granted – power to nominate who would succeed him in the event of incapacity or death. He tells us that after some trouble he succeeded in obtaining it, but the royal order he cites as proof tells a different story. The King accepted the argument about the importance of an orderly transition but cautiously gave power of nomination to the Viceroy of Peru. Quiros interpreted this to mean that at least until he reached Lima the power was his. At face value, Quiros' concern was to ensure that the expedition would proceed whether or not he survived as far as Lima to lead it, but there is another possible explanation. He was shipwrecked crossing the Atlantic, but was able to make his way to Caracas in 1604, where he 'found' three orphaned children of his dead brother. The two boys, who would be putative heirs-on-voyage, he took with him to Panama and Peru.[8]

He found that his royal orders and authorisations carried little weight with the colonial officials from whom he sought assistance in Panama and elsewhere. When he arrived at Lima in March 1605 he was so destitute that he had to sleep in the shop of a charitable potter until the newly-arrived Viceroy could receive him. The Count of Monterey had been transferred from Mexico and was unenthusiastic about providing ships for another cross-Pacific expedition. It seemed to him that it would be better for Quiros to depart from Manila (or indeed anywhere other than the Viceroyality of Peru).

He was not alone in his reservations. Doña Ysabel and her husband were now living in Peru and Fernando de Castro protested that the expedition would infringe on the rights to the Solomon Islands that he had inherited from Mendaña through the Governess. Quiros regaled Castro with the arguments that had persuaded the King, until 'the good cavalier was convinced by my pious reasoning, and he said that, as he understood it, he would condemn the soul who pretended to disturb me'.[9] History does not record how Don Fernando was received when he explained his change of heart to Doña Ysabel.

For someone who was sceptical about the expedition, Monterey made thorough preparations, while Quiros became increasingly anxious as the best months for sailing slipped by. The King had authorised two ships; Monterey added a *zabra*, or launch, so that news of success could be brought back to him while Quiros continued the circumnavigation. Monterey told Quiros that he wanted to nominate a next-in-command, as ordered by the King. Quiros represented that he would not wish to sail with anyone who knew that he had been so nominated, 'an arrangement fraught with obvious danger'. He claimed that his only purpose in raising the issue with the King had been to ensure that the expedition would reach Lima even if he did not, but here he was, fit and well, so the Viceroy could leave the selection to him 'when it appeared necessary'.

And there, as far as Quiros knew, the matter rested. The Viceroy contented himself with appointing a young gentleman of impeccable breeding and good education but little relevant experience, Don Diego de Prado y Tovar, 'as a person necessary for the carrying out of the enterprise'.[10] Luis Vaez de Torres, an experienced Breton seaman,[11] was given command of the *almiranta*, nicknamed *San Pedrico*. Against the wishes of Quiros, Monterey selected as Chief Pilot Juan Ochoa de Bilboa, who was given the choice making this voyage, without pay, or of serving the six years in the galleys to which he had earlier been sentenced. The second pilot, Pedro Bernal Cermeño, was placed in charge of the *zabra*, *Los Tres Reyes*. The expedition, 136 persons in all, including Quiros' nephews, sailed from Callao on 21 December 1605. A notable omission was Juan Luis Arias, who had applied in hopes of verifying the discoveries of Juan Fernandez. Quiros embarked in poor health and would remain in that state for much of the voyage.

At sea, Quiros outlined his plan of exploration and gave Torres the orders to be followed in the event of separation. The ships would proceed WSW to 30°S, where the southern continent should lie. If no land were seen, the course would be changed to north-west until they reached the latitude of Santa Cruz. Thence they would hold due west to the island. If one ship reached Santa Cruz but the other did not, the survivor would steer south-west to 20°S, thence north-west to 4°S. There it would turn west to find the coast of New Guinea, which it would follow before proceeding to Manila.

On 19 January 1606 land was seen from Torres' *almiranta* and the fleet steered south to investigate, but on the following morning there was nothing in sight. The wind became variable and bad weather set in. A great swell rolled in from the south and some of the crew became anxious. 'Whither are they taking us, in this great gulf, in the winter season?' they cried.[12] In 26°S Quiros abandoned the push south. Torres protested in writing that there was no obvious reason for not adhering to the plan, but the ships were turned north-west. Prado was of the opinion that Quiros had listened to the advice of some who were more concerned to get to Manila and make a profit on the wine they had brought aboard than to explore. It was even suggested that Quiros had a financial interest in the goods. Quiros later blamed the decision on the delayed departure from Callao, which had cost them several weeks of good weather.

The new course quickly took them to land but the initial discoveries were only islands, and uninhabited ones at that. Their very abundance reinforced Quiros in the view that 'the mother of islands' could not be far away but, as usual, the longer the voyage went on the louder the crew grumbled. Prado suspected Ochoa of plotting mutiny and informed Quiros, who took no action other than to promise the crew as much silver and gold as they could carry, and pearls by the hatful, if they could find an island with even two 'Indians' to save.[13] It did not satisfy Ochoa, who declared in public that they had already sailed 2,200 leagues from Peru, which was 350 beyond where Quiros had said Santa Cruz lay. He was implying that they were lost. Quiros quickly convened a meeting of the pilots, which unanimously agreed that Ochoa had grossly overestimated.

At the inhabited island of Taumaco, Prado removed himself to the *almiranta*, 'seeing the little remedy that was to be expected', but Quiros had only been biding his time. Ochoa was seized and sent across to the *almiranta*, accompanied by an oral instruction to Torres that he was to be garroted on arrival. Torres, counselled by Prado, declined to act without a written order.

Taumaco's headman, a friendly and informative native named Tumai, told them that they were only five days sail from their destination. He knew of Mendaña's visit eleven years earlier, and about Spanish firearms, and was eager to co-operate. Quiros asked him what he knew of other lands in the vicinity and Tumai answered by pointing to the ground under his feet, then to the sea, then to various points on the horizon. He held up his fingers and counted off as many as sixty islands and a very large land, which he called Manicolo. To explain the distances, 'he pointed to the sun, then rested his head on his hand, shut his eyes, and with his fingers counted the number of nights one had to sleep on the voyage'.[14]

The next day Quiros assembled a throng of natives on the beach and read from a paper all that Tumai had told him, with which they concurred. Some were amazed at the recital and examined the paper on both sides. Not all of the Spaniards were as careful as Quiros when it came to verifying information. One day some natives were seen eating meat and a Spaniard, perhaps suspecting cannibalism, asked what it was. He was shown hide with hair on it and the native put his hands on his head. This was taken as evidence that cattle were to be found in the 'great lands'. Everything seemed to point in the same direction – south. All thought of watering at Santa Cruz was dropped. The southern continent was within reach.

The Spaniards repaid Tumai's hospitality by kidnapping four of his subjects, three of whom jumped overboard and swam to shore at the first opportunity. As the ships proceeded south, the islands seen grew in number and size. While making for one of them, Ochoa's replacement as Chief Pilot, Gaspar Gonzalez de Leza, noted a 'great land bearing south'. They continued west but two days later, on 27 April, 'at five in the afternoon we discovered a great land with high mountains, which promised to be no less than mainland.'[15] The first sighting had been of Margaritana Island and the second, also south of their track, was known locally as Ireney. Quiros assumed that these northernmost islands of the New Hebrides group (today respectively Maewo and Santo) were connected to each other and to other lofty land seen further south.

Santo presents a deceitful face to anyone approaching from the north. A great bay, estimated by Quiros to be twenty leagues in circuit, four leagues wide at the entrance and three at its head, bites deep into the island. Chief Pilot Gonzales described it as large enough for all the fleets of the world to enter. Big Bay, as it is known today, is certainly grand enough to be the gateway to a continent, but the impressive mountains at its back fall steeply away to the southern shore. As continents go, Santo is a hollow sham. Tumai's Manicolo (Malakula), slightly smaller, is the next substantial island to the south. Quiros explored the bay and grew more and more confident that here was what he had set out to find. The inhabitants were reluctant to accept him as the agent of their deliverance and salvation, probably because the Spaniards again resorted to kidnap as a means of establishing communication and extorting food.

The natives were hostile rather than dangerous, but among Quiros' early acts was to create officers of war and marine. One of his nephews, Lucas de Quiros, was elevated to the dignity of Royal Ensign. He and all the other officers were made Knights of the Holy Ghost, an order of chivalry personally created by his uncle. The pantomime continued with an act of possession on the following day, when Quiros made a speech that would not have been out of place at the Academy Awards. He called on the heavens, the earth, the waters with all their creatures, and all those present, to witness that he was taking possession in the name of the Holy Trinity, Jesus, the Virgin Mary, Saints Peter and Paul, the Apostles, the Pope, the whole Catholic Church, 'all pious and just persons who have a right to these possessions', St Francis and his Order, John of God and his Order, the military of the Order of the Holy Ghost and – almost as an afterthought – Philip III. The bay was named for St Philip and St James, its port was Vera Cruz and the city to be erected nearby was New Jerusalem. Two leagues distant, the River Jordan flowed into the bay. The whole, 'all these islands and lands newly discovered, and that I shall discover as far as the Pole', was to be known henceforth as Austrialia del Espiritu Santo. Quiros declared that it had more than two thousand leagues of coast and was thickly populated.

Obviously such a grand declaration had to be followed by a grand act and so Quiros convened his council of war to create the Municipality of New Jerusalem. Most of the senior people who had not been made Knights of the Holy Ghost were now given one of the 21 magistracies, but there was one glaring anomaly. Don Diego de Prado y Tovar, a genuine Knight of Calatrava, added to the expedition by the Viceroy to give it some tone, was made Storekeeper-General, senior only to the Custom House Guardians, who were glorified pound keepers. Prado was scornful.

> It was all wind, both walls and foundation, for he sought to cover up thus what he had promised on the way and was mistaken … I said to him before his friends … God has given you Indians, not only two but thousands as in the islands … and now this of Ireney (Peace) which you call the great Australia of the Holy Ghost. We have only found the black devils with poisoned arrows; what has become of the riches? We quite understand that all your affairs are imaginary and as such have gone off in wind.[16]

Sphere der Winde

Von den vier Winde vnd jrer zwölff Ecken.

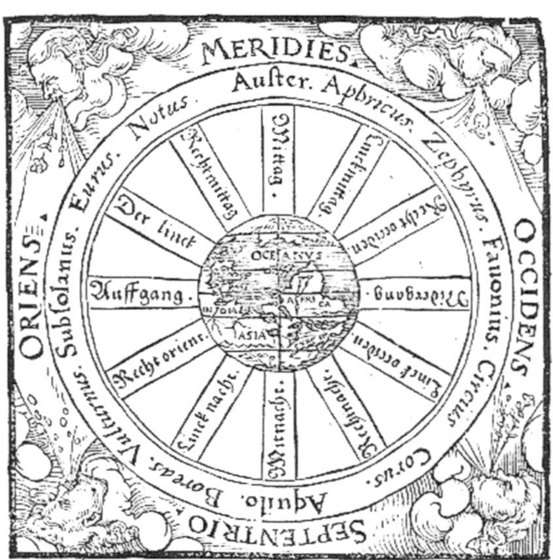

Diß Spher der Wind/ zeigt an wenn Mars regiert das denn Wind vnd wolcken kommen von mitag/So aber Jupiter regiert/so kommen sie von dem Nord/vnd so Saturnus regiert so kommen sie von Ost/NordOst/vnd von Nord/NordOst/ vnd also fürbas.

Teutsch's Australia anticipates Antarctica

Prado wrote Australia as we spell the word today. Quiros coined the extended form Austrialia in homage to the ancestral home of the Hapsburgs, but he also described it as part of Australia Incognita.[17] They had been anticipated by the Teutsch *Astronomia* of 1545, which had claimed the word for a notional continent around the Antarctic Circle, presumably extending south from Tierra del Fuego.

After a month in the bay, Quiros was keen to discover whether Espiritu Santo extended towards Chile, as the published maps promised. He gave orders to explore to windward, south-east, expecting to find

200–300 leagues of coast that they would survey for ports and anchorages, noting soundings, rocks, banks, and latitudes. No sooner had they left the bay than a great wind blew in their faces and forced them to reduce sail. Torres said that they should seek shelter and Quiros authorised a return to the bay. Entering it against the wind proved to be difficult and for two days the ships were on a beat from one side of the bay to the other, making little headway towards Vera Cruz. In the evening of 11 May the *zabra*, most weatherly of the three vessels, made the port. The *almiranta* followed but the *capitana*, making shorter tacks, had lost ground. As the wind was freshening, Quiros consulted his pilots. Cermeño said the ship could not reach the anchorage. He advised anchoring under one of the capes until the wind moderated. Quiros, who was ill, agreed and went to bed.

When he next came up, at noon the following day, the ship had been blown from the bay and was to leeward of its west cape. He sought to reduce leeway by ordering more sail but was told the ship's seams would open under the pounding. The drift to leeward continued and after three days the land was no longer in sight. Quiros' faithful secretary, Luis de Belmonte y Bermudez, believed that advantage had been taken of his master 'owing to the Captain being disabled by illness on this and other occasions when the pilots wasted time, obliging him to believe what they said, to take what they gave, measured out as they pleased'.[18]

The picture is of a man no longer in charge, but the situation may have been even worse than Bermudez was prepared to admit. Some of the crew afterwards told Prado that the long-threatened mutiny had taken place. When Quiros had asked why the ship had not been anchored behind the cape, 'he was told to shut his mouth and go to his cabin, where they put the Portuguese grocer and his nephews with guards', but seeing how submissive Quiros was they had refrained from throwing him into the sea.[19] This goes some way towards explaining what happened next. No further attempt was made to return to the bay. Instead, the ship ran north with the wind for Santa Cruz, the expedition's originally appointed rendezvous. Given that Quiros had redirected the expedition to Espiritu Santo, it was a forlorn expectation that Torres would go looking for him at Santa Cruz.

When the latitude of the island was reached there was uncertainty about whether it lay east or west. Some aboard said that they should sail to Manila, which was the Viceroy's order in the event of separation, but by vote of the whole ship's company it was decided that they would head for Acapulco. Quiros consoled himself that at least he would survive to report his finding of the southern continent to the King. For the rest, he was confident that Torres, if safe, would follow the instructions he had been given and 'discover more lands'.

The west coast of New Guinea

As Quiros was preparing to sail from Callao a small vessel slipped quietly out of the port of Bantam on the north coast of Java. The event did not escape the notice of a temporarily resident Englishman, John Saris, whose business it was to keep an eye on the activities of commercial rivals like the Dutch. He reported that on 18 November 1605 'a small Pinnasse of the Flemmings' had departed for New Guinea 'which, as it is said, affordeth great store of Gold'.[20] The Dutch had been in the East Indies for only a few years, but as early as 1602 had sent Willem Cornelisz Schouten from Banda to Ceram in that same pinnace or *jacht*, the *Duyfken*, with instructions to learn what he could of New Guinea. It was little enough. The Ceramese could only say that there were white people living on the south coast, which they believed was inhabited by Portuguese although they had seen none of their ships.[21]

In fact no trace remains to indicate that the Portuguese had penetrated so far. In the push to displace their rivals the Dutch were aggressively probing the limits of the archipelago in ways that the Iberians had scarcely troubled themselves about, Eredia excepted. The 1605 voyage of the *Duyfken* was part of an ambitious program of commercial exploration under a new flag, one bearing the initials of the *Vereenighde Oostindische Compagnie*. The letters became famous throughout the world, identifying the United East Indies Company even to people who knew no Dutch. Similarly, it was sufficient to speak of 'the Managers' when referring to the Company's central administration. *Duyfken*'s new captain, Willem Jansz, was tasked with finding what there was of trading value on 'the lands east of Banda unto Nova Guinea'.[22]

A copy of his chart, the only surviving record of the voyage, shows a departure from Banda, the nutmeg island, on an easterly course that took the *Duyfken* north of the Kai and Aru Islands. She made landfall on the New Guinea coast north of False Cape, which is a treacherous lee shore during the north-west monsoon. It was not possible to make much offing until the cape was rounded, when the sheets could be eased and some distance put between ship and shore. Jansz chose to try his luck in deeper water. He left the coast and proceeded in a south-easterly direction, towards the islands of Mendaña and Quiros.[23] On some undetermined date early in 1606 an extensive coast came into view, stretching north and south as far at the eye could see. The mouth of a small river beckoned. Gold and spice could wait, for here was the promise of wood and water, always the mariner's first thought at landfall.

There was nothing to indicate that this one was special. Although they did not know it, Jansz and his crew were looking at Australia, and in so doing were the first Europeans to set eyes on a continent entirely confined to the austral hemisphere. The river is called the Pennefather now, but Jansz named it for the wood and water he was able to obtain there – *R. met het Bosch*. He placed this 'River with the Bush' in about 11°45'S, half a degree short of its true latitude. He sailed south, scanning the dry, baked shore for anything of value and in 14°S paused to take stock. His supercargo, Jan Lodewycksz van Rosingeyn, had seen nothing from which a Dutch merchant could make a guilder. Cape York aboriginal tradition recalls early white visitors and their strange conveyance. If it is Jansz they are remembering, he had nothing they wanted either, so honours were even. He would have been astonished to learn that the common red earth that looked so sterile would be precious to later generations. It was bauxite, the mineral that smelts into aluminium.

Cape Keerweer (Turnabout) marks the furthest south achieved on the voyage, but the matter-of fact name does not give us a reason for the event. If the traditional aboriginal account is to be believed, the Dutch landed a party to dig for water, conscripted aboriginals to help and abused two of their women. In the resulting skirmish, five or six Dutchmen were killed.[24] As the numbers amounted to as much as a third of his crew, Jansz would have found it difficult to continue with the voyage, but continue he did. Rather than sail directly for Banda, he retraced his track to the Pennefather River and began exploring northwards. At the tip of the Cape York Peninsula he found shoal water but continued northward, expecting again to fall in with mainland, always keeping west of the numerous reefs and islands. In 9°S he found his course barred by a particularly ominous stretch of discoloured shoal water. He charted it as a 'foul bank' and turned west, shadowing the New Guinea coast without seeing it as far as False Cape. A more detailed examination of this part of the coast was followed by an excursion to Os Papua, north of the Aru Islands.

Jansz had encountered three landmasses, more or less equidistant from each other, stepping from south-east to north-west. The northern one, Os Papua, he knew to be part of New Guinea. He had no reason to suspect that his middle and southern landfalls were any different and labelled the last accordingly, thus misrepresenting a new continent as the extension of a long-known island. Whatever, it was a useless discovery. In June 1607 the news came to Saris in Bantam by way of an Indian captain newly arrived from Banda.

> … he told me that the Flemmings Pinnasse which went upon discovery for Nova Ginny, was returned to Banda, having found the Iland: but in sending their men on shoare to intreate of Trade, there were nine of them killed by the Heathens, which are man-eaters; so they were constrained to returne, finding no good to be done there.[25]

Contrary to the aboriginal account, the reference to cannibals points to the New Guinea coast rather than the Cape York Peninsula as the scene of the *Duyfken*'s losses. It may be significant that Jansz's chart shows no coasting along Os Papua, but only a single, possibly disastrous, landfall. Certainly Os Papua was the end of Jansz's exploration, which is what one might expect in the event of serious crew loss. At Banda, Jansz was transferred to command a larger ship. The *Duyfken* may have made a further voyage to New Guinea[26] but at Amboyna in May 1607 she was added to the fleet being assembled for an assault on the Moluccas. Her exploring days were over.

The summit of the Antarctic Pole

It is an ironic coincidence that just as Jansz was mistaking Australia for the island of New Guinea, Quiros was abandoning the island of Santo, which he had declared to be the southern continent Austrialia. The men that he left behind at Vera Cruz had not seen the *capitana* leave the bay. Some suspected that she had been wrecked, and Torres took out the *zabra* and a boat to look for signs. Prado told him not to bother, 'for the crew had determined to mutiny if they saw an opportunity, the wind had invited them and they had mutinied'. Torres was less sure and waited in the bay for 15 days in case Quiros should return. Then he produced a sealed envelope that the Viceroy had given him before departure. Because of Quiros' concern that no successor be publicly identified, the envelope was only to be opened in the event of his separation or incapacity. Torres probably expected that he, as Admiral, would succeed, but Monterey had made sure that there would be a Castilian gentleman available: his orders named Prado.

It was not quite that simple. The orders assumed that Prado was with Quiros in the *capitana*. Any ship that separated, the *capitana* included, was ordered to proceed to 20°S to see if there was land. If no land was found, the ship was to go to Manila and wait four months for the others. In the absence of any evidence to the contrary, Torres had to assume that Quiros was following orders and heading for Manila. Only if he failed to show up there would the succession come into effect. Until then, Prado's responsibilities in respect of discovery could be exercised where the *almiranta* went.

Prado seems to have accepted the ambiguity of his position. He simply records that he 'accepted the charge as committed to him, and thenceforth executed his office', noting particularly that *after* Manila the expedition was to sail to Spain via the Moluccas and the Cape of Good Hope, carefully charting the route. What the new command relationship meant in practice became immediately apparent at the officers' council convened to discuss the orders. A majority was for ignoring them, but Torres insisted that they be fulfilled. He prevailed because 'my condition was different to that of … Quiros'. Thereafter Prado raised banners, cowed natives, claimed possessions and charted harbours, but only where Torres took him.[27]

South, the orders said; south-west, the wind and currents allowed. Torres was unable to circumnavigate Santo, but before the shore receded from view Prado was satisfied that Quiros had been mistaken. It was after all only another island, about 30 leagues in circumference. Torres pushed on to 21°S, one zealous degree further than instructed, and 'would have gone further if the weather had permitted; for the ship was good. It was right to act in this manner for these are not voyages made every day'.[28] Holding south-west for a few days longer would have brought him to the Australian coast somewhere between Keppel Bay and Moreton Bay, or to a grinding halt on the coral ramparts of the Great Barrier Reef. Instead, Torres turned northwards and found the Louisade Islands off the coast of New Guinea. On reaching the mainland, Prado charted the islands that enclose the south of Milne Bay but Torres was unable to weather its eastern point.

There was no knowing how long they might have to wait before a change of wind allowed passage along the north coast of the great island. Torres did not accept the delay. He turned west, along what appeared to be a southern coast. Prado was doubtful. He believed that New Guinea was connected to the south polar regions. Was Torres about to freeze them all to death trying to find a new route to Manila? Some maps showed a channel between New Guinea and the reputed southland they had been seeking at Santo. Was the fact that they had found no southland at Santo, or south-west of it, evidence for or against the existence of a strait? Even the most recent map of New Guinea, which showed a strait, had the honesty to admit that it was *incertu*.[29]

The first indications were reassuring. The coast trended WNW, and they followed it for 300 leagues, the latitude diminishing from 11½° to 9°S. At an offshore island Prado repeated the act of possession he had performed at Milne Bay, but here he gave the land a name, Magna Margarita, after the Queen of Spain. The vessels were then entering the Gulf of Papua, the start of a great shoal covered with as little as three fathoms of water and nowhere more than nine. On the other side of the Gulf, with the water continuing shallow, the coastline turned south. One can almost hear Prado muttering 'told you so'.

Even when the coast resumed its westward course, in 9°S, the seaman's aversion to shoals caused Torres to stand out from the land in search of deeper water. Instead he found islands, rocks and reefs that forced him south-west, where 'there were very large islands and they seemed more on the southern part'. His laconic account glosses over the difficulty of the navigation. The ship's boat earned its keep by feeling the way ahead. Torres used tidal currents to counteract the wind's persistent attempts to strand the ships. Without expendable shallow-draught tenders it is most unlikely that he would have proceeded so far into the labyrinth. This was no place for ships to be wrecked, particularly as potential rescuers would not know where to look for them even if they were so inclined. As it was, the *San Pedrico* had at least one bumping and only escaped serious damage because the bottom was mud. It took the two vessels about a month to cover 50 leagues.

Torres cited shortage of provisions as the reason for abandoning his attempt to find the southern end of the bank, but he was also daunted by the 'infinity of islands … for I doubt if in ten years it would be possible to inspect the coasts of all the islands we saw'. In 11°S the south-west course finally carried them clear of the islands and Torres turned north-west as soon as open sea presented itself, west of what is now Prince of Wales Island. Not until the expedition reached western New Guinea, after two months on the bank, was there again deep water under the keel.[30] There can be little doubt that among the 'very large islands' seen on the way to 11°S were parts of Cape York, the northernmost point of the Australian mainland. Without realising it, Torres had been looking at the continent that Quiros had hoped to discover, albeit some distance from where he had expected to find it.[31]

Although the expedition was now encountering natives who possessed goods of Chinese manufacture, Prado remained sceptical about the alleged strait south of New Guinea until they encountered an Italian-speaking Moor of Mediterranean origin. He told Prado that they were five days sail from Bachan in the Moluccas.

> It is impossible to exaggerate the pleasure we all felt at such good news, and certainly for us he was like an angel, for we already gave ourselves up for lost. And as in the modern maps they colour [New Guinea] as mainland of the summit of the Antarctic pole, we thought it was so until this man told us where we were.[32]

The remark speaks volumes for the quality of Torres' seamanship and leadership. He could have waited at Milne Bay for the wind to change but chose instead to test the mapmakers' theory, confident of his ability to retrace his course should their strait prove to be a chimera. With subordinates disinclined to follow the Viceroy's sealed orders, a disrated Chief Pilot who had been condemned as a mutineer, and Monterey's appointee looking over his shoulder, he nevertheless persevered and prevailed.

The Moor also told them that the Governor of the Philippines had seized the Moluccas and carried the King of Ternate to Manila. The islands were insecurely in the hands of Camp Master Juan de Esquivel. It was now November 1606, and as the expedition neared Bachan, a man in a canoe gingerly approached the ships and asked what nationality they were. Portuguese, the Spanish lied, at which the man accused them of being 'nothing but Dutchmen'. Torres then admitted that they were Spanish, much to the relief of the canoeist, a Portuguese himself.

Eight days earlier a Dutch ship had left the island. It had 24 guns but only ten men, and those very sick. The man in the canoe had thought that these new visitors might be her consorts, equally unwelcome.[33] Philip III's loyal Spanish subjects might have succeeded in reinforcing Philip III's reluctant Portuguese subjects in the Moluccas, but both were now under threat from Philip III's rebellious Dutch subjects. The King of Bachan, a Spanish client, sought Torres' help to put down a rebellion and it was some time before the expedition could proceed to Ternate. There the hard-pressed Esquivel commandeered the *zabra*. Torres sailed on in the *almiranta* to Manila, not arriving until May 1607.

Nine days after his arrival a familiar ship entered the bay. It was the lost *capitana*, the *San Pedro y San Pablo*. Quiros was not aboard but some of his expeditioners were. They told Torres and Prado of the decision to sail to Acapulco and of safe arrival there, and of the disintegration of Quiros' authority. The word mutiny was not used, but they were unsparing of Quiros, saying that in Mexico City some of the crew had publicly condemned him as a fool and a madman, following which the Viceroy had dismissed his 'discovery of the southern continent' as a deception.[34] There were those in Manila who were also willing to put in a bad word. The Chief Justice of Cavite at the time was none other than Felipe Corzo, who had deserted the second Mendaña expedition with the *galeot*, and who now told Prado that Quiros had been responsible for the loss of that fleet and Mendaña as well.

The denigration of Quiros did not influence Torres. As ever, he made up his own mind about the proper course to pursue. He saw it as his duty to report events subsequent to separation of the ships and on 15 June 1607 wrote to his erstwhile commander. The letter had to chase Quiros across two oceans and took two years to reach him.

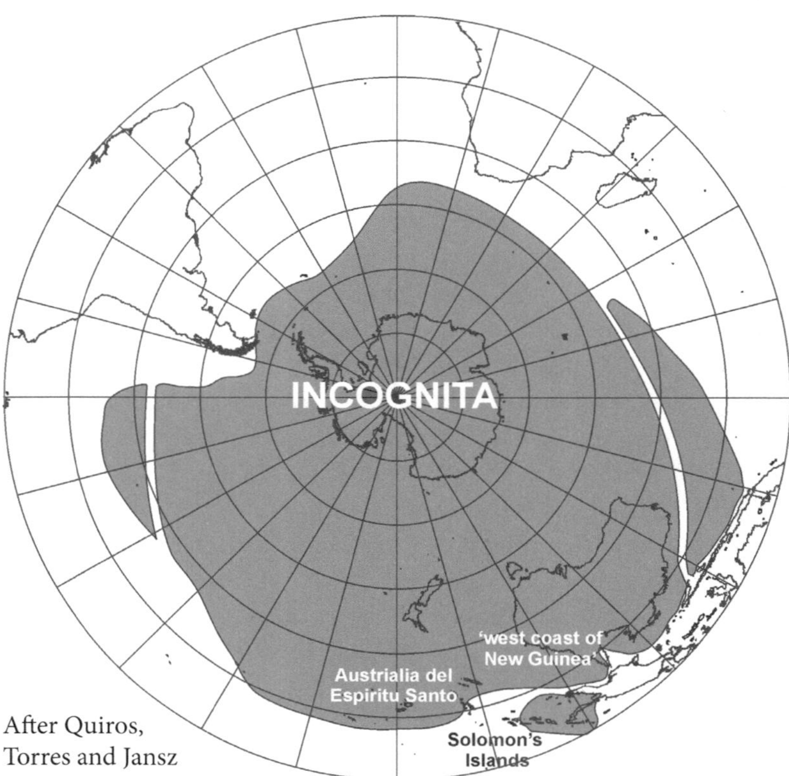

After Quiros, Torres and Jansz

The augmentation of the Indies

> Geographers, in austral maps
> With country-fables fill their gaps;
> And in place of mighty oceans
> Delineate fantastic notions.
> (after Jonathon Swift)

John Saris, the English factor at Bantam in Java, was a merchant adventurer, with the emphasis on merchant. The sailors' gossip he filtered for news about discoveries by foreigners was a poor substitute for the information that had been gained first-hand by Drake and Cavendish. English ships now went to the Orient to trade, not to explore, but the Elizabethan imagination was not to be thwarted by anything as prosaic as lack of transport when it came to penetrating the unknown south. In *Twelfth Night*, Shakespeare describes Malvolio's face as 'more lined than the new map, with the augmentation of the Indies'. The map was that of Edward Wright, published in 1599 to illustrate Hakluyt's *Voyages*. It was crazed with rhumb lines, a spider's web of sailing courses. The augmentation in question was Sarmiento's Solomon Islands.

Although the bard had turned cartographers' work to literary ends, he was referring to a real map. Not so Bishop Joseph Hall, who in 1605 drew his own. In the tradition of Thomas More, Hall has his narrator's friend, Beroaldus, propose an exploratory voyage to the largest unknown portion of the globe, partly in pursuit of fame and partly because

> It has always disturbed me to meet constantly with *Terra Australis Incognita* on geographical maps, and indeed, is there anyone who is not completely senseless who would read this without some silent indignation? For if they know it to be a *continent*, and a *southern* one, how can they then call it *unknown*? And if it be unknown, why have all the geographers described the form and location to me? They are idle men who say it to be thus and still claim not to know it themselves! And finally, who will not be vexed to remain ignorant of that which it is profitable for us to know.[35]

He condemns the indolence of the times, supposing that there are yet to be discovered other men like the Chinese, 'perhaps no less cultured than we'. He conjures up Solomon's Ophir, and equates it with Atlantis. He recalls a prophecy by the Roman philosopher Seneca – that in time Ocean will 'relax the bond of circumstances' and reveal a great continent – and denies that it has been fulfilled by the discovery of America. He persuades his friends to accompany him, their reservations swept away on the flood of his rhetoric: 'Behold, my world, I am coming to you now … full of hope and confidence, and in my boldness either to share you with the world or to share my body with you'.[36] Regrettably, Beroaldus' enthusiasm carries him only as far as France, where he allows himself to be diverted to home and family. He leaves the narrator to make the voyage alone, warning him that to abandon it will lead to ridicule after raising so many expectations! After two years, the narrator arrives at a land south of the Cape of Good Hope.

Whereas More's Utopia had been no more than a small offshore island near the southern continent, Hall appropriated the mainland and labelled every corner of it. Like More, he wrote in Latin. The title of his satire translates as *Another World and Yet the Same*, and in it the vices of Europe, specifically England, are amplified to make this world a dystopia. One of its countries is Viraginia, or Nova Gynia, a land where women rule in a very misanthropic manner. Viraginia is where geographers place the Land of Parrots, says Hall, and Nova Gynia ('which others incorrectly call Guinea') is the extreme east of the southern continent, 'very near to Maletur and Beach'. The continent is twice the size of the rest of the Earth's landmasses combined, thus making the geographers' neglect even more culpable.

Hall's Another World and Yet the Same fills the southern hemisphere

The significance of Hall's geography is that, although by 1605 no-one would have been deceived by the Mandevillean marvels his narrator claimed to have found, they were irrefutable for the very good reason that their alleged location was unexplored. Furthermore, Hall continued the old tradition that whatever had still not been sailed over in the southern hemisphere must be land. With New Guinea he came up against the boundary of the known but, after making his Nova Gynia pun, he neatly side-stepped the issue by insisting that this was not New Guinea but a separate place found in the same part of the world. His map shows it to the south and west of New Guinea, with its southern province named Eugynia, the land of Good Women, whose inhabitants are honorable and virtuous.

When he translated Hall's book into English, John Healey rendered Eugynia as Black Swan province. If latitude and longitude are superimposed on Hall's map, one finds that Eugynia is very near what later became known as Swan River in Western Australia. Did Healey know that black swans – birds unknown in Europe at the time – would be found there? Hardly. Healey had found his swans in the library. To satirise the satirist, he borrowed a simile from Juvenal, who in a celebrated jibe had characterised the virtuous wife as 'a rare bird on earth, as rare as a black swan'.[37] It is a pity that Healey and Hall did not live to view the specimens brought to Europe by Vlamingh at the end of the century, living metaphors of antipodean inversion.

Although the southland continued to figure as a rhetorical device in English writing as the century progressed, geographical invention flagged as the maritime glory of Elizabeth's reign faded into memory. Francis Bacon's *New Atlantis* was posthumously published in 1627. The philosopher-statesman was promoting the creation of an academy for scientific research, an idea that the next generation would realise in the form of the Royal Society. Bacon chose a part of the South Sea 'utterly unknown' in which to discover his ideal academy partly to make a point about the self-cancelling advantages of solitude for intellectual pursuits. The inhabitants of Bensalem, descendants of the Atlantians, deplore visitors as disturbers of their peace, but regularly send spies abroad to keep the Society of Solomon's House in touch with developments in the outside world.[38]

That same year John Speed published *A New and Accurat Map of the World*. He had nothing to add to Drake and Cavendish except a rather plaintive label affixed to 'The Southerne Unknowne Land', which complained that 'this south part of the world containing almost the third part of the globe is yet unknown, certain sea coasts excepted: which rather show there is a land than descry either land, people or commodities'.[39] This is implicit criticism, but it is not accompanied by advocacy or remedy; there is a curious fatalism about it that would have been anathema to the Elizabethans. Large projects had fallen into disfavor with the failure of Raleigh's Guiana venture, and the execution of its projector in 1618 was not calculated to encourage others. Sir William Courten's 1625 request for a grant of all *Terra Australis incognita* eastwards and westwards from the Strait of Le Maire was not even acknowledged. His large ambitions were played out on the tiny island of Barbados.

The spirit of the times was introspective. By 1638, when playwright Richard Brome staged *The Antipodes*, a Jonsonian comedy of deception, he did not even feel obliged to take his characters beyond the limits of London. An antipodean voyage is feigned to cure a wife-neglecting husband whose head is stuffed with Mandeville. Inversions are represented as conventional behavior in the southern world to which he has ostensibly been transported. Healey's black swans take flight again, here accompanied by white ravens. The play treats interest in exploration as a form of insanity, bound to distract a man from his domestic obligations. It foreshadows the civil war and European quarrels that would be a demanding reality for Britain over the next half-century. Beyond the seas, the first British Empire would begin to take shape in North America, but exploration to augment the Indies would fall to others.

5
Zyderlants

Determination to face down opposition can degenerate into obsession, and one symptom of the slide is selective use of evidence. When Luis Vaez de Torres' letter reached Spain, more than two years after it had been written, Pedro Fernández de Quiros seized on it. He was trying to persuade his sovereign to give him a thousand men with which to colonise Austrialia, and he did not scruple to misrepresent Torres.

> Touching the extent of these regions newly discovered, grounding my judgment on that which I have seen with my own eyes, and upon that which Luis Vaez de Torres, admiral of my fleet, has presented to your Majesty, the length thereof is as great as all Europe and Asia the less, unto the Sea of Bachu, Persia, and all the isles, as well of the Ocean, as of the Mediterranean Sea, taking England and Ireland into this account. This unknown country is the fifth part of the Terrestrial Globe, and extends itself to such length, that in probability it is twice greater in Kingdoms and Seignories, than all that which at this day do acknowledge subjection and obedience to your Majesty ... The land which we have discovered is all seated within the Torrid Zone, and a great tract thereof reaches to the Equinoctial Circle ... And if success proves answerable to hope, there will be found Antipodes to the better part of Africa, to all Europe, and to the greater portion of Asia.[1]

What is more, Quiros argued, even the lands we have discovered in 15°S are better than Spain, so the others lying further south 'must by proportion and analogy prove some terrestrial Paradise'. To read Quiros, all of the lands of Torres' 'confused report' appear to be adjacent to Espritu Santo – if not actually part of it – but the King's advisers knew better because Torres had also written to the King. His purpose in writing was to apologize for not coming home. He complained that the Manila administration would not provide food for his crew, much less the assistance he needed to continue the voyage. He had no idea when he would be able to leave Manila but he had followed his instructions to the letter, as His Majesty would see from this brief account of the voyage so far, and he would report in person as soon as the colonial authorities obeyed the royal order to assist him on his way.

Torres' unvarnished account threw Quiros' wishful thinking into sharp relief, and did the latter no good. The Council of the Indies was dismissive, and the Council of State agreed. Spain did not have manpower to spare, fresh discoveries drew more men away and were open to enemies to occupy, the treasury had difficulty supporting what had already been discovered and, anyway, they were not sure that 'with good conscience' they could conquer heathens that did not disturb or attack Spain. But how were they to deal with Quiros?

> That [he] has got it into his head to be a second Columbus, and seeing that from what is aforesaid his design cannot be encouraged, it is not desirable to drive him to despair on account of what he has seen and discovered, and the risk that there would be that he might have recourse to Your Majesty's enemies to occupy it; and therefore, taking for granted that it will be best not to discuss this fresh discovery, [the Council of State] is of opinion that this man being so experienced should be retained here as cosmographer in order that he may be of service in marine charts and globes… [2]

And so Quiros went into unofficial and honourable house arrest and remained there for years, agitating the whole while – by his own count he presented fifty memorials to the King. One of his difficulties was that whenever word got around that he was again asking for a new expedition, often because he was as indiscreet as the Council feared that he would be, there always seemed someone ready to object. In 1608 Fernando de Castro, backbone presumably stiffened by Doña Ysabel, petitioned the King not to allow any concession that would injure his rights in the Solomons, and declared that Quiros' 'discovered land' was nothing more than part of New Guinea. Furthermore, he wrote, Quiros was not to be relied upon: he had not obeyed his instructions on the first expedition, turning away in 25°S when a few hours would have brought him to the land he sought.[3] In 1610 the King was moved to order Quiros to retrieve the memorials that he had published because they would inform foreigners of things they should not know. Nevertheless, Quiros wore down the objectors at Court and was eventually authorised to prepare for return to Peru 'to prosecute the discovery'.

In 1613 this reached the ears of Prado, long parted from Torres and far away in Goa.[4] In two blistering denunciations sent to Madrid, Prado referred the Court to the map that he had prepared of the Torres voyage[5] and pointed out that Quiros, 'the imposter', had discovered only reefs and small islands. He was 'low and mendacious', 'a liar and a fraud' who 'did not discover that which the Count of Monterey most desired, namely, the crown of the Antarctic Pole, though we were so near to it'.[6] The King had already decided that Quiros should accompany a new Viceroy, the Prince of Esquilache, to Peru, but Prado's letters could only have further undermined his former commander.

Just nine days after the letters arrived in Madrid, Esquilache informed Quiros that he had orders to send him to people the 'Austral Land' when convenient and when the state of affairs in Peru would allow. 'And with this the business of this man at the Court was considered finally dispatched.'[7] Quiros could have had no illusions that this was other than a formula for indefinite delay. In 1615, on passage to Lima with the Viceroy, he died at Panama. Esquilache did not even trouble to notify Madrid, but four years later he made amends by appointing Quiros' son Francisco to the post of Cosmographer Major.

Quiros was mistaken in most of his beliefs about the whereabouts of land in the South Pacific. He did Spain a disservice by holding them so strongly, by publishing them so widely, by persisting with them for so long, and by misrepresenting contrary evidence, but he thereby kept them alive. Spain had turned a deaf ear, but further north there were others who had heard his arguments and were more willing to give them credit, notably Isaac Le Maire, merchant of Amsterdam.

The Australian Company

Le Maire was a trustee of the VOC (Vereenigde Oost-Indische Compagnie (United East India Company)) and one of its largest

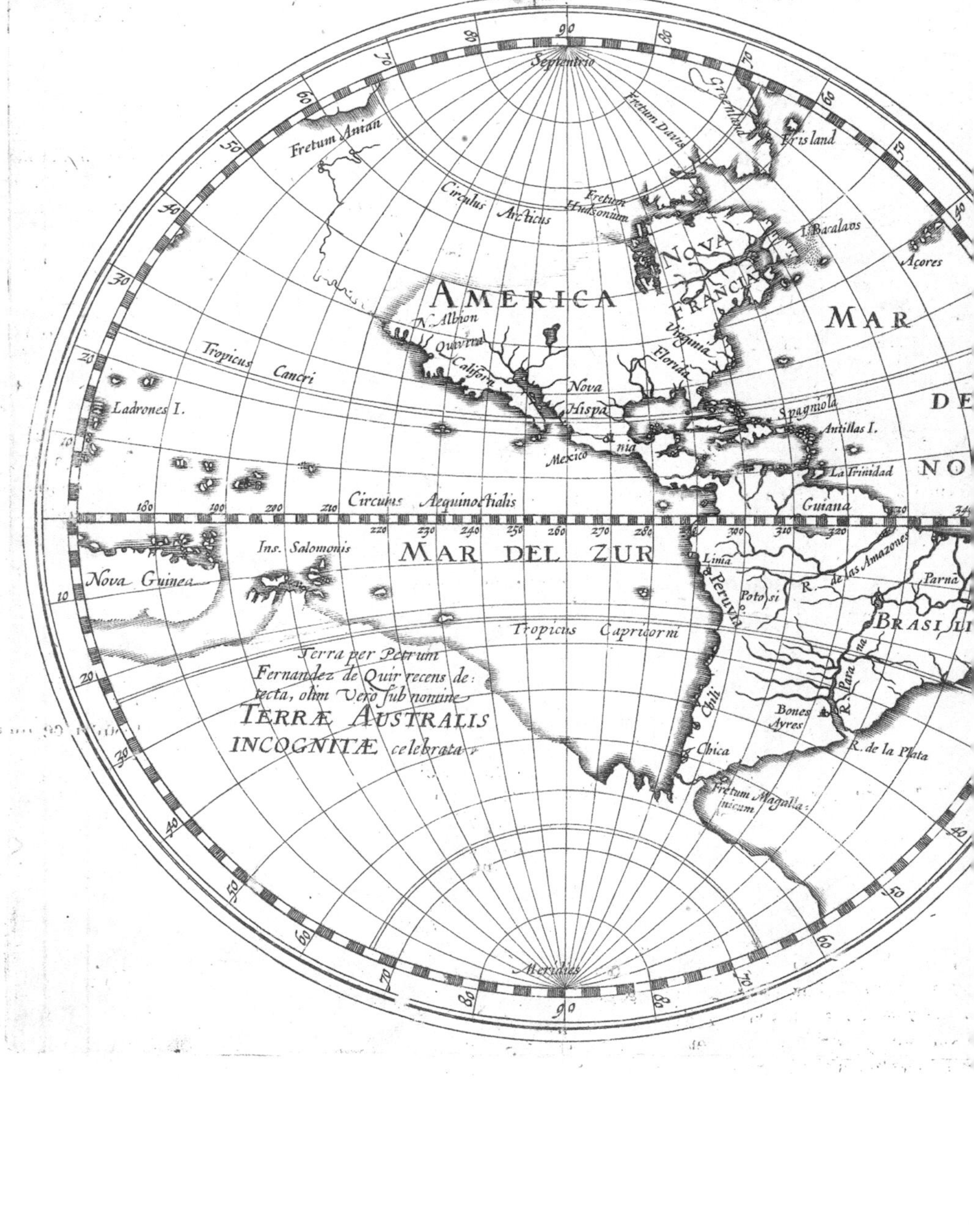
Septentrio
Fretum Anian
Fretum Davis
Groenland
Frisland
Circulus Arcticus
Fretum Hudsonium
NOVA FRANCIA
I. Bacalaos
Açores
AMERICA
N. Albion
Quivira
Californ
Virginia
Florida
MAR
Tropicus Cancri
Nova Hispania
Ladrones I.
Spagniola
Antillas I.
DE
Mexico
La Trinidad
NO
Circulus Aequinoctialis
Guiana
MAR DEL ZUR
Ins. Salomonis
Lima
Peruvia
Potosi
R. de las Amazones
Parna
BRASIL
Nova Guinea
Tropicus Capricorni
Terra per Petrum Fernandez de Quir recens de: tecta, olim Vero sub nomine TERRÆ AUSTRALIS INCOGNITÆ celebrata
Chili
Bones Ayres
R. Parana
Chica
R. de la Plata
Fretum Magallanicum
Meridies

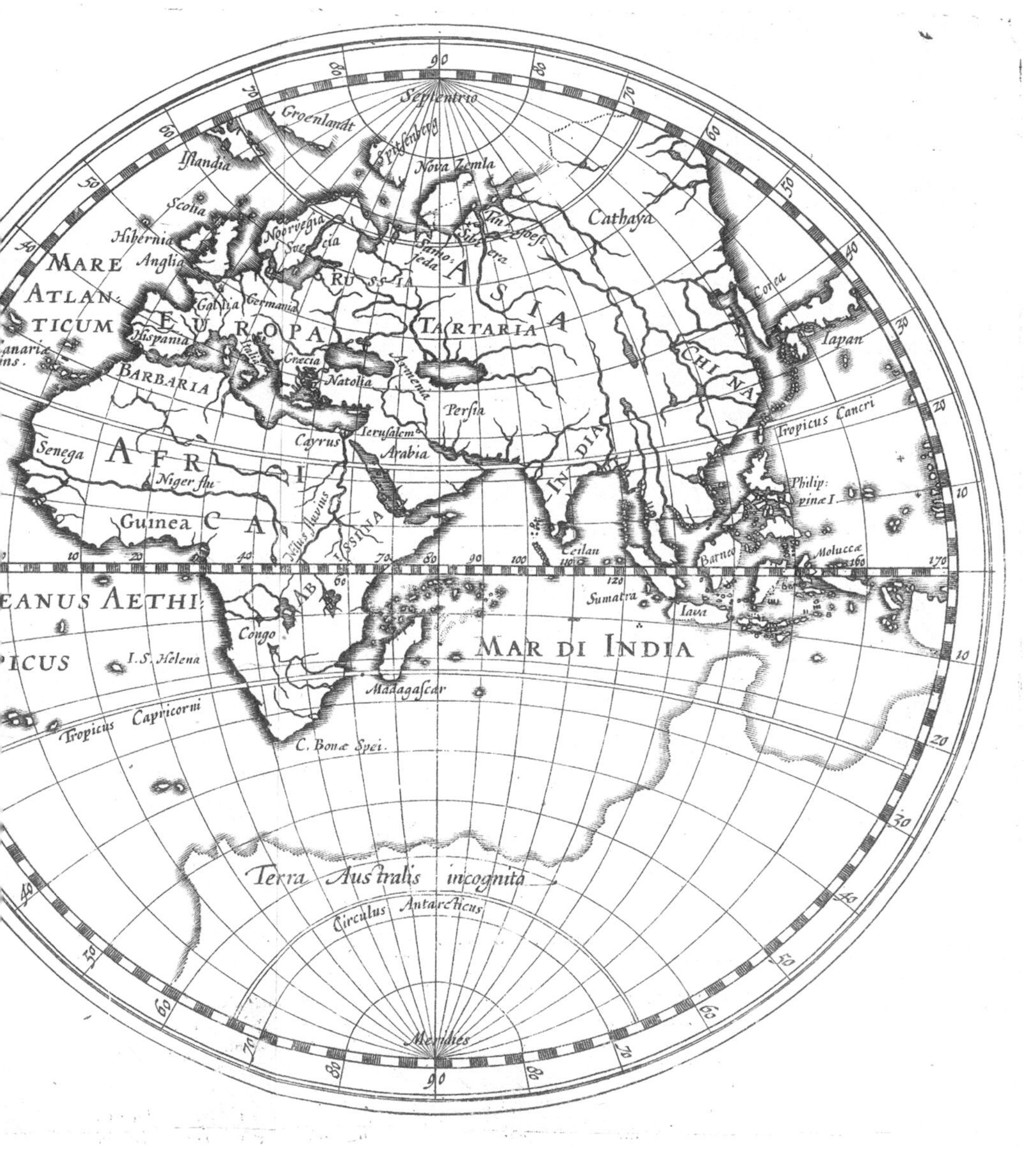

'Things they should not know': Hessel Gerritsz's reading of Quiros, Amsterdam 1612.

shareholders, but he chafed at the Company monopoly which prohibited his private trade. He urged on the Company's directors the riches to be had by breaking the Spanish hold on the western route to the Indies. They gave him no better a hearing than Quiros was getting in Madrid but, just as Philip III's advisers had feared, Le Maire had also read Quiros' published account of the vast lands of Australia Incognita, as yet beyond the Company's reach. In 1614 he agreed with Willem Cornelisz Schouten, the man who had sailed the *Duyfken* to Ceram in 1602, that they would each raise half of the capital needed to create their own *Australische of Zuid Compagnie*.

The States-General of the United Provinces of the Netherlands were not prepared to interfere with the privileges they had granted the VOC, but they could see that it would be in the national interest to have another route to the Orient. They decreed that Le Maire could send his ships into the Pacific under the Dutch flag provided that he did not use the routes reserved to the VOC, including the Strait of Magellan. If he found a new route his company would have exclusive use of it for four years. Exclusion from the Strait of Magellan did not perturb Le Maire. He had read the accounts, from Magellan and Drake onwards, and knew that many maps showed a speculated passage between Tierra del Fuego and the southland.

That summer the VOC also prepared a fleet for the East. Its primary mission was to counter a Spanish naval threat to the Dutch position in the Moluccas, but the instructions drawn up for Joris van Spilbergen also required him to raid Spanish possessions in the Americas on the way. Perhaps Le Maire's criticism had struck home and the Company was making a two-fold demonstration, exercising its right to the Magellan Strait route and at the same time exploiting neglected regions notionally within the bounds of its monopoly. Significantly, Spilbergen was prohibited use of all other routes to the East; if time had been uppermost in the directors' minds he would have been directed to use the Cape route. He sailed on 8 August 1614.

Le Maire was too old for voyaging. He appointed his 29-year-old son Jacob as president of the fleet and supercargo. Schouten, then about 47 years old, sailed as patron of the expedition and master of the larger of the two ships, the *Eendracht*. The smaller, *Hoorn*, was commanded by his brother Jan. They sailed from Texel on 14 June 1615, intending to reach Terra Australis in ten months. The Netherlands Captain-General, Prince Maurits of Nassau, had given the expedition official blessing by naming Jacob Le Maire as its Captain-Major. Of more substantial benefit was permission to recruit from the Dutch naval fleet because, like Le Maire and Schouten's shareholders, the seamen were not to be let into the secret of the expedition's destination. Sailors being sailors, they soon dubbed their ships the Goldfinders, and when at the equator they were told that they would be finding a new route into the South Seas and on to India, most were delighted at the prospect of private profit. At Port Desire in Patagonia the expedition paused to refresh and refurbish. The *Hoorn* caught fire while being defouled and was burnt to the waterline, but the *Eendracht* sailed on, crossing the entrance of Magellan's strait to reach its southern shore, the coast of Tierra del Fuego.

As the expedition was prohibited use of the Strait, the ship went east looking for the extremity of the land and found it in 65°W. There a narrow strait opened to the south. Le Maire named its eastern shore Staten Land. He could see only a few kilometres of coastline but to him it was part of the southland, his first sight of the vast connected territories that would open to view in the Pacific, 'whereat we were very glad, holding that a way had been discovered by us which till then had been unknown to man, as we afterwards found to be the truth'.[8] Confirmation had come quickly. Four days after leaving the little strait they sailed past a promontory they named Cape Hoorn. For a place that would give pause to the hardiest of sailors for the next 300 years, particularly when making passage from the east, the Horn on this occasion was remarkably benign. Once through Drake's Passage, the expedition headed north to reach 18°S on 15 March 1616 when, 'by common consent', the ship stood west.

Le Maire's first objective appears to have been the fabulous continent of Juan Fernandez. Not having found it within three days sail on the westerly course, he had the ship's council agree to make WNW for 'the higher southern land', by which he meant Quiros' discovery. By 24 March they were in the indicated latitude 'looking out eagerly for the southern land, but almost despairing and fearing there was no such' because of a prodigious swell from the south. An island was seen on 10 April and from there they again steered directly west 'towards the Islands of Solomon'. Two days later, almost ten months into the voyage, Le Maire gave charts of Terra Australis and New Guinea to the pilots 'to the end that they should direct themselves by them'. At the next island, in 14°30'S, there was no swell and Le Maire thought that the Solomons or Terra Australis must be very near.

On 16 April they descried a third island, where they watered. Le Maire was now anxious to hold west exactly in 15°S, fearing that they

Le Maire shows his Staten Land, east of Tierra del Fuego, as a cape of the great southland

would otherwise pass Quiros' Bay of St Philip and St James, 'reckoning that we were not far from the continent'. By the 23 April the swell from the south was again so pronounced as to suggest that any land to the south must be far distant, but smooth water on 9 May raised Le Maire's hopes and the following day proved him right. Two islands, one boasting a volcano, agreed 'very well to Quiros' description, which made us hope to find also the rest ahead, and very soon should see the Terra Australis'. On 14 May another island came into view. Le Maire named it Good Hope, in expectation of finding water and provisions, but the natives were hostile and his plan to force a landing was overruled 'by a plurality of voices'. This appears to have been Le Maire's first important setback in council, but he was allowed to keep the ship's head south of west against the wishes those who favoured a north-west course.

The ship reached 16°S, still looking for the mainland, but there was more grumbling. Water and provisions were very short. On 17 May Le Maire had to issue of one-eighth of a pint of Spanish wine in lieu of water at breakfast. The council nevertheless agreed to a WNW course, the best Le Maire could ask of the ship against the wind. On the following morning the pilot came to the stern gallery, where he pressed Le Maire to cease fighting the wind and turn directly north. As Le Maire would not agree, the pilot then went to Schouten, who would have ordered the helm altered immediately had not Le Maire advised holding course until noon, when a sun sight would give them a better idea of their latitude. His delaying tactic failed. The ship's council convened and Schouten argued that they should go north looking for the north coast of New Guinea and thence to the Moluccas, as they had now sailed more than 1,600 leagues from Peru without having seen anything of the southern land. They had also seen nothing 'of advantage' although they were already much further west than they had intended.

Le Maire made a skilful rebuttal. He pointed out that Schouten's was the highest estimate of distance sailed. Averaging the estimates of all those aboard who were qualified to navigate gave a figure of 1,550 leagues. The expedition should at least continue west to the 1,600 league mark, he said, 'for [I] imagined it a thing certain' that a south part New Guinea would be found on that course. Schouten invoked the spectre of a lee shore: continuing west would undoubtedly take them to the southward of New Guinea 'and in case of not finding a passage to the south (which was very dangerous and uncertain)' the ship would certainly be lost, as it would not be possible to sail back against the prevailing easterly winds.

Le Maire might have pressed his case but there were signs that the westerly wind would not last much longer and he could see that he would not be able to persuade the council, let alone the sailors. He tried to salvage what he could by proposing to alter course to the north-west, towards 'the point' of New Guinea, 'hoping that by this means both parties would be satisfied, and that in doing this [I] could not fail to find the [Santa Cruz] islands which are to the north of the bay [of St Phillip and St James] in 13°S'.

The pilot gave the attempted compromise short shrift. A north-west course would lead to the middle of New Guinea, not to the point, causing them to pass by any place where provisions might be obtained. Le Maire, probably wishing he had kept his charts to himself, decided not to undermine his authority further by futile dissent. The council unanimously agreed to go NNW to 11–12°S. That evening the threatened change arrived, shifting the wind to the south. For Le Maire, the rain it brought to replenish the water jars was little consolation. The coast of Quiros' continent was just over the southern horizon, he was sure, and his Bay not far to the west, but this contrary wind would keep them beyond his reach.[9]

To this point Le Maire had held steadily west through nearly a hundred degrees of longitude to 178°W, certain that the course would eventually bring him to Quiros' Bay. It would have, but he was yet 320 leagues short of the goal. On 19 May the expedition came across two islands and traded with the natives for pigs, fish and coconuts. Fresh water was obtained from a little river that could be reached without going beyond the protection of the ship's guns, although the main threat posed by the natives was their propensity to theft.

Schouten was so pleased with what he took to be vindication of his judgment in coming north that he declared this to be the true Terra Australis. Even Le Maire, so recently disappointed in his search for a southland with commercial possibilities, wondered at what seemed to be a survival from the world before the Fall: '… they are without religion, as brute beasts, and have no knowledge of merchandise, living like the people of the first world, without labouring, having for food the fruits of the trees and fish quite raw'.[10] The natives called their paradise islands Futuna and Alofi. Le Maire charted them as the Horn group.

By now relations between Le Maire and Schouten were strained. In their published accounts, each belittles the contribution of the other. Le Maire refers to himself as president, but in Schouten he is merchant or supercargo. Schouten calls himself master or skipper, but Le Maire describes him as patron.[11] Le Maire believed that the islands of Good Hope and Horn were the Solomons, on the grounds that they corresponded well with Quiros' description, adding wistfully that he had 'no doubt but the Terra Australis was very near'. He had ceased to have any faith in Schouten's navigation. On 1 June the master held that, according to his noon sight, the latitude was 13°15'S. Le Maire, who relied on the pilots, made it 13°40'S, a difference of 25 miles. Two days later Schouten reckoned that the ship was 1,730 leagues from Peru and far beyond the point of New Guinea. His reckoning was compared with that of the two pilots and two other sight-takers on board. Their highest figure was 1,665 leagues and the mean, even with Schouten's figure included, was 1,660 leagues.

For all that, no-one was sure where the point of New Guinea was and so they proceeded to search for it, unwittingly tracking parallel to the eastern littoral of the Solomon Islands. On 25 June New Ireland came into view and Le Maire made for it, 'presuming that it might chance' to be New Guinea. The longitude seemed a little suspect but the coast was running SE-NW, as it should, and the latitude was about right. They rounded Cape North and headed west across what is now the Bismarck Sea, unaware that they had left 'New Guinea' behind. Island after island in the Admiralty group led them on until on 5 July they came within sight of a very high mountain to the south-west. Schouten, who a month earlier reckoned that they had already overshot the point of New Guinea, was 'half inclined to think that it might be Banda', but changed his opinion when a closer approach disclosed three or four similar peaks further north.[12] They saved him from a great embarrassment. The mountain was Vulcan, on Manum Island off the north coast of New Guinea: Banda was 15° further west.

Every league that the ship logged westwards along the coast strengthened the conviction of those aboard that this was, finally, New Guinea. At length the expedition came to the Moluccas. On 17 September they anchored off Ternate alongside the *Morgenster* of Rotterdam, one of Spilbergen's vessels. His fleet had arrived six months earlier after plundering its way along the coasts of Brazil, Chile, Peru, Mexico and the Philippines. While passing through the Strait of Magellan, as instructed, Spilbergen had seen a gap to the south that appeared to open into 'the Chilean Sea'. He would have investigated but his only vessel small enough for the purpose had become separated from the fleet.

Le Maire went ashore with the letter of introduction that his father had written to the VOC Governor-General, but was told that the addressee had died ten months earlier. Fortunately the successor, Laurens Reael, was present in Ternate with his Councillors, who together comprised the Council of India. They were courteous but firm: the Australian Company was not to trade in Ternate but it could sell surplus ship's gear. Fifteen of the *Eendracht*'s crew decided that the VOC offered better prospects and sought release, which Le Maire granted. With exploration at an end and trade prohibited, the ship sailed for Java. It arrived in Batavia at the end of October. Le Maire had no reason to expect that his reception would be any less cordial than it had been at Ternate – after all, he had the Governor-General's leave to sail here unescorted – but everything changed with the arrival of a ship carrying the President of the VOC's Bantam council, Jan Pieterszoon Coen.

Coen wasted no time. On 2 November he invited Le Maire and Schouten to attend him in council. Their ship was not associated with the VOC or under its orders. To get here they must have 'come south of Magellanes'. The quoted words are Spilbergen's. They attempt to reconcile his loyal support of the VOC's charter rights with his belief that an alternative passage did exist, and a suspicion that it might have been found by Le Maire. Spilbergen was probably present at the council interview, but he seems to be interviewing himself when he sets out at length the reasons for the council's scepticism about the expedition's log.

> On a voyage of such long duration they had with this vessel discovered no unknown nation, no countries of fresh intercourse, nor anything that might be for the common weal; although they claimed to have found a passage shorter than the usual one, yet this was without any probability, since they had spent on their voyage as far as Ternate just fifteen months and three days, and that too (according to their own admission) with a favourable wind and only one ship, which is not called upon to wait for others, as happens in a whole fleet. These claimants to the discovery of a new passage through the South Sea were greatly surprised that the fleet under Commander Spilbergen had been so long before at Ternate ... [13]

Spilbergen's voyage had taken nineteen months, a belligerent cruise along the Spanish Pacific littoral via Valparaiso, Acapulco, Manila and points between. Apart from the delay inherent in keeping six ships together, he had spent time defeating the Spanish in two pitched battles. And Le Maire had done only four months better than this on a direct voyage? There was no evidence here of a short cut.

Spilbergen may also have been hesitant about contradicting Coen. There can be little doubt that the President was not the least interested in the justice of his proceedings. The promptness of his arrival at Batavia, council in tow, when even a short interval would have seen the *Eendracht* gone with no harm done, testifies to his determination and ruthlessness. Not for him the gentlemanly behaviour of Laurens Reael. An ambitious servant of the Company, Coen was out to make an example of these trespassers. They had violated the Company's charter and so their ship, its papers and its cargo were forfeit. The seamen would be transferred to the Company's ships. Le Maire, Schouten and the officers would return to the Netherlands. There was no appeal and no remedy. Le Maire and Schouten meekly submitted inventories of the *Eendracht* and its cargo and embarked in Spilbergen's ships.

They sailed from Batavia on 14 December. Before the month was out, Le Maire was dead. Away from Coen, on his own quarterdeck and with opportunity to talk, Spilbergen had come to respect his passenger and grieved at his passing, 'since he was a man endowed with remarkable knowledge and experience in matters of navigation'.[14] Le Maire senior was bitter when he learnt of his son's treatment in Java, attributing his death to 'the affront and harshness put upon him'.[15]

On arrival in the Netherlands Schouten, anxious to retrieve some of his losses, rushed into print with an account of the voyage. Its title page did not even mention Jacob Le Maire, although it seems to have drawn heavily on the younger man's writing. Isaac Le Maire was incensed, but was partly mollified the following year when Spilbergen's journal was published 'with the Australian Navigations of Jacob Le Maire, who passed through a new strait in the south'.[16] It would be nice to believe that Spilbergen himself was responsible for the acknowledgement, but it is more likely to have been his publisher, who admitted that he had appended Le Maire because of Spilbergen's mention of a new 'thoroughfare' into the South Sea from Magellan's strait. Spilbergen himself says no more than that Le Maire commanded 'throughout the passage of the South Sea'.[17]

Isaac had a care for his property as well as his son's reputation. He took the VOC to court and throughout two years of litigation maintained that Jacob had indeed discovered a new route and that therefore Coen's confiscation of the *Eendracht* was illegal. Even if Jacob's was a new route, the VOC argued, the Australian Company should nonetheless be excluded from the southern hemisphere between Ceylon and the meridian a hundred leagues east of the Solomon Islands. This could not be considered virgin territory as the VOC 'had repeatedly given orders for discovering and exploring the land of Nova Guinea and the islands situated east of the same'. The Company cited the discoveries of Willem Jansz and Jan Rosingeyn, 'who did several explorations on the same coast of New Guinea, as shown extensively in their journals'.[18] Asserting priority, the Company was laying claim to the southland for which Le Maire had been searching.

In the outcome, the Le Maires were comprehensively vindicated. The VOC was ordered to restore the vessel and its cargo to the owners, to meet all costs, and to pay interest since the date of the seizure. It might be imagined that the VOC would be less than pleased with the expense Coen had put it to. Rather, it promoted him to Governor-General. The episode had served its purpose. The Australian Company might have an exclusive route but the court case had taken so long that its four years of monopoly were all but up. Isaac lived to see his son's relation published in its own right in 1621, but three years later the ambitions of the Australian Company to all intents and purposes died with the old merchant. His tombstone wryly records that his trading life in all quarters of the globe had 'been so richly blessed by God that in thirty years he lost over 1,500,000 guilders'.[19]

The fairway to Java

Given that the priority of the VOC was to displace Spain and Portugal from markets already known to be profitable, it is not surprising that the only action taken on Willem Jansz's disappointing reports was to file them away. They nonetheless enhanced his reputation as a reliable servant of the company and, as we have seen, they had other uses.

A much more valuable discovery than Jansz's 'west coast of New Guinea'[20] was made in 1610 by Hendrik Brouwer. Time was money to the Company and a quick voyage was a good voyage. Instead of relying on the seasonal south-west monsoon after rounding the Cape of Good Hope, Brouwer demonstrated that if the company's ships ventured south to the Roaring Forties at any time of year they would find mighty winds to hurry them a thousand leagues across the Indian Ocean. They should then turn north to find the trade winds that would bear them to Sunda Strait. The route added much distance to the voyage but Brouwer had made it in five months and 23 days, saving a good year. He recommended 'this fairway' to the Managers.[21] It was a radical proposition that the Company was slow to accept, but in 1617, at the urging of Coen, it issued new Sailing Directions that required skippers to make their easting from the Cape in 35–36 or 40–44 degrees south. Article 14 assured them that 'steady westerly winds blow here and because the degrees [of latitude] are considerably shorter … one makes up for the distance apparently lost …'[22]

There was a difficulty; how did one know when to turn north? Finding longitude was a matter of experience and judgment rather than science. Most skippers relied on reckoning deduced from an estimate of distance sailed. The first skipper to underestimate in a big way on Brouwer's route was Dirk Hartog of the *Eendracht*.[23] In 1616, the year before the new directions became mandatory he ran across the Indian Ocean to 113°E, fetching up against an extensive coastline. Hartog was able to make a safe landing and left an inscribed pewter plate recording his mistake.

In Java, his report of an unknown coast struck a chord. Le Maire's arrival in the Indies had already concentrated the Council's mind on the need for pre-emptive exploration of the Company's domain and it now considered sending the *Morgenster* in search of 'Southland-New Guinea'.[24] The conjunction of terms indicates a belief by the Council that Hartog had found the fabled southern continent and that it was connected to Jansz's 1606 landfall, still unexplored below 13°S.

Before news of Hartog's landfall could reach the Netherlands another Company ship had seen the same coast further north. The supercargo of the *Zeewolf* complained that the chart there showed nothing but open ocean. The skipper, van Hillegom, noted that it was probably mainland and 'a fit point to be made by ships coming here with the eastern monsoon in order to get a fixed course for Java'.[25] Hartog had given no name to his find but by 1619, when Frederik de Houtman came upon the same coast in 30°S, it was already referred to as Eendracht's Land. Although Houtman knew this he identified the whole as 'the Southland Beach' – Polo's Locach – possibly because his supercargo, Jacob Dedel, remarked that the red, muddy coast might prove to be gold-bearing.[26]

Houtman also could see the usefulness of this coast as a way-mark on the course from the Cape to Java but warned that in 28°S he had unexpectedly come across an extensive shoal that he charted as Abrolhos, a Portuguese term which translates as 'keep awake', and it did not take long for the hazards of this new navigation to become apparent. From the Company's perspective it was a double stroke of good fortune that the first victim was English rather than Dutch. In 1622 the *Tryal* was wrecked near the Montebello Islands on rocks that today bear the ship's name. The survivors made it to Java in the ship's boats and told Coen that they had been following Brouwer's route. They said that they intended 'to dissuade their countrymen from imitating their example, and that their masters are sure to take other measures accordingly'. Coen passed this good news on to his masters in Amsterdam but warned that there had also been two Dutch near-misses and that he intended to make further discovery of the lands as among 'best measures taken in order to avoid such accidents as befell the English …'.[27]

Coen planned to send two vessels. The instructions he issued reveal a large conception of the possibilities. The ships were to sail to 32–33°S, ‘where sundry ships coming from the Netherlands have accidentally come upon the *Zuyderlant*’, and follow the coast to its southern extremity or 50°S, whichever was reached first. The expedition would then backtrack to ‘near the northern extremity and the east coast of the Southland’, where its leaders were to enquire after sandalwood, nutmeg, cloves and other spices. The instructions assume that the coast extends north to a latitude where such commodities might be found but they do not mention New Guinea. It seems, then, that the ‘east coast’ was now thought to lie somewhere further west than Jansz’s ‘west coast of New Guinea’. The expedition was to follow the east coast as far as was practicable with the provisions aboard, ‘even if in so doing you should sail round the whole land and emerge to southward’.[28]

The voyage did not take place but in the following year the Governor of Ambon, Herman van Speult, sent Jan Carstensz off on a complementary mission. If the Southland could be circumnavigated, as Coen supposed, and the Jansz coast was not part of it, where did that coast terminate? Carstensz started out along the south coast of New Guinea. His ships, *Pera* and *Arnhem*, had not sailed very far before they were attacked by natives who killed some of the crew. Continuing eastwards along the coast, they came to the shoals that mask the entrance to Torres Strait. After failing to find a way through, the expedition turned south. Carstensz wrote that they had been trapped in a ‘drooge bocht’ (shallow bight). The term implies enclosure by land but his chart leaves open the possibility of a passage to the east.

When Cape York was sighted, Carstensz recognised it as Jansz’s New Guinea. He followed the coast to 17°18’S but there the fleet council, fearful that the ships might be sailing ever deeper into a bay where the north-west monsoon would trap them, resolved to proceed no further. Shortly thereafter the *Arnhem* separated ‘and seems to have set her course for Aru (to have a good time of it there)’.[29] Carstensz turned north to make a more detailed examination of the coast and bestow names on its features, ignoring (or ignorant of) those given by Jansz. He noted seven rivers, the most northerly of which he named for van Speult.[30]

The deserters, sailing the *Arnhem* north-west for home, came across the land that today bears the name of their ship. Rudder failure left them drifting near Banda but they were seen and brought in. The Governor of the island reported to Batavia that the expedition had been worthless, ‘for at the place where the chart … led them to expect an open passage, they did not find any such, so that they could not get to the island they wished to reach'.[31] The deserters' expectation strongly suggests that van Speult was as interested in finding a passage into the Pacific as in exploring Jansz's find. The 'island' being sought was probably the Solomon Islands or Quiros' Austral Land. As for the 'west coast of New Guinea', Cartensz could find nothing positive to say.

> … we have not seen one fruit-bearing tree, nor anything that man could make use of; there are no mountains or even hills, so that it may be safely concluded that the land contains no metals, nor yields any precious woods, such as sandalwood, aloes or columba; in our judgement this is the most arid and barren region that could be found anywhere on the earth; the inhabitants, too, are the most wretched and poorest creatures that I have ever seen in my age or time.[32]

The expedition was clearly a failure, but when Carstensz wrote his journal he did not know of the *Arnhem*'s landfall. Might this be the east coast of Coen's Southland?

Two Southlands?

By 1627 most of the south-western quarter of the Australian coastline had been charted by the skippers of VOC vessels, using it as a way-point for the turn north to Java. The trick was to find it without hitting it. Frans Thijszoon of the *Gulden Zeepaert* discovered another difficulty: if one crossed the Indian Ocean too far to the south it was possible to miss the coast altogether. On 26 January 1627 his ship made landfall at Point Nuyts on the Southland in 116°40'E. Here the coast unexpectedly ran east-west, athwart the course to Java. The wind that had served so well for crossing the Indian Ocean was now the ship's enemy, preventing a backtrack. East then, and Thijszoon, with the sanction of his senior passenger, VOC council member Pieter Nuyts, sailed 1,500 kilometres across the Great Australian Bight, led on by a coastline that edged ever so slightly northwards. It presented a cliff-face of uniform height to the sea, a tabular landberg without the least promise of penetrability.

Even after it hooked south they persevered, hoping that this was only a temporary setback, but in 133°E the trend became more pronounced and the Dutchmen paused at a small offshore archipelago. This coast was becoming a lee shore. The attempt to reach the Indies by outflanking whatever land it was that they had found would have to be abandoned. At Point Nuyts they had not been able turn back and here at the islands of St Peter and St Francis it was hazardous to go forward. As they thereafter somehow contrived to reach Batavia only 74 days after first sighting the Australian coast, it can only be assumed that they were favoured by an autumnal easterly that allowed them to recross the Bight.

The Company might dismiss this inconvenient country as worthless to trade but it could not ignore such a large hazard to navigation. Coen, returning to Batavia in 1627 to resume the governor-generalship, was storm-driven towards Houtman's Abrolhos. The steersman's chart showed no land for 300–350 leagues, but dead ahead, less than half a league distant, were breakers. As Coen complained to the Company, 'if we had come on this place in the night-time, we should have been in a thousand perils with our ship and crew'.[33]

He recommended that the chart be amended but the fates were too quick for him. Gerrit de Witt's *Vianen* almost came to grief on the north-west coast and in 1629 the *Batavia* was wrecked on the same islands that had threatened Coen's fleet. Mutiny and massacre added to the horror of the *Batavia* shipwreck, but not the least cause of the Company's dismay was the failure to recover a chest of silver, the indispensable medium of eastern trade. Ship and treasure were written off and the route continued to be used, but sightings of the Southland fell away. In the thirteen years between *Eendracht*'s landfall and the wreck of the *Batavia* there were twelve reported sightings; in the thirteen years following there were only two, apart from discovery voyages. An early turn to the north might cost time, but that was preferable to losing a ship.

The man who gathered, collated and charted the available information about this bleak coast was Hessel Gerritsz, the first Cartographer-in-Ordinary to the VOC. Company voyages provided much of the data with which he revised his work over the years, but he did not confine himself to Company sources; indeed, he had published Quiro's eighth memorial in Dutch. His masterwork, dated 1622, was a general chart of the Pacific in which he sought to rationalise the reports of all navigators. It incorporates a three-portrait hall of fame – Le Maire is up there with Balboa and Magellan, even though his Staten Land is dismissed as no more than a small island adjacent to Tierra del Fuego.[34] Jansz's discovery, labelled 'Nueva Guinea', appears for the first time on a large-area map, in approximately the same latitude as the Solomon Islands and Le Maire's Horn Islands. Gerritsz knew that the Spanish claimed to have sailed west 'in 10°S' which, if true, would make Jansz's land separate, 'differing from the other New Guinea', with a strait between.[35]

South of the Tropic of Capricorn, only South America breaks the surface of Gerritsz's Pacific. If there is a Southland, it is hidden beneath a mass of text in which he attempts to reconcile Mendaña, Quiros and Le Maire. By placing the western margin of his map at about longitude 115°E, Gerritsz also excuses himself from revealing the recent Dutch landfalls on the west coast of Australia. By 1626 he had become a little more forthcoming. On the title-page of Jacques L'Hermite's journal, which Gerritsz published to record a recent circumnavigation, he printed a small map. It shows a gulf joining the Jansz and Hartog discoveries. To the north of it there is a fragmentary New Guinea, while to the south it fades into a shadowy and incomplete Terra Australis.

But that was all he made public. Gerritsz continued to refine his regional chart of the west coast of the Southland for VOC confidential use but the armed struggle for control of the Malay archipelago gradually absorbed much of the Company's strength and attention, leaving little for exploration further south. A major exception was the dispatch of two ships in 1636 to follow up Carstensz's efforts. In almost his first act as Governor-General, Anthony van Diemen instructed Gerrit Thomaszoon Pool to make for the 'vast lands' of Arnhem and van Speult and from there to 'cross over' to the 'west coast of New Guinea' (Carpentaria).[36] From Carstensz's furthest south Pool was to follow the coast to the Houtman Abrolhos.

The instructions assume that neither Arnhem Land nor Speult's Land is connected to Jansz's find, but take it for granted that the two form 'one whole with the Southland'. Clearly, there are thought to be at least two austral landmasses and a third should New Guinea proper be found not to connect to Jansz's find. Pool was specifically tasked to look for passages into the Pacific, which van Diemen surmised would be found in the north rather than the south.[37]

Pool fared even worse on the coast of New Guinea than his predecessor. Along with some crewmen he was killed by natives not far from where the Carstensz expedition had been attacked. Pool's successor in the command, Pieter Pieterszoon, could not make headway east against the winds and turned south to the Aru Islands. After revictualling, the expedition sailed south again 'in order to get eastward by some means or other'. In 11°S they reached a coast that they identified as Arnhem's Land and Speult's Land and, despairing of getting further east, resolved to follow it west, which they did before returning to Banda. They named the new length of northern coast for van Diemen. It was a poor return for the personal hopes and Company funds that the Governor-General had invested in the expedition.

Anthony van Diemen nevertheless remained determined to promote the Company's interests by every means at hand. Consolidation by conquest and expansion by exploration were his themes. Year after year his fleets besieged or blockaded the Portuguese. The key event was the fall of Malacca in 1641, which unhinged the Portuguese communications and isolated their posts further east. Shortly thereafter emissaries brought word that Portugal had re-asserted its independence from Spain and wanted to negotiate a settlement with the Netherlands. Van Diemen looked forward to a peace dividend: with an end to hostilities he would have more ships than were needed just for trade and policing. He could pursue exploration further afield.

He had two instruments for the purpose, one blunt, the other keen. The first was Abel Janszoon Tasman, a no-nonsense skipper who for years had confronted the Company's competitors throughout the East. He was the tough man for a hard voyage, as he had already demonstrated in the search for the islands of gold and silver rumoured to lie east of Japan. The other man, Frans Jacobszoon Visscher, was more thoughtful than forceful but he too had run his share of risks in the Company's service. He combined the skills of a practical pilot with extensive knowledge of navigational science. Although he had not been promoted beyond steersman, his abilities had commended him to Hendrik Brouwer and during the latter's term as Governor-General at Batavia he had been employed on improving maps of the East. When Brouwer returned to the Netherlands in 1636 Visscher had gone with him, and it was probably on his patron's recommendation that he was rewarded with promotion to upper steersman (first mate), sometimes referred to as pilot-major. Back in the Indies in 1637, Visscher found that he was no less highly regarded by van Diemen, Brouwer's successor.

Within two months of the conquest of Malacca, van Diemen told Visscher that he was to be employed on 'discovery of the Southlands'. Peace did not break out as quickly as expected, however, and for the next ten months van Diemen had to detain the pilot-major in Batavia waiting for a ship. Visscher chafed at the inactivity but made good use of his time. In January 1642 he submitted a voyage plan of great audacity, predicated on the Unknown Southland. The starting point would be Le Maire's Staten Land. As 'there is no want of westerly winds there', the ships could follow the coast in to establish its limits and proceed to the longitude of the Solomon Islands, thus becoming 'acquainted with all the utterly unknown provinces of Beach', and returning northward of

New Guinea.[38] Alternatively, a start might be made south of the Cape of Good Hope or Mauritius.

Visscher believed that it would take too long and be too difficult to continue eastward of the Solomons in the one voyage, and dismissed as impractical the idea of making the voyage in reverse, west against the winds. The Pacific gap would be best explored by sending ships on a second voyage via Chile to the Solomon Islands, whence they should go south to 50° or until land was met, then on to Le Maire's Strait with the westerlies, 'by which method one will be enabled to discover the southern portion of the world all around the globe, and find out what it consists of, whether land, sea or icebergs …'[39] All, that is, except for the north side of the Known Southland from 22°S to New Guinea's False Cape. That would require a third voyage, from Banda or Ambon eastwards into the large bay that Carstensz had penetrated in 1623.

Visscher conceives that there are two southlands. One encircles the pole below 50°S; the other is greater New Guinea, with a 'west coast' that extends to Eendracht's Land and probably to Nuyts' Land. A circumnavigator starting from 52–54°S would have to reach the

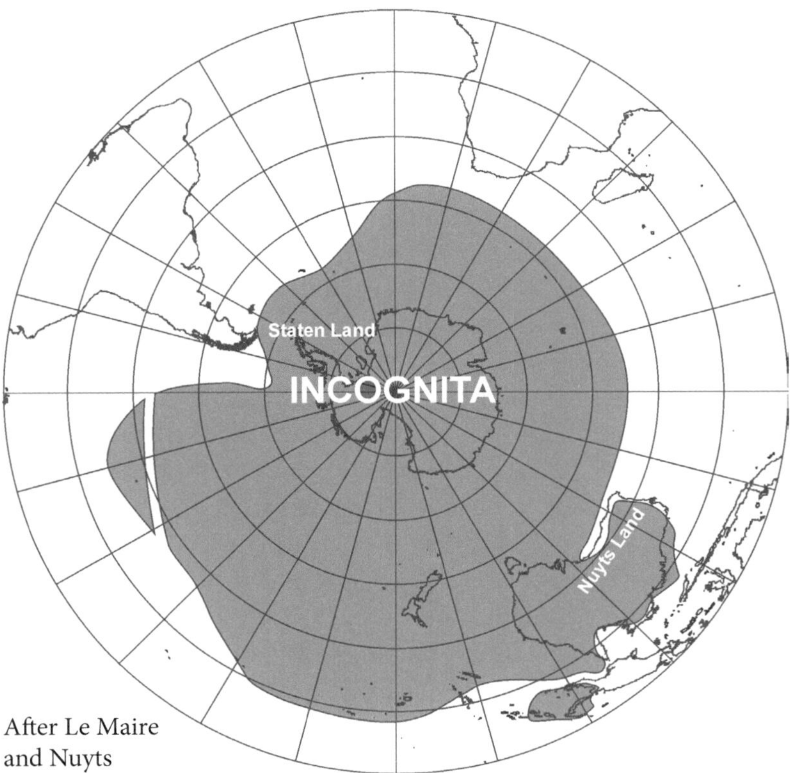

After Le Maire and Nuyts

longitude of the eastern point of greater New Guinea before turning north-west to fetch up with its east coast. Visscher does not mention Arnhem's Land or Pieterszoon's Van Diemensland, thereby dismissing them as mere islands, and gives no indication that he suspects the existence of Torres Strait.

The Council of India debated how best to adapt this expert but naive advice to the Company's purposes. There could be no question of a start from Staten Land: that was beyond the Company's charter and van Diemen's authority. And if there had to be more than one voyage, were these the most economical itineraries? The Council thanked 'renowned and highly experienced pilot' Visscher for his advice, opted for Mauritius as a departure point and, after weighing up the naval situation, decided that 'without detriment to the Company's ordinary trade and military interests', it could afford to send two ships on one voyage.[40] Visscher would be pilot-major, with a voice second only to Tasman's in the fleet.

The conundrum of Staten Land

For those who do not know their port,
no wind is favourable – Seneca

Anthony van Diemen was a successful servant of the Company. He knew he was in the Indies to make money and he did, but there was more to him than that: he had an eye to his place in history. The explorations he initiated were expansive beyond the Company's requirements and beyond its capacity to exploit. To the managers in Amsterdam he justified his latest venture by appealing to their avarice. He had 'hardly any serious doubts' that the expedition would find a shorter route from Java to Chile which, if practicable, would enable the Company 'to do great things with the Chilese, and have opportunities … to snatch rich booty from the Castilians in the West Indies, who will never dream of such a thing'. He was uncertain whether the charter of the West India Company included Chile. If it did, that would prevent the VOC from establishing factories and engaging in mercantile operations there. Would the Managers please advise him? Meanwhile, if Tasman was successful, he would send a trial cargo to Chile to test the market.[41]

If this forthright explanation had formed the preamble to his instructions, Tasman would have been in no doubt about what was expected of him. Instead, he was given a history lesson. For 150 years, the Council of India told him, European monarchs had been discovering lands in the northern hemisphere that had enriched their kingdoms and spread the light of Christianity.

> Nevertheless up to this time no Christian kings, princes or commonwealths have seriously endeavoured to make timely discovery of the remaining unknown part of the terrestrial globe, although there are good reasons to suppose that it contains many excellent and fertile regions, seeing that it lies in the frigid, temperate and torrid zones, so that it must needs comprise well-populated districts in favourable climates and under propitious skies. And seeing that in many countries north of the line equinoctial (in 15-40 degrees latitude), there are found many rich mines … there must be similar fertile and rich regions south of the Equator, of which matter we have conspicuous examples and clear proofs in the gold- and silver-bearing provinces of Peru, Chili, Monomotapa or Sofala [in southern Africa] … so that it may be confidently expected that the expense and trouble that must be bestowed in the eventual discovery of so large a portion of the world, will be rewarded with certain fruits of material profit and immortal fame.[42]

So was Tasman expected to find a way to Chile or was he not? It is difficult to say. The instructions sent him to discover and explore 'the known and unknown Southland … the south-east coast of New Guinea [Australia], and … the islands circumjacent', a confused composite of Visscher's first and third proposed voyages. Tasman was to proceed south from Mauritius until he found the Unknown Southland. If he did not find it, on reaching the latitude of Staten Land he was to steer east and, if unimpeded by land, go as far as 200 leagues beyond the supposed longitude of the Solomon Islands (192°E). If he could achieve this, the Council would be more confident that there was a southern route from the Indian Ocean into the Pacific, and his voyage would 'prepare the way for *afterwards* conveniently finding a short route to Chili'.[43]

The Council gave Tasman some leeway. If he had not found land in the latitude of Staten Land by the time he reached the longitude of Nuyts' islands of St Peter and St Francis, he could go north, find Nuyts' coast and follow it eastward to see if it joined New Guinea near

Jansz's Cape Keerweer.[44] If it did not, Tasman should sail through the passage between them and follow the coast westward to Willem's River at the north end of Eendracht's Land, thus completing the Company's chart of the Known Southland. Having opened this door, the Council then shut it by opining that New Guinea and the Known Southland were 'most likely' joined, and that the winds would prevent Tasman coasting as far as New Guinea, leaving him with no option but to go south, back to the westerlies, 'or otherwise to return to Batavia by [Nuyts'] westward route along the land of Eendracht'.

The Council concluded this debate with itself by declaring that, after all, the route they had first proposed was the more eligible. Tasman must have seen that no matter how faithfully he tried to follow these multiple-choice instructions, some members of the Council were going to be unhappy with the outcome of the voyage, whatever it might be. In the mind of the Council, Staten Land was probably a continent-sized landmass that extended in about 52–54°S from Tierra del Fuego at least as far as Nuyts Land, and possibly around the world.

So, having directed Tasman east of the longitude of the Solomons in high southern latitudes, the Council next instructed him to run before the south-east trades to those islands, and from there sail to the north coast of New Guinea. That was not the end of it: somewhere along that coast he would probably find a passage that would take him directly south to Cape Keerweer. From there he was to follow the coast to Willem's River, being particularly on the lookout at those two places for evidence of passages south-east into the Pacific, this being a matter 'of the utmost importance'. All to be done in nine to eleven months.

6

New Netherlands

The yacht *Heemskerck* and the flute *Zeehan* sailed from Batavia in August 1642, bound for Mauritius, and the southern voyage began from there on 8 October. Tasman ran due south for a fortnight, reaching 40°S. Although still well short of the latitude indicated by his instructions, southerly and westerly gales forced the ships to head south-east for the next fortnight. By 7 November they were in 49°S, but hail and snow set in, the only canvas they could carry was a furled foresail, and the men began to suffer badly from the extreme cold. Tasman consulted Visscher, who advised that going east in 44°S would suffice to show whether there was open sea beyond 150°E. That established, they could reach the Solomon Islands (assuming that Le Maire's Horn Islands were part thereof) by zig-zagging north to 40°S, east to 220°E, north again to 7–17°S, and then west.

Subsequently, Tasman was careful to get the fleet council's endorsement of this deviation from the instructions, and he recorded his own view that there was unlikely to be any 'great mainland' to the south given the high seas that continued to roll in from that direction. On 17 November Tasman estimated that they had passed the known eastern extremity of Nuyts' Land. If he had considered pursuing the Council of India's alternate route he did not share the thought with his journal. Six days later he estimated that they had reached the longitude of Jansz's 'west coast of New Guinea' and on the following day, 24 November, high mountains and an extensive coast came into view. Tasman was sure that land here, in 42°30′S, was 'known to no

European peoples' and he named it for van Diemen. Posterity would rename it Tasmania. He fixed its longitude by polling the navigators of the *Heemskerck*, whose reckonings averaged out to 163°50′E of Tenerife.[1] This he mandated as an established point of departure for all subsequent reckoning and charting.

Ashore there were numerous signs of human inhabitants but not a single figure was seen amid the shadows of the forest. Baffled, Tasman had the ships follow the coast of this new Van Diemen's Land anti-clockwise until it turned north and then north-west. Prevented by a contrary wind from coasting further, the fleet council resolved to quit the land and continue east. Again Tasman noted heavy swells rolling in from the south-west and he remarked that no mainland could be expected to southward. Proceeding across the sea that today also bears his name, on 12 December Tasman saw 'a large, high lying land' to the south-east. The ships sailed towards it until evening came on, when the council, fearful of 'the high open sea running there in huge hollow waves and heavy swells', instructed the steersmen to head east should the breeze freshen. Freshen it did, and the steersmen turned the ships from the dangerous shore. Daylight disclosed that the coast was trending north-east and the ships had no choice but to track along it. If Tasman had intended to sail around the south of this new land, as he had Van Diemen's Land, the opportunity was lost.

For five days they coasted northwards seeing neither boats nor smoke, but when on 18 December they approached the shore looking to anchor and find a watering place, the inhabitants soon made their presence known. The 'gruff, hollow voice' with which the Maoris made their challenge from two outrigger canoes signified nothing to the Dutch, who were not surprised to find that Le Maire's vocabulary was useless 'seeing that it contains the language of the Solomon Islands, etc.' Compounding the danger, Tasman ordered a crewman to sound his trumpet in response to conch calls from the canoes.

Things became much clearer the following day. The Maoris returned, intercepted one of the ships' boats and attacked its crew. The canoes were driven away by cannon and musket fire and the boat was retrieved, but only after three of its crew had been killed and another mortally wounded. One body was taken ashore by the Maoris for purposes the Dutch did not venture to guess. They were so stunned that they did not even attempt recovery or reprisal, but quitted this Murderers' Bay. They did not doubt that from it they would have

The Maoris challenge and then attack, from Tasman's Journal

found 'a passage into the open South Sea, but this turned out to our hearts' pain very much otherwise'.[2]

The otherwise soon became apparent. After midnight the wind turned north-west and for the remaining hours of darkness the ships tacked to avoid the shore assumed to lie under their lee. Morning on 20 December revealed land on all sides. Tasman reckoned that they must have sailed more than thirty leagues into a bay, and for the next four days stormy weather from the west confined them to it. As the coast now appeared to be more extensive than first thought, Tasman named it Staten Land 'because it could well be, that this land would be joined to [Le Maire's] Staten Land'. Joined or not, he 'trusted' that he had found the main coast of the unknown Southland. If it was, here was no passage to Chile, but the evidence was far from conclusive.

Indeed, when a brief calm on the 24 December allowed the fleet council to assemble, Tasman informed it that 'we' (presumably he and Visscher) had observed that the tide was running from the south-east, which was likely to indicate a passage through, and the council agreed that when wind and weather permitted they should investigate. Permission appeared to be forthcoming the following evening, when calm fell, but on the 26th the light breeze that sprang up quickly stiffened into a south-easterly and there was no more thought of passage-hunting in that direction. The ships escaped the bay as they had entered it: on a following breeze. Tasman named the bay Zeehan's Bight, and his chart shows a single, western entrance. Visscher's chart shows an additional opening, to the south-east. More than a century later, James Cook would validate Visscher's judgement by sailing through the strait that separates the main islands of New Zealand. At 41°S the strait was within the belt of westerlies that the VOC believed were reliable winds for Chile. Further, the islands offered the prospect of refreshment – the inhabitants permitting – which would have made possible the all-southern route that Visscher's plan had reluctantly dismissed as too arduous. The Company would be presented with a choice: which to accept, Tasman's chart or Visscher's?

The ships continued coasting north-east into the New Year. On 4 January 1643, while crossing from the land to an island, a strong current carried them west. It was combined with a heavy sea from the north-east and hopes rose that they had found a passage to the east. As they left the island on Twelfth Night they named it Three Kings and resolved to proceed to the Solomons in accordance with Visscher's revised plan. The further north they went, clearing New Zealand, the more the swells swung southwards, and on 8 January Tasman was confident that he had found a route from Batavia to Chile, and as there was nothing in the way to prevent a traverse, 'we shall hereafter write instructional proceedure concerning this waterway, but leave it at present for some reasons'.[3] This was promising more than he could deliver and Tasman knew it. Although he does not say what his reasons were, they probably had much to do with the fact that the winds had become variable; the ships had left the dependable westerlies of the roaring forties behind them. From the uncertain thirties, Chile would be a problematical voyage.

On 20 January the ships reached Tongatapu and Eua, as friendly then as when Cook later so named them. In the Tonga group they were able to water and revictual and there, inevitably, discipline broke down in the face of temptation. Although nothing of trading value to the Company was found, the ships lingered in lotus-land for nearly a fortnight. Draconian punishments had to be posted to enforce watch-keeping and keep natives off the ships. Tasman believed that Tonga was well to the east of the Horn Islands, which he took to be outliers of the Solomons. When the voyage was resumed, at the beginning of February, he took the ships north to 17°S and then, as earlier resolved, turned west to look for the Horn Islands.

On 6 February, they came across three islets set amid extensive shoals and for two days were forced to feel their way through. The weather was very rough as the south-east trades contested with the monsoon at the turn of the season. Visscher believed that these Heemskerck Shoals were the islands shown south-west of the Horn Islands on Gerritsz's large chart.[4] He advised holding as strictly northwards as the wind would allow so as to stay clear of the coast of New Guinea, which he feared might not be too far under their lee. Tasman summed up their predicament; their present latitude agreed with that of the islands on the large chart, but those islands should have been 200 leagues further west according to ships' reckoning. It was very vexing: 'thus it is that one says as a proverb, estimating is indeed missing'.

The consensus of the fleet council was that they should go north until they could be sure of avoiding the unknown east coast of New Guinea. That meant sailing beyond the latitude of the Solomon Islands, which Visscher acknowledged would be 'partly' contrary to the expedition instructions although not in breach of any precise order. Tasman nevertheless obtained his subordinates' views in writing, which revealed a range of views about how far one had to go to be safe. The low bid was from one of the steersmen, De Ratte, who wrote that they need not sail beyond 6–7°S before turning west. The weather continued to be execrable and Tasman was at a loss to account for the north-west winds that often thwarted their progress. For a month they struggled northwards, with Tasman complaining that 'if one should describe all this weather and the wind, one would have nothing else to do but write'.[5]

Their next landfall was Ontong Java in 5½°S. Had the wind been more amenable and De Ratte's advice more acceptable the expedition would have rediscovered the northern Solomons, unvisited since Mendaña three-quarters of a century earlier. As it was, they had tracked north-west in parallel with the Solomons' coast and, like Le Maire, they came to New Ireland instead. Far from finding the Solomons, Tasman was not even sure whether he had passed them to the east or the west of his track but at least he and Visscher had found their bearings, courtesy of Le Maire, and turned their attention to that part of the instructions that required them to find a route to Cape Keerweer. On 8 April they rounded the northern tip of New Hanover and endeavoured 'to get to the south, both for the discovering of the lands and to find passage the earlier the better to the south'.[6]

Tasman was hoping that the gap in Le Maire's chart of the north New Guinea coast might offer a short cut. The coast of New Britain came into view on 13 April. They closed with it the following day and when land could be seen to the SSW and WSW 'thinking to find there between the two (although vainly) a passage but coming nearer found it to be a bight and the land to the west continuous therewith …'[7] They then proceeded to convert this last remark into a self-fulfilling prophecy by sailing west out of sight of the coast, thereby missing the strait that divides New Britain from New Guinea.

Although the ships surveyed west along the north New Guinea coast for the next month looking for a passage south, Tasman also failed to identify the strait between New Guinea and Waigeo Island off its north-west extremity. There was still time and provision enough for him to try for Cape Keerweer by way of the south coast of New Guinea but the south-west monsoon was due and that would have made return to Java difficult. By then he felt that he had done enough, 'holding ourselves content to have found a good passage which in the future can become serviceable for the Company coming at the time of the east monsoon from Peru and Chile'.[8] With these complacent words he turned on its head the underlying task he had been given. The winds north of New Zealand that had barred the way *to* Chile were represented as facilitating voyages *from* Chile. Furthermore, the possibilities and limitations of the route that he was recommending had already been demonstrated by Le Maire. Nothing of value to the Company had been found along the way, but by shortening the survey of New Guinea Tasman could at least get back to Java within the timetable laid down by the Council of the Indies.

He obscured the significance of his singular achievement, circum-navigation of the Known Southland, by speculating that there was an Unknown Southland – Staten Land – still waiting to be explored. The first reaction of the Council at Batavia was positive. They were critical of the failure to establish the northern limits of Van Diemen's Land and to make contact with its inhabitants, but interpreted Tasman to be saying that favourable winds persisted north of Staten Land, 'consequently a passage from the Indian Ocean into the South Sea has been found, it having been ascertained that in this parallel, where the westerly trade wind is blowing, there is a convenient passage to the gold-bearing coast of Chili …' The crews were rewarded with extra pay; two months for Tasman and his officers, one month for the common seamen.

Planning commenced for a trading voyage to be made along the same southern route that October, but detailed scrutiny of Tasman's account created doubts. Van Diemen became more critical: Tasman had been 'somewhat remiss' and 'as regards the main point has left everything to be more closely inquired into by more industrious successors'. Clearly Tasman would not be a commander of choice for the second voyage, but it was not a matter requiring immediate decision. Growing

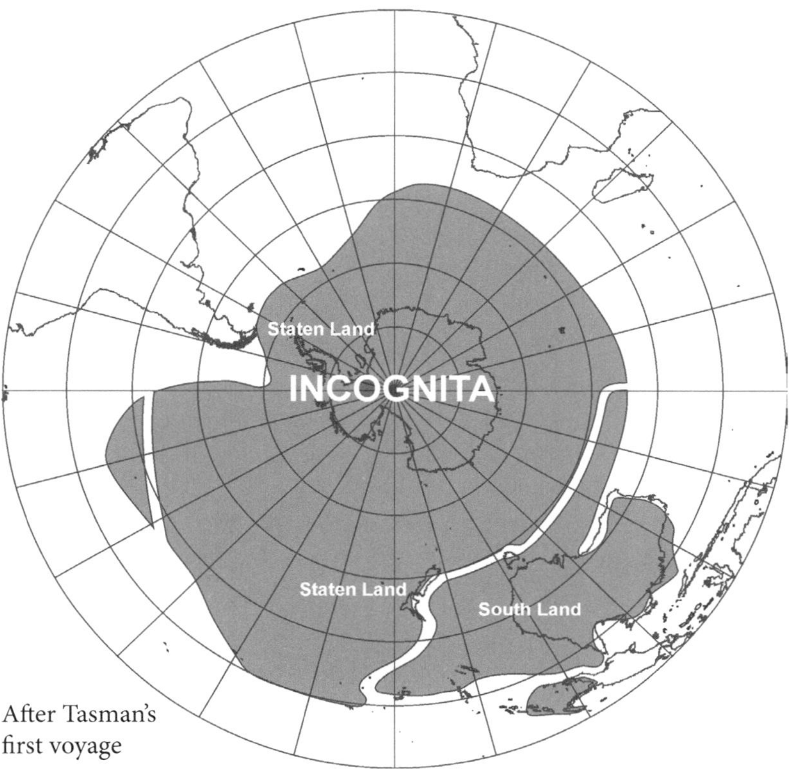

After Tasman's first voyage

Portuguese intrigue was forcing van Diemen to resume hostilities in the Indies. Exploration lost its priority and by the time ships could again be spared there was another consideration. Van Diemen had learned that Hendrik Brouwer was headed for Chilean waters 'which might have given rise to unexpected encounters on both sides'.[9]

The fairway to Chile

The Governor-General's concern about his predecessor's presence in Chile was well-founded: Hendrik Brouwer had defected to the opposition. After more than thirty years' VOC service, including three as Governor-General in Batavia, he had placed his skill and knowledge at the disposal of the Dutch West India Company. His new employers wasted no time in sending him to exercise its charter rights. In November of 1642, barely a month after Tasman had sailed from Mauritius, Brouwer's fleet had departed for South America.

By March 1643 Brouwer was off Le Maire's Strait, where he quickly established that Staten Land was only a small island, unconnected to

Terra Australis. Tasman's theory that Staten Land extended to New Zealand had been demolished even before he could report it. Brouwer rounded Cape Horn and proceeded to Chile, where at first the Dutch were welcomed as liberators from Spanish oppression. It did not take long for the Araucanian Indians to learn that their new allies were as avaricious for gold as any Spaniard. They withheld provisions and starvation loomed. In the midst of these difficulties Brouwer died. The expedition lingered off Chile for a while but in December 1643 was forced to return to Brazil.

Ignorant of these developments but concerned to cover himself against being accused of unilaterally violating the West India Company's rights, van Diemen advised the VOC that unless it was countermanded he proposed to mount a voyage to Chile in September or October 1644, 'this time arms in hand'.[10] In the interim, so that Tasman and Visscher would not be idle, he resurrected Visscher's earlier proposal for a separate voyage towards Cape Keerweer. If Keerweer were not connected to the Known Southland, the passage between might be factored into the route for the proposed Chilean voyage. Two yachts, *Limmen* and *Zeemeeuw*, and the galiot *Bracq* were available.

Tasman was probably both surprised and relieved that van Diemen again asked him to command, given that the Governor-General had been critical of his first voyage. As it was, the new command came with very limited discretion. The Council of India set out in great detail what was known and what was not after the explorations of the previous 37 years. Its instructions attempted to foresee all possible turning points and provide ready-made decisions binding on the commander.

First, Tasman was to proceed with the south-west monsoon to False Cape. From there he was to coast eastwards along New Guinea to 9°S and 'next cautiously cross the shallow bay situated there' to make landfall at High Island or Speult's River (on Cape York Peninsula). The yachts should be anchored for two or three days while the shallow-draught, fore-and-aft rigged *Bracq* examined the bay 'for the purpose of ascertaining whether … there is any passage to the South Sea, a fact which may in a short time investigated and settled either in this way, or by the direction of the current'.

Second, the ships should follow Jansz's 'west coast of New Guinea' (Cape York Peninsula) south beyond 17°. If it trended to the south-east, every effort should be made to follow it, even against the trade wind that probably blew there, 'that it may once for all decided whether this land is separated from the great known Southland, a fact that might easily be ascertained from the heavy and slow swells of the sea …'. Heavy swells would indicate open passage to Van Diemen's Land. Making from there to Nuyts' Land would disclose how far to the north Van Diemen's Land extended and whether there was a passage to the South Sea between the two. Nonetheless, having made so far south by this route, return should be along the east coast of the Known Southland, following it as it swung west towards Eendracht's Land, 'after which the whole of the known Southland would have been circumnavigated and found to be the largest island in the world'.

Alternatively, if from 17°S New Guinea were found to be a whole with the Known Southland, the south-east trades would permit a continuous voyage along the coast to Eendracht's Land, and so much time would have been saved that the ships could go further south to Houtman's Abrolhos and there recover the chest with 8,000 silver dollars left behind in the wreck of the *Batavia*. They should also recover the cannon that lay across the chest, preventing its earlier retrieval, and look for the two mutineers marooned on the mainland fifteen years earlier!

Third, if the season were too far advanced to permit a *Batavia* excursion, the ships should try to get north-east from Eendracht's Land to Arnhem's Land and the Pieterszoon discoveries of 1636 to see if the latter were connected, and if there were any other islands between Bali–Sumbawa–Timor and the Known Southland. 'All of which having with God's help having been successfully performed', van Diemen expected the ships to be back in Batavia in July 1644, five months after departure.[11]

The instructions had been drawn up by Justus Schouten of the Council with 'the advice and concurrence' of Tasman and Visscher, but it is not to be doubted that Visscher's was the main influence, at least in matters of navigation. Tasman might still be useful as the necessary hard man, but it was Visscher who had been promoted to skipper after the last voyage and who was now made master of the flagship *Limmen*. Confidence, however, only extended so far and he was not nominated to command the expedition in the event of Tasman's death – that distinction would devolve upon the skipper of the *Zeemeeuw*.

Tasman may also have read lack of confidence in a particular instruction that appeared to be critical of his previous voyage. He was directed to husband wood and water carefully, 'that you may not come to be in want of them, or forced to defer your voyage to seek for them, or to return from such search unsuccessfully, which would redound to the serious detriment of the Company … and to the discredit of you all.' It is ironic that the only record of this voyage, for which the purposes and preparations are so well documented, is Tasman's chart. His journal is lost. The chart, which delineates the entire northern and north-western shoreline of the Known Southland, is a remarkable achievement in spite of a fundamental flaw, the joining of New Guinea to the Southland. We have no way of knowing whether the *Bracq*, as instructed, entered Torres Strait or observed its currents, but we can be certain that it failed in its mission. Indeed, Visscher recklessly went so far as to claim as a 'first discovery' that the two landmasses were one, joined by the shallow bay.[12] The Council of India's report to the Managers was critical.

> The said yachts … found no open channel between the half-known New Guinea and the known land of Eendracht or Willem's river … they however found a large, spacious bay or Gulf … What there is in this Southland, whether above or below the earth, continues unknown, since the men have done nothing beyond sailing along the coast: he who makes it his business to find out whatever the land produces must walk all over it, which these discoverers pretend to have been out of their power, which may be true to some extent.

The Council refused to believe that there was no profit to be made in a land so vast. It promised to have a further search made by 'persons more vigilant and courageous than those who have hitherto been employed on this service'. This judgement should have put paid to Tasman's already slim prospects of commanding the proposed trading voyage to Chile but, as after the first voyage, van Diemen told Amsterdam one thing and did another. The Council of India resolved to raise Tasman's monthly salary from eighty guilders to one hundred, he having given 'reasonable contentment' by duty done and service rendered. As if this were not sufficiently two-faced, the Council added that it found in Tasman 'the courage required to do additional good service to the Company on similar occasions'.

Soon after Tasman's return from the second voyage, the managers responded to van Diemen's query about the Dutch West India Company's charter rights in Chile. The managers were in no doubt that the rival company would assert such rights. Van Diemen interpreted this to mean that he should not establish a settlement in Chile ('which could easily be effected and maintained there') unless so directed by the VOC, but that he was not forbidden an expedition to trade for gold or even take it as loot should the Spanish be taken unawares.[13] The Governor-General was hair-splitting, holding that VOC 'mercantile operations' were permitted in Chile provided that they were not conducted from a VOC factory. He continued with preparations for his trading voyage, which would establish whether Tasman's 'new short passage' was 'quite free' or had 'more large lands lying across or in front of it'.[14]

It can be assumed that the voyage would have commenced in the spring of 1645 and that Tasman would have commanded, but van Diemen died in Batavia on 19 April 1645 and with him died Dutch interest in far-flung exploration. That September, at about the time Tasman should have been sailing on his third and most audacious voyage, the managers in Amsterdam wrote to extinguish whatever residual enthusiasm might have lived on in Batavia. The search for gold and silver mines, they grumbled, was costly and unlikely to yield favourable results. Extraction too was not without expense, as some would seem to imagine. The plans of the Council of the Indies were aiming 'somewhat beyond our mark'. On a self-satisfied note the managers called a halt to VOC exploration. 'The gold and silver mines that will best serve the Company's turn, have already been found, which we deem to be our trade over the whole of India, and especially in Taiwan and Japan'.[15]

When a consolidated chart of the two Tasman voyages was drawn up in Batavia in 1644, the known southland was given the name of Company's New Netherlands.[16] Notional coastlines were dotted in to join Nuyts' Land to Van Diemen's Land and the latter to New Guinea. There was less confidence about the unknown southland: no dotting extends Staten Land towards South America or anywhere else. The one place where dots of uncertainty would have been wholly appropriate, across the suspected gap at the south-eastern corner of Zeehan's Bight, is rendered as continuous coastline, as it is in the Netherlands State Archives copy of Tasman's 1642 journal.[17]

There is, however, another depiction, the so-called Eugene map. According to the inscription, it is derived from Visscher's chart of the 1642 voyage. It calls the Known Southland 'Nova Hollandia'. More significantly, Staten Land is now labelled 'Nova Zeeland', an act that decouples it from Tasman's unknown Southland without actually repudiating the concept.[18] There are no notional coastlines: Visscher has even been careful not to close Zeehan's Bight. In this we might read a conviction that no land had yet been found that definitely blocked his 44°S route to Chile. Thus ended Dutch East Indies Company's efforts to find the Unknown Southland, although the Known Southland – New Holland – continued to claim their attention from time to time as ships ran afoul of its coasts.

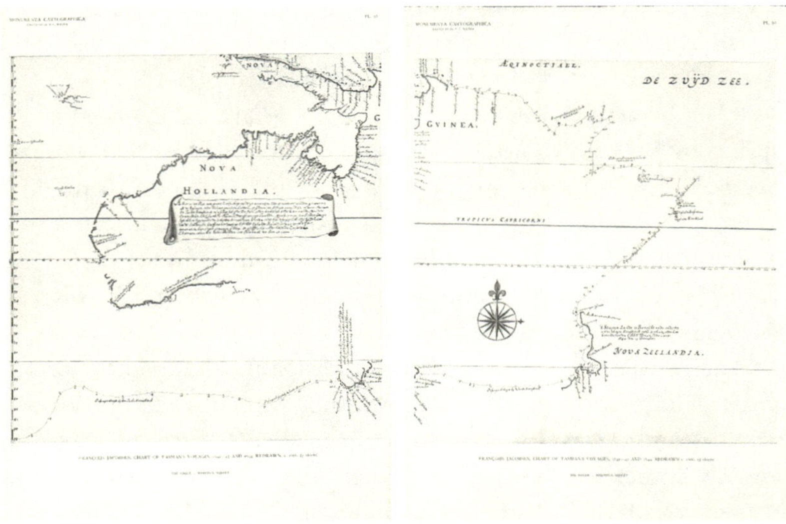

On his first voyage Tasman added Tasmania and New Zealand to the map and on his second he charted the north-west coast of Australia. Pilot Visscher has left Cook Strait open but closed off Torres Strait.

The competitors hover

The VOC's appetite for exploration might have been sated but there was no shortage of hungry rivals still looking for a place at the table. The French were late to the feast in the South Seas, and might have been even later had they not been reminded that there was an inheritance to be claimed and an obligation to be fulfilled. In 1663 a memoir dedicated to Pope Alexander VII called for a mission to be sent to the *Terre Australe* reported in 1504. Its author inscribed himself J(ean) P(aulmier) D(e) C(ourtonne) *Prêtre Indien*, and he was indeed related to Essomericq, the 'Indian' taken to France by Paulmier de Gonneville. Courtonne had compiled an account of the voyage from family papers. In it he asserted that Gonneville had rounded the Cape of Good Hope and sailed to a hitherto unknown land in the Indian Ocean that he called Southern India, whose inhabitants Courtonne referred to as Australians.[19]

Nothing came of the project, probably because Gonneville had declared that the return voyage in 1504 had taken just three months which, as any experienced seaman knew, was out of the question for a voyage beyond the Cape. Nonetheless, in 1664 a French Company of the Indies was chartered and began to compete with its English and Dutch counterparts on the sub-continent. The Essomericq story also became more plausible when a merchant seaman, Antoine de la Roché, was blown east of Cape Horn to land in the vicinity of Vespucci's Antarctic coast. It was inaccessible, but NNE of it la Roché said he had come across an 'Ile Grande' that had a good port and abounded in timber and fish. Although apparently uninhabited (and therefore incompatible with Essomeriq's homeland), it joined the list of southern lands awaiting further discovery.

In addition to the French and British challengers, there were some at home who were impatient of the complacency of the Netherlands-chartered monopolies. In 1676 a teacher of mathematics and navigation named Arend Roggeveen persuaded the States-General that he should be allowed to find lands with which to trade in the South Pacific Ocean. The West India Company, whose charter allowed it to claim commission on all voyages after the first outwards, sought a guarantee that the ship would not visit places within the Company's monopoly and stipulated that the voyage must begin within eighteen months of approval. All this Arend agreed to, but he could not raise the finance. He died in 1679, his dream unrealised but not forgotten.

Meanwhile the VOC continued charting the west coast of New Holland, but the Masters could not be stirred further afield by their men in Java. In 1697 Vlamingh reported good land along the Swan River, but nothing followed and his was the only serious attempt at exploration beyond the coast for decades. In 1718 Jean Pierre Purry, a Company servant, unsuccessfully urged the VOC to colonise Nuyts' Land as a source of wine and wheat for its Java establishments,[20] but the Company convinced itself that even if there was anything of value the finding would not be worth the effort. Not until 1756 was there an attempt to revisit the matter of the 'shallow bight' on 'the west coast of New Guinea'. For all the confidence with which the bight had been drawn on Company charts since Frans Visscher had dismissed the idea of a strait more than a century earlier, no Dutch navigator had yet set eyes on its supposed shore. And there was still an unexplored opening just south of the bight.

In 1756 the barquentines *Ryder*, commanded by Jean Etienne Gonzal, and *Buys*, under Lavienne Lodewijk van Asschens, were sent to the Gulf of Carpentaria. The full purpose of their voyage is unclear, but at the least they were expected to explore inland and kidnap a few natives. The ships were separated during a storm off Banda and the *Ryder* continued alone to the High Island north of Speult's River. The account subsequently compiled by VOC cartographer Gerrit de Haan – the only surviving record – is light on navigational data, but it appears that the ship then crossed to the mainland. Gonzal and his crew reconnoitred ashore until 26 April, when, 'shaping their course ENE close to the wind … following the trend of the coast till they had got into 10°30'S latitude', they again came to anchor 'in order to to explore the land also in this latitude'.[21]

If this means what it says, Gonzal had sailed through what is now Endeavour Strait to arrive at Peak Point,[22] thus becoming, without realising it, the first navigator to transit Torres Strait from west to east, 150 years after Torres had done so from the other direction. For 15 days he waited expressly for the purpose of allowing the *Buys* to rejoin, which implies that this southern entrance to the 'shallow bight' had been appointed as a rendezvous. The ship's council then resolved to continue the voyage, 'shaping their course along the land as high as they could in order to keep the same alongside; but they lost sight of the land all the same, and became aware that the said land lay at least one degree more to the southward than the chart had led them to believe'.[23]

These are the impressions of men who expect the coast to lead them north and east beyond Peak Point – which it does as far as Cape York – but are surprised to find that their ENE course thereafter takes them away from the land. They do not doubt that the 'shallow bight' exists but believe that they have found it to be deeper to the south and east than their chart shows. The land of which they became 'aware', one degree further south than shown on their chart, was the east coast of Australia, and therefore first seen by Europeans fourteen years before James Cook sailed by. There is no indication that Gonzal had the least notion of his achievement.[24] There is then a gap in Haan's account but it is apparent from what follows that Gonzal subsequently returned to the Gulf of Carpentaria and followed its west coast south to 13°S. As soon as he had trapped two natives for Company questioning he carried them back to Batavia.

After separation the *Buys* made landfall at Cape Keerweer on 24 April and proceeded northwards to the vicinity of Speult's River. There van Asschens sent a boat to sound ahead, as one would expect him to do were he attempting to reach a rendezvous within the supposed bight. The boat got well ahead of the ship and did not respond to a recall gun. It was soon lost to sight, perhaps carried into Endeavour Strait by the tidal stream. Neither the boat nor its eight men were seen again, although at that time the *Ryder* was only a few kilometres ahead at Point Peak, waiting for her consort. Van Asschens did not attempt to follow but lingered for 12 days hoping that the boat would return. Without even having landed, he then abandoned the voyage and returned to Batavia.

In cartographer Haan's estimation, Gonzal had done as he was directed 'so far as the shores of the Land of Carpentaria are concerned', even if he had neglected to explore inland. Van Asschens had reported nothing 'worth any serious consideration'.[25] There is no indication that Haan considered altering his charts to take Gonzal's easterly excursion and southern vista into account. The shade of Anthony van Diemen would have been very unquiet that year.

The Buccaneer's Archipelago

Even though the VOC was now passive so far as exploration was concerned, it was too well entrenched in the eastern archipelago to be seriously challenged by any of its emerging rivals. There were easier overseas targets and, as the Dutch themselves well knew – for they had made it so – the easiest of all was Spain. When the British put an end to their domestic broils by restoring Charles II to the throne in 1660, maritime enterprise underwent something of a revival. Its most dubious manifestation was buccaneering, in which licensed pirates joined in the near-universal pastime of picking at the carcass of the Spanish Empire.

One of these buccaneers was William Dampier, who had first gone to the West Indies to cut logwood. Subsequently he went a-buccaneering with an expedition that crossed the Isthmus of Darien, seized Spanish ships and began raiding the Pacific coast. In 1681 they called at Juan Fernandez, then uninhabited save for descendants of the founder's goats. The unexpected arrival of three Spanish ships forced the expedition to depart in such haste that a Mosquito Indian from the coast of Honduras was left behind. Dampier soon thereafter left the expedition himself and recrossed the Isthmus, but in 1683 he again signed up for a Pacific raid. Under Captain Edward Davis the *Bachelor's Delight* rounded Cape Horn and put into Juan Fernandez. It was March 1684. The first man ashore from Dampier's boat was another Mosquito Indian, anxious to learn the fate of his compatriot. When the abandoned one appeared, clad only in a goatskin, the two greeted each other like long-lost relatives. Robin prostrated himself before Will, who helped him to his feet. It was then Will's turn, and Robin reciprocated.

> We stood with pleasure to behold the surprise, and tenderness, and solemnity of this interview, which was exceedingly affectionate on both sides; and when their ceremonies of civility were over, we also that stood gazing at them drew near, each of us embracing him we had found here, who was overjoyed to see so many of his old friends come hither, as he thought purposely to fetch him. He was named Will, as the other was Robin. These were names given them by the English, for they had no names among themselves; and they take it as a great favour to be named by any of us; and will complain for want of it, if we do not appoint some name when they are with us: saying of themselves they are poor men, and have no name.[26]

With his gunpowder spent, Will had survived by making a saw of his knife to cut a musket barrel into pieces. Over a fire started with gun-flint and steel he had forged harpoon and lance heads, hooks and a long knife. He had manufactured fishing lines from sealskin thongs. Goatskins had served as clothes, hut-lining, bed and bedclothes. His self-sufficiency was typical of Mosquito Indians in their own country, where they were accustomed to making fishing and hunting instruments without forge or anvil.

After an unsuccessful attempt to take Spanish treasure ships off Panama in May 1685, Edward Davis cruised the South American coast. In 1687 he refreshed at the Galapagos Islands and sailed again for Juan Fernandez, intending to quit the Pacific. One night a great roar, as of the sea breaking, was heard coming from ahead of the ship. Alarmed sailors implored Davis to stand off until morning, which he did. Daylight revealed a small, flat island. The surgeon's mate, Lionel Wafer, recorded that they closed to within a quarter of a mile. It was unimpressive, but further west they could see what they took for a range of islands about 14 or 16 leagues in extent, from which issued great flocks of birds. Some of the crew wanted to explore but the captain would not permit it.[27]

Wafer placed the small, flat island in 27°20'S, 600 leagues from the Galapagos Islands and 500 leagues almost due west of Copiapo in Chile. The latitude given is exactly that of Copiapo and good to within a degree for Sala y Gomez Rocks (26°28'S), which are in fact about 480 leagues from Copiapo and 520 leagues from Chatham Island in the Galapagos. If the identification is correct, the high land seen beyond the Rocks could have been Easter Island, which lies 56 leagues further west. Mirage may have caused Wafer to underestimate the distance. As if anticipating scepticism, he was adamant that the morning was clear, 'neither foggy nor hazy', and his publisher was sufficiently persuaded to annotate the passage 'New Land discovered'. It was hardly convincing as a potentially continental discovery but Dampier advertised it as such on the frontispiece map to his immensely popular *New Voyage Round the World*. So it was that Davis Land joined the headlands of Terra Australis, or at least it did so if one believed that Magellan had passed between Davis Land and the mainland of South America. If, on the other hand, Magellan had tracked west of Davis Land it could not be part of a continent. There was insufficient room.

Dampier had separated from Davis just before the 1685 Panama raid. Ironically, he had transferred to the *Cygnet* because he 'had still a mind to make further discoveries', and Captain Swan's declared intention was to cruise north to Mexico and then cross to the East Indies to trade. After an unhappy transit with a crew reluctant to give up buccaneering, Swan was deposed as captain and abandoned in the Philippines. At the end of 1687 the ship cleared the Malay Archipelago, 'intending to touch at New Holland, a part of *Terra Australis Incognita*, to see what that country would afford us'. They made landfall on the north-west coast, 16°50'S, in the vicinity of Lacepede Channel. Dugongs and turtles were plentiful but there was nothing of value and Dampier marvelled that human beings should live there.

> The inhabitants of this country are the miserablest people in the world. The Hodmadods [Hottentots] … although a nasty people, yet for wealth are gentlemen to these; who have no houses and skin garments, sheep, poultry, and fruits of the earth, ostrich eggs, etc. as the Hodmadods have: and setting aside their human shape, they differ but little from brutes.[28]

Dampier was uncertain whether New Holland was an island or a continent; whichever, he believed it to be a very large tract of land unconnected with the other great landmasses of the world. When he attempted to convince his fellow crewmen to make for an English trading post they threatened to maroon him there on New Holland, so he kept his counsel and waited for a more convenient place to leave. On 12 March 1688 the ship sailed for India. Dampier's opportunity came in the Nicobar Islands. There he left the ship and buccaneering, but it was September 1691 before he was able to return to England, and with nothing more to show for a twelve-year absence than his battered journal and a tattooed Filipino to exhibit for money.

He was cheated of his 'painted prince', but the book he wrote from his papers was the making of him. *A New Voyage Round The World* was published in 1697. It brought Dampier fame, an appointment to the Customs and the patronage of Charles Montague, Chancellor of the Exchequer, who recommended him to the Earl of Orford, First Lord of the Admiralty. Orford asked the author to draw up a proposal for a voyage of exploration. Dampier the author naturally recommended a voyage to the Southland, of which Dampier the seaman had more experience than any other English navigator.

Dampier believed that a coasting expedition could hardly fail to find 'lands, continent or islands, or both', productive of the fruits, drugs, spices and perhaps minerals found in the same latitudes elsewhere. He planned to get there by sailing westwards 'that I might [begin] my discoveries upon the eastern and least known side of the Terra Australis'. Not if the Royal Navy could help it. Dampier was first offered a totally unseaworthy vessel, the *Jolly Prize*. The second, HMS *Roebuck*, was not much better but even a rotten ship was a lesser difficulty than the fact that it was His Majesty's ship, and in the opinion of the professionals should have been commanded by a naval officer. As it was not, they made sure that Dampier had a second-in-command who could show him how a holder of the King's commission should comport himself.

The uneasy relationship between Pirate Captain Dampier and Lieutenant George Fisher RN survived only as far as Brazil. In March 1699 Dampier put Fisher ashore in irons and had him imprisoned at Bahia on a charge of mutiny. Dampier judged that he could not now pass Cape Horn before the onset of winter and took the *Roebuck* around the Cape of Good Hope instead. Seven months later the ship made landfall on the west coast of New Holland in the vicinity of the Houtman Abrolhos. Even then Dampier might have sailed south-about to the east coast, but he excused himself on the grounds that land in higher latitudes would not be 'so well worth the discovering as the parts that lay nearer the line and more directly under the sun'. Besides, his crew did not like the cold. Instead, he made it his intention to return from the north via the unexplored east and south coasts in the summer months.[29]

Coasting northwards along the west coast, to Shark Bay and beyond, Dampier found himself in the coastal archipelago that today bears his name. He began to experience great tides that led him to suspect that here, in 18–20°S, there might be a route to the Pacific eastward through New Holland, but shortage of water deterred him from attempting to find it. He was also sceptical of Tasman's chart at this point, which showed continuous coast where in Dampier's opinion it should have shown islands, but he accepted the Dutch view that the part of New Holland north of this possible passage was connected to New Guinea.

With the north-west monsoon momentarily expected and scurvy beginning to ravage the crew, the expedition quitted the coast in 15°S and made for Timor. Five weeks and three landings had revealed to Dampier lands no more inviting and natives no more appealing than those he had seen eleven years before. He was remorseful at having had to kill an Aboriginal man during a skirmish but did not refrain from criticising them on aesthetic grounds: 'They all of them have the most unpleasant looks and the worst features of any people that I ever saw, though I have seen a great variety of savages.'[30]

After refreshing in Timor, Dampier sailed north of New Guinea to what his chart told him was its north-east point (in fact the northern tip of New Ireland) and proceeded south along what he took to be the east coast of New Holland. When the coast turned abruptly south-west, south of Le Maire's discoveries, Dampier knew that he was in unexplored territory. He failed to identify the passage that separates New Ireland from its neighbours, but a few days later came to a wide strait. He suspected that he had been coasting around an island and named it New Britain. New Guinea was 40 miles to the westward. The hydrographers showed them as joined, but here was a passage. Should he enter or should he continue south-west, where there appeared something like land? After all, according to his geography that land would most likely be the desired east coast of New Holland. Alternatively, if he followed the coast of New Britain through Dampier's Passage (for so it became named) he could confirm that it was an island.

He did neither, but he makes a point of telling us that he had been ill for three days. The *Roebuck* passed through the strait and, after noting that the coast of New Britain held north, Dampier went west along the known north coast of New Guinea, where there was little new to discover. He was conscious that he had allowed an opportunity to pass. In the preface to *A Voyage to New Holland* he pleaded a fouled ship, a pinnace beyond repair, an incompetent carpenter and a reduced crew wanting to go home. Home it would have to be.

The existence of Dampier's Passage led its discoverer once again to query Tasman's notion of a continent-sized New Holland. If New Britain were not part of New Holland, did that not lend weight to Dampier's theory that there might also be an east-west channel across New Holland in 18–20°S? A sun-sight taken when the ship was near Schouten's Island provided further reinforcement. It revealed that Dampier's dead reckoning had been nearly half a degree out. He suspected that he might have been deceived by a current issuing from a passage through to the southward, further sub-dividing New Guinea, 'but this being at best a probable conjecture, I shall insist no further upon it'.

But he would test it if he could. After clearing the western extremity of New Guinea he sailed south past Timor, intending to reach the west coast of New Holland again in 20°S. This is not the way home, the crew would have muttered. Dampier gives no reason for the diversion, but the latitude is that of his supposed east-west strait through New Holland. Again, illness confined him to his cabin for a crucial few days and no land was seen (or at least none was reported to him). Dampier then resolved to chart the rocks on which the English ship *Tryal* had been wrecked in 1622 but failed to find them, 'my people being very negligent, when I was not upon deck myself'. Seeing no prospect of his health recovering at sea, Dampier altered course for Java and home.[31]

The *Roebuck*, deteriorating faster with each passing mile, held together as far as Ascension Island in the Atlantic where she sprang a leak that could not be controlled by the pumps. Attempts to repair the hole were futile, the plank being so rotten that it crumbled away like dirt. The ship was warped into the shallows and abandoned after personal possessions, sails for tentage, and some provisions had been rafted ashore. There were abundant goats, birds, land crabs and turtle which, with good water, allowed them to subsist in reasonable comfort until rescued by a passing British flotilla six weeks later.

Dampier's reception in England was frosty. He was court-martialled twice, once for losing his ship and again at the instance of Lieutenant Fisher, who had made his own way back to England. The court members, hearing a complaint by one of their own against an interloper, tut-tutted about Dampier's 'irregular proceedings' and he was found guilty, it being the opinion of the court that he was not fit to be employed as commander of a naval vessel. He was also fined his voyage pay, which left him so impecunious that he was obliged a few months later to ship out again as a Pacific privateer.

This expedition, like many before it, ended in dissension and recrimination but it subsequently became noteworthy for something that had nothing to do with privateering. Dampier's ship was joined by another, the *Cinque Ports*, whose sailing master was a Scot, Alexander Selkirk. He fell out with his captain and asked to be put ashore on

Juan Fernandez. That was in 1704, 20 years after Dampier and Robin had rescued Will from the same island. Four years later, the time loop closed again: Dampier, then serving as a pilot with the privateer Woodes Rogers, was present when Selkirk was rescued. Dampier told Rogers that the castaway had been the best man on the *Cinque Ports* and Rogers took him aboard.

Selkirk had survived in much the same manner as Will, but there was a significant difference. After his powder was gone, the Scot had set aside his musket and caught his goats by running them down. He could not make fire with flint and steel, lacking tinder, but succeeded by rubbing pimento sticks together. By the time of his rescue in 1709 he was reverting to the wild, with soles tougher than shoes and words spoken 'by halves'. Will, with fewer pretensions to civilisation, had maintained himself in a material sense rather better, but Selkirk was of opinion that in his own case solitude and leisure to read his bible had made him a better Christian than he had ever been before or, he feared, would be again. Rogers had similar reservations about the impact of resocialisation on this now 'natural' man.

> … he [had] found means to supply his wants in a very natural manner, so as to maintain his life, though not so conveniently, yet as effectually as we are able to do with the help of all our arts and society. It may likewise instruct us how much a plain and temperate way of living conduces to the health of the body and vigor of the mind, both of which we are apt to destroy by excess and plenty, especially of strong liquor … for this man, when he came to our ordinary method of diet and life, though he was sober enough, lost much of his strength and agility. But I must quit these reflections, which are more proper for a philosopher and divine …[32]

The repatriation of Robinson Crusoe

> God forbid that we should give out a dream of our own imagination for a pattern of the world. – Francis Bacon

Woodes Roger's account turned Alexander Selkirk into a celebrity. Daniel Defoe was neither a philosopher nor a doctor of divinity but as a journalist he knew a good story when he heard it and as an earnest dissenter he could see its potential for religious and moral instruction. Will, Robin and Selkirk became the inspiration for his most famous adventure story and the first realistic novel in English. They are the reality behind a fiction that Defoe pretends is true. His Robinson Crusoe is Alexander Elsewhere – Defoe has shifted the main action from Juan Fernandez to the mouth of the Orinoco River. His aim, beyond mere entertainment and moral uplift, is to revive British interest in the Guianas, dormant since Sir Walter Raleigh's doomed expeditions in search of El Dorado a century earlier.

So in place of Will the survivor and Selkirk the voluntary exile there is Crusoe the colonist, carrying the banner for British empire in Spanish America. He is dependent on Western technology, especially gunpowder.[33] Will and Selkirk had soon expended theirs and had fallen back on ingenuity, but from his wrecked ship Crusoe is able to get 'so many necessary things as will either supply my wants, or enable me to supply myself, even as long as I live'.[34] When, 25 years later, the cannibals bring Man Friday ashore, Crusoe is living in reasonable circumstances by Western standards and still has sufficient powder to deal with any number of savages. Furthermore, with Friday and the persons they subsequently rescue he can people his little empire.

At the outset Defoe swore that Crusoe existed and the story was true but, as if to expiate the lie, like Sir Thomas More he provided his readers with clues to his sources. Crusoe writes that he was shipwrecked in 1659 – exactly 50 years before Selkirk's rescue – and resided on the island for 28 years, which happens to be the period between the stranding of Will in 1681 and Selkirk's rescue in 1709. In any case, the parallels were undeniable: Crusoe's staple for food and clothing is goat, as it was for Will and Selkirk; Man Friday prostrates himself at Crusoe's feet, as Will did before Robin(son); Crusoe gives Friday a name, albeit less respectful than those given to Dampier's Mosquito Indians.[35]

The island story formed the core of the *Adventures*, and was so immediately popular that the *Further Adventures* appeared later in the same year, 1719. A third volume, *Serious Reflections*, was published the following year. Seriously reflective from end to end, with no new adventures, it was doomed to literary oblivion, but in it Defoe came to close to admitting his fiction, justifying it by moral purpose.

> … here is the just and only good end of all parable or allegorical history brought to pass, viz. for moral and religious

> improvement. Here is invincible patience recommended under the worst of misery; indefatigable application and undaunted resolution under the greatest and most discouraging circumstances … [36]

For all its circumstantial realism, Defoe's romance has echoes of the late medieval travellers' tales, most obviously in Crusoe's *Further Adventures*, in which he sails to the East Indies and returns overland to Europe via China – Marco Polo in reverse. His tropical island adventure validates the more recent past, in which European powers claimed to have brought civilisation and religion to benighted heathen. The story's most modern element, the dichotomy between natural man and his civilised counterpart, is paradoxical. Crusoe is the fitter to rejoin society by having purged himself of the corruptions of civilised life but now he has to develop a new and truly moral sense of responsibility that reconciles personal selfishness – individual integrity – with social altruism. To relapse, as Crusoe arguably does on release from the island, is to fail.

Defoe sought to promote self-improvement – individual and national, material and moral – but fable is more potent than propaganda and homily. The vehicle has dumped its baggage. *Robinson Crusoe* retains its grip on the Western imagination because it is a ripping yarn, not because it is a moral tale. What is left is popular literature and, incidentally, popular geography. In 1966 the government of Chile, looking to promote tourism, repatriated the castaway from the Orinoco to Juan Fernandez. *More Landwards*, the scene of Selkirk's exile, was renamed Robinson Crusoe Island. *Further Off*, which the Scot probably never saw, became Alexander Selkirk's Island.

7

South Sea Bubbles

Selkirk's rescuer, Woodes Rogers, had brought home a fortune for his investors. Commerce raiding during the War of the Spanish Succession was immensely rewarding for a few individuals but that was no consolation for a British government deep in war debt and getting deeper. Robert Harley's Tories began manoeuvering for a peace that would leave the Spanish Empire largely intact and independent as a counterweight to the ambitions of Louis XIV. Along the way they hoped to extract trade concessions that would help to repair the national finances.

In 1711 the government chartered a South Seas Company, granting it rights of 'sole trade and traffick' from the Orinoco to Tierra del Fuego, and in the Pacific to the northernmost part of America 'unto, into and from all countries in the same limits, reputed to belong to the Crown of Spain, or which hereafter shall be discovered'.[1] Harley had calculated that such a potentially profitable monopoly would be irresistible to the government's creditors, who could exchange what they were owed for shares in the Company. Although Defoe was a propagandist for Harley at the time there is no direct evidence that the scheme was his, but it was consistent with a project for colonising Guiana that he claimed to have laid before King William III some years previously.

The 1713 Treaty of Utrecht brought only limited concessions from Spain and even the Company's temporary monopoly of the Spanish slave trade was not profitable. The directors saw more opportunity in financial manipulation and in 1719 elaborated Harley's scheme with an offer to take over most of the national debt. By talking up future trading profits, by engaging the self-interest of politicians with free shares, and by lending ordinary investors the money to purchase them, the directors inflated the price ten times over par and even further beyond any prospect of a reasonable return on investment.

There was a similar speculation in France, where the Mississippi Company was built on a foundation of paper money. When the bubbles burst many of those caught with grossly overpriced shares were ruined. Defoe was among the deluded, intellectually if not financially. In a brief history of Raleigh's schemes he had represented to the South Seas Company 'how that rich country [Guiana] might now be with ease, possessed, planted and secured to the British nation, and what immense wealth and increase of commerce might be raised from thence'.[2] He had challenged the directors, if unwilling to act themselves, to licence a group of London merchants that, Defoe assured them, stood willing to subscribe a million pounds sterling for the venture. It could not fail. Here were millions of naked people just waiting to be clothed in English woollens, with nothing but gold to pay for them. Now he sadly reflected that the English and French speculations had been 'overturned by their own bulk, the unperforming machines blew themselves up by the force of their own motion, and the projectors are overwhelmed with them'.[3]

The gold of New Zealand

The siren call of gold also helped reawaken a dormant Dutch project. When Arend Roggeveen died in 1679 his young sons had showed no inclination to pursue his South Seas ambitions, but in the course of a long legal career one of them, Jacob, served seven years at Batavia as a judicial officer of the VOC. What finally inspired him to go exploring at the age of 62, 42 years after his father's death, is obscure, but we know that he placed great store in Lionel Wafer's supposed Davis Land. If it could be found, presumably his father would be vindicated. His brother Jan was more interested in Tasman's New Zealand, which, as it was in the same latitude as Chile, should be similarly rich in gold. In 1721 Jacob approached the West India Company, which agreed to provide three ships to find Davis Land and the land supposed by Willem Schouten to lie further west in 15°S. The ships would sail by Cape Horn, both outwards and homewards, to avoid infringing the monopoly of the VOC.

Jacob Roggeveen's reprise of the Le Maire voyage, with similar father-and-son origins, met with initial success. The expedition rounded Cape

Horn in 60°S and sailed north-west from Juan Fernandez, looking for Davis Land. Failing to find it, they held west from its supposed location and discovered Easter Island on 5 April 1722. Roggeveen wrote that with proper cultivation the island could be made an earthly paradise but that it did not answer Wafer's description of 'high land'. After a diligent search to the east and west he recorded his frustration.

> ... one must be greatly astonished at finding people who contrive to become famous through ... writings in which they seek to establish embellished lies as clear truth, as applies to a so-called Captain Davis, William Dampier and Lionel Wafer ... Now when the narration is compared with our observation, nothing else remains to be said but that these three (for they were English) were as much robbers of the truth as of the goods of the Spanish.[4]

Having failed its first objective, the expedition headed north-west on a 'second voyage' in search of the islands where Schouten had reported smooth water with no hollow swells from the south. To their dismay, they found one of Schouten's islands by running their smallest vessel, the *African Galley*, aground on it. Very little food was salvaged from the wreck, which was a major setback. Continuing, they passed many islands unreported by Schouten. Roggeveen concluded that Le Maire and Schouten must have tracked further north than indicated in their log. These islands south of their track, and not a continent, must have been responsible for calming the waters. At Makatea in the Tuamotu Archipelago he wrote 'our voyage in this sea comes to an end' and on 3 June 1722 he convened the fleet council and placed before it options for the voyage home: they could run south or south-west to seek the 'changeable winds' that would carry them to Cape Horn; they could sail north and west to the East Indies, trespassing on the area of VOC monopoly; personally, he favoured making for New Zealand, there to refresh before running to Cape Horn.

Jan Koster, skipper of the *Arend* and a veteran East-Indiaman, flatly declared the New Zealand option to be impossible. Assuming that they could make the right latitude, when they got there they would still be unsure whether the land lay east or west. The ravages of scurvy, which had left only 30 men fit to handle both ships, ruled out Cape Horn. There was no reason to fear the VOC on the Indies route. The Company was only concerned for its trading privileges, which would hardly be threatened by the expedition's trifles, 'which are not sought after by any peoples except the worst sort of blacks in Africa, whom we put equal with those whom we might have found in the South Sea if we had discovered any considerable land'. Koster's logic carried the day.[5]

Many more islands were seen, but it was now June and Roggeveen feared that the north-west monsoon would set in before they could reach the Indies, forcing them to wait for six months until the South-East Trades returned. On 18 July the coast of New Ireland came into sight. As far as Roggeveen knew it was New Guinea. Here he ended his journal so as to leave no written record of the landings on VOC territory that would have to follow. He appears to have been less confident than Koster about how the Company would receive them.

When they reached Batavia it was Le Maire all over again: the ships were confiscated and Roggeveen was shipped back to the Netherlands in 1723. The West India Company eventually received compensation for its ships and was no doubt relieved that a failed experiment had not been a more expensive one. Into the limbo of might-have-been went Roggeveen's hopes of finding gold in New Zealand, but it was a near thing. From Makatea, the South-East Trades might just have sustained a WSW course to 35ºS at that time of year. On the other hand, a slightly more southerly course would have run the ships parallel to the east coast of New Zealand, so fulfilling Koster's dire warning about missing land altogether.

Roggeveen was the not the first to doubt the unknown southland but he had better cause than most. He had not been chasing classical or biblical references. His method had been to follow up reported sightings of land by English predecessors and he had been disappointed at every turn. Speculation, presented as such, could be excused, but Roggeveen believed that he was dealing with deceit. To what end, he did not say.

A new English nation

In London, deflation of the South Sea Bubble in 1720 was quickly followed by financial distress and political recrimination. South American trade and colonisation were no longer topics for polite conversation. It might also have been put to Defoe that the natives of tropical Guiana did not wear clothes, woollen or otherwise, for good reason. He skillfully changed carriage without changing horses, shifting his focus from the Orinoco to more temperate climes and reverting from the propaganda of Raleigh's history to the realistic fiction that had served him so well in *Robinson Crusoe*. He steered his writing desk south on an imaginary voyage of discovery that 'might discover unto the Pole itself, and find out New Worlds and new Seas, which had never been heard of before'.[6] It could, among other things, remedy his friend Dampier's failure to find the east coast of New Holland.

He took the title of Dampier's book, *A New Voyage Round the World*, and added *by a Course never sailed before*. The course was that sailed by Le Maire, but further south and in reverse. Defoe wanted to respect what was already known about Terra Australis, but to do that he had to reconcile Tasman with Quiros. How had the Dutchman been able to sail from New Zealand to New Guinea without encountering the continent of Austrialia? Defoe took refuge in the uncertainty of everyone's longitudes. Austrialia must be the east coast of New Holland, and Tasman had passed further east. Like Visscher, Defoe correctly assumed that by running with the westerlies across the Pacific it would be possible to explore much further south than hitherto. He recommended a transit in 56–60°, promising 'new inexhaustible funds of wealth and commerce, such as were never yet known to the merchants of Europe'.[7]

His imaginary excursion into the Pacific starts from Guam with the northern monsoon in September, steering south and east, not expecting 'to do something respecting discovery' until he has crossed Le Maire's track. In 17°S the expeditioners find land that they take to be an extension of New Guinea, remarking that is still unknown whether the latter is 'an island or the continent'.[8] They sail eastwards for 120 leagues, at which point the coast is lost to sight, but whether it terminates or runs southwards Defoe cannot tell (so providing a possible passage for Tasman between New Zealand and New Guinea). After another couple of days they turn south to seek the land. They fail, go east again, and south yet again until, in precisely 27°13'S and approximately 161°E, they succeed where, for all anyone knew, it might yet be so. Here, beyond contradiction by the map-makers, Defoe finds tractable natives who possess, we are not surprised to learn, quantities of gold. His co-ordinates indicate a place in the Tasman Sea 7° east of where Brisbane now stands. He refers to it as the Gold Coast.[9]

Defoe's voyagers are enlightened explorers. Although they boast of trading trifles for gold and sum up the prospects for exploiting their hosts, they do their best to avoid offending them. Six of the crew are so taken with this land of gold, oranges, flax, maize and llamas that they choose to stay, although warned by their captain that it is likely to be permanent exile. Still, he reflects, it is a wonderful place, now wanting only English women to raise up 'a new nation of English people'. What the absence of this civilising influence might lead to, however, he can only guess.

> I doubt not, but the natives will bestow wives upon them, but what sort of posterity they will make, I cannot foresee; for I don't find by enquiry, that the fellows had any great store of knowledge or religion in them, being all Madagascar men; that is to say, Pyrates and Rogues; so that for aught I know, there may be a generation of English heathen in an Age or two more.

The captain elaborates on the commercial possibilities. In such a temperate climate it should not be at all difficult to sell woollens to the natives 'especially when civilised by our dwelling among them, and taught the manner of clothing themselves for their ease and convenience'. From them, Britain would receive gold and perhaps spices, 'the best merchandize and return in the World'.[10]

It was Defoe's view that most of Britain's eastern imports were either unnecessary or injurious to domestic industry. Spices were one exception and pearls were another, so it is unsurprising that by continuing on to 49–50°S the captain finds a chain of islands rich in pearl. These he takes to be the Solomon Islands on the grounds that 'we can read of nobody that ever went on shore of them; except such as are Romantick, and not to be depended on'.[11] South and east the captain presses, to within the Antarctic Circle, the furthest south reached by a European vessel in those seas. His Pacific crossing ends at Juan Fernandez, where begins the 'chief design' of the voyage, an overland trek from the mines of Chile to the east coast of America south of the River Plate to establish a colony. The most striking thing about Defoe's imaginary geography of the far South Pacific is that while on its western side, towards New Holland, there are numerous populated lands and islands, to the east, from 165°W to South America there is practically nothing.

The dark face of empire

Some of Defoe's countrymen were less certain about the advantages of empire, whether for the colonisers or the colonised. Shortly after the *Voyage* appeared, Jonathon Swift published Lemuel Gulliver's *Travels into Several Remote Nations of the World*, a project he had been working on for many years. All of his nations are located in the Pacific; two of them in unknown parts of the South Seas. The locations are vaguely plausible but Swift himself undermines them by a reference to critics who whisper that these nations exist no more than Utopia does. Gulliver claims to have assisted Dampier with his writing, but seems to have relied on Jean Pierre Purry for his geography. Lilliput lies near 30° 02′S, north-west of Van Diemen's Land but supposedly south of the Nuyts' archipelago.[12] The country of the Houyhnhnms is approximately 45°S, west of the south-west coast of New Holland, but only a day's sail from its south-east point, which Gulliver explains by supposing that the charts place Van Diemen's Land at least three degrees too far east.[13]

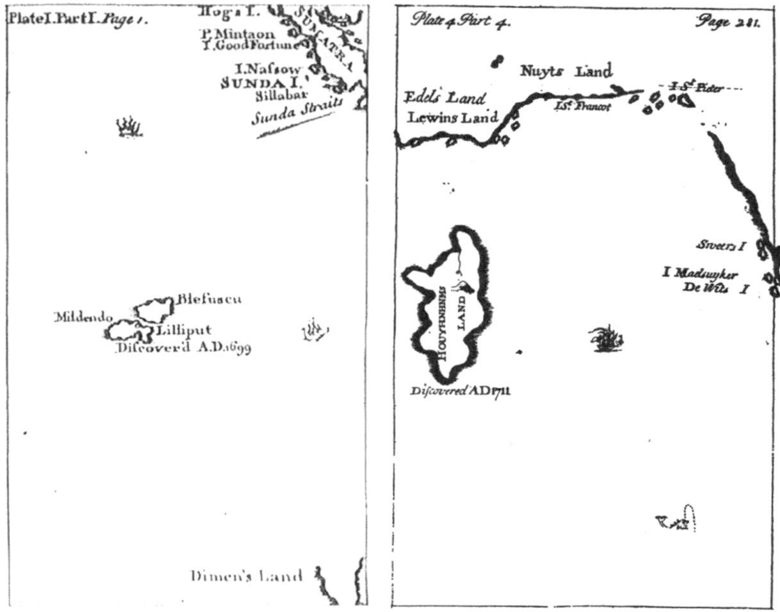

The Lilliputian Terra Australis is charted near a misplaced Van Diemen's Land south of Sunda Strait. The Land of the Houyhnhnms (and Yahoos) is rather better related to the known parts of New Holland.

The where, of course, is not nearly as significant as the what. Swift's islands are all inhabited by people with European manners, but European manners seen through the eyes of an outsider, Gulliver. As Lilliputians we are insignificant, treacherous and pretentious; as Brobdingnagians, arrogant, coarse and unfeeling; as Laputans, Struldbruggs etc., fantastic, exploitative, unfair and unhappy. Last and darkest, Swift shows us how we would appear to the eyes of truly rational beings. We are Yahoos, grossly inferior to a race of talking horses with which we share an island somewhere west of Van Diemen's Land.

It has been suggested that the Yahoos were modelled on Dampier's 'miserablest people in the world', but that seems unlikely. Gulliver, having been educated by the equine Houyhnhnms to recognise himself as a Yahoo, subsequently reaches Van Diemen's Land where he encounters naked savages and flees from them, only to return when he sees a Portuguese ship, 'choosing rather to trust myself amongst these barbarians than live with European Yahoos …'[14] Yahoos are unfit to rule themselves, much less others, and Gulliver is led to condemn imperialism as one of the crimes and follies of his countrymen. He protests that even though the British 'may be an example to the whole world for their wisdom, care and justice in planting colonies', yet

> … as those countries which I have described do not appear to have a desire of being conquered, and enslaved, murdered or driven out by colonies, nor abound either in gold, silver sugar or tobacco; I did humbly conceive they were by no means proper objects of our zeal, our valour, or our interest.[15]

In 1762 the British gained a slice of Guiana and half a century later they became masters of Crusoe's Orinoco island, Tobago. The trading privileges conceded by Spain in 1713, like many others extorted in peace negotiations, in the long run proved to be worthless. The negative aspect for Spain was that, not having become a respectably-bedded partner of Britain, she remained an object of lust. When hostilities again broke out between the two countries, with a comic-opera overture called the War of Jenkin's Ear (which unfortunately Swift was no longer alive to satirise), British thoughts inevitably turned to raiding Spanish colonies in the Pacific.

In 1740 a British fleet of seven ships under Commodore George Anson sailed for Cape Horn. His primary mission was to incite Chile and Peru to rebel, but there was much spoil to be had along the way. Scurvy ravaged his crew, but at Juan Fernandez they were able to refresh on Selkirk's goats and seals. Amongst the latter they saw a previously unrecorded large species with 'a large snout or trunk'. Anson called it a sea lion and it was initially classified as *Macrorhinus leoninus*, but the Commodore had in fact found the only pachyderm of the South Seas, the elephant seal.[16] The Spanish colonists were unmoved by the British overtures and Anson lost most of his force, but he intercepted the annual Acapulco-Manila galleon and after a four-year circumnavigation brought home treasure to the value of £400,000.

In the Devil's accounts that was £66,666 for each of the ships that failed to return, or £300 for every man lost to scurvy, dysentery, typhus and shipwreck. It is best thought of as a profitable disaster. The wreck of HMS *Wager* in Chile, an early adventure for midshipman John Byron – grandfather of the poet – became a byword for South Sea hazard. Anson drew attention to Britain's lack of a way-station where ships could refresh before tackling Cape Horn, and suggested that the Falkland Islands might be suitable. In 1748 plans were made to explore the islands, but they were dropped when the Spanish objected.

The patrimony of Essomericq

Having suffered through the Mississipi Company speculation of 1719, sobered French investors focused on their nation's growing trade with India and a diligent employee of the Compagnie des Indies disinterred Courtonne's memoir about the land of the Australians – *Terre Australe*. Jean-Baptiste Bouvet de Lozier persuaded the company that it was overlooking a great opportunity. It gave him two ships, *L'Aigle* and *Marie*, the latter commanded by one Duclos-Guyot, and he sailed south. Failing to find *Terra del Vista*,[17] the Cape of the Southern Continent, where expected, he ran south and east. On New Year's Day 1739 he sighted fog-bound land to the east and named it Cape Circumcision for the festival of the day. It lay in 54°20'S and 9°13'E, extending from north-west to south-east. The ships stood along the discovery in fog and ice for twelve days, willing it to be land, down to 57°S. On 25 January, 'despairing at length to find an inlet hereabouts, we quitted the Austral land, which seemed inaccessible', and steered north-east to look for Gonneville's land.[18]

That search was equally unsuccessful. Bouvet Island, as Cape Circumcision is now known, is so small and Bouvet's longitude for it was so inaccurate – 6° too far east – that it was not seen again until 1808, but it joined the list of continental headlands. In his 1752 survey of progress in the sciences, Pierre Maupertius, mathematician and astronomer, regretted that the discovery had so soon been 'laid aside'.

> The Southern continent is certainly entirely divided from the others, since the tour of the globe has been frequently made in that hemisphere, in a course parallel to the Equator, leaving the Terra Australis always on the same side … in the New Austral world, cut off from communication with the Ancient, and where long voyages are certainly unknown, we

> must find many things of different kinds absolutely unknown to us, many branches of commerce intirely new, and many wonderful objects, moral as well as physical.[19]

He recommended looking for the continent east of Africa rather than east of America, as the 'capes' there projected closer to the Equator and the ice that had thwarted Bouvet could be avoided.

A hemisphere for the taking

By the end of the seventeenth century a fundamental shift in the balance of oceanic power had occurred. The Iberians were over-extended, the Dutch defensive. The coming maritime powers, Britain and France, jostled each other on the frontiers of uncertain spheres of influence that extended from the Bay of Bengal to the banks of the Ohio. In spite of Anson's voyage, it was the French who displayed the greater interest in the South Seas. The dynastic compact between the Bourbon rulers of France and Spain gave the French East Indies Company limited access to trade with Peru and Chile.

One of the Company's captains was Alexander Duclos-Guyot, possibly the same Duclos-Guyot who had sailed with Bouvet. In 1756, returning from Lima to Cadiz on the Spanish merchantman *León*, he appears to have persuaded the captain, Gregorio Jerez, to hold east into the Atlantic in 54ºS, the latitude of Cape Circumcision. On 28 June land duly appeared, but well to the west of Bouvet's discovery. If they were connected, it would be have to be an immense tract of land but this appeared to be an island. They named it St Pierre. It was probably Vespucci's Antarctic coast and la Roché's first discovery – South Georgia.

In 1756 Charles de Brosses, President of the Parlement of Dijon, published his *Histoire des Navigations aux Terres Australes*. Not just another collection of voyages, it brought a new sophistication to austral geography. De Brosses divided the remoter parts of the southern hemisphere into Australasia, Polynesia and Magellanica and consolidated the information on each that could be extracted from navigators' accounts. Dampier's two voyages, for example, were disjointed into four geographical parts. De Brosses' purpose was to weigh up the prospects of each region for trade and colonisation, and he came down in favour of Australasia because it was better known than the other two, and because Dampier had sung the praises of New Britain. Furthermore, Australasia included, so de Brosses thought,

Quiros' Land of the Holy Spirit which, although unvisited for a century and a half, 'promised advantage'.[20]

To locate it in Australasia was a logical deduction, consistent with Quiros' claim that he had found a continent. If Tasman had cut across Quiros' track east of Santo, as he suspected he had, the Spaniard's continent must lie west of Polynesia, in the vicinity of New Holland. It might even be the east coast of New Holland itself, and that is how Jacques Nicolas Bellin, *Ingenieur de la Marine*, showed it in the official charts he drew up for the Ministry of Marine. In the conjectural tradition of the Dieppe school, he dotted in a coastline that connected Van Diemen's Land and Carpentaria to New Holland, taking in Quiros' discovery along the way. Some reconstruction was necessary: he reoriented the entrance to the Bay of St Philip and St James north-south and relocated Vera Cruz and New Jerusalem outside of it, creating fully four degrees of coastline for which even Quiros provided no authority. Robert de Vaugondy, Geographer-in-Ordinary to Louis XV, took the same approach when he came to illustrate de Brosses' work but with one significant difference: he did not join New Guinea to New Holland. This might indicate that he was familiar with Torres' voyage as well as that of Quiros but if so he would also have known that New Guinea extended much further east than he showed.

De Brosses proposed that France should send three ships from Pondicherry to establish a settlement on New Britain. From there, one of the ships would reconnoitre to discover if Carpentaria was separate from New Holland, to see if Quiros' land was as he had reported it, and to circumnavigate Australasia more deliberately than Tasman. The commanders of the ships must, of course, be proficient professionals, but beyond that they should be of sympathetic character, looked up to by their men and firm but not arrogant. They should not be temperamental, impatient or brutal in their dealings with natives. Where might such paragons be found? The Spanish were fierce and cruel, the English lawless and piratical, the Dutch avid for profit. It was to be regretted that the French, sociable at home, were so disputatious with each other abroad. Nevertheless, their flaws of impatience, indiscipline, presumption, insubordination, pretension, infatuation with false honour and murmuring against authority could be forgiven, said de Brosses. They were directed against Frenchmen and not inflicted on others.[21]

In the same year that de Brosses' work was published, 1756, the confrontation between Britain and France degenerated into all-out hostilities. Winston Churchill liked to describe the Seven Years' War as the first world war but, like that twentieth-century conflict, it was essentially a European war with global sideshows. Far from expanding the number of her colonies, France was hard pressed to defend those she had. In the face of Frederick the Great's expansionism, which was supported by British subsidy, the effort required of France to maintain her position in Europe reduced her capacity to respond overseas. In the outcome, military humiliation was complete. France lost Canada to the British and was weakened in India, but the world still was wide and full of opportunity for those who could see beyond a temporary setback.

As a young man before the war, Louis Antoine de Bougainville had been secretary to the French ambassador in London, where he met Anson. He knew de Brosses. During the war he had served as a colonel in Montcalm's defence of Quebec. When he was sent back to France to plead for reinforcements he was told that as the house was burning no water could be spared for the stables. As chance would have it he returned to Canada on the frigate *Chézine*, commanded by Nicholas-Pierre Duclos-Guyot. Nicholas was a former East Indies pilot who, thanks to his brother Alexander, was also well-informed about South American waters. He and Bougainville discussed what might be done to restore French power.

As early as 1761 Bougainville was formulating plans to create new empires in the southern hemisphere to replace those lost in the north. He recalled Anson's advice about the strategic merits of settling the Falkland Islands and took up the cause of the Acadians, French colonists expelled by the British from Canada. He put it to Choiseul, the foreign minister, that resettling them on the Falklands would place them in country much like that they had lost and give France a possession from which it could control passage from the Atlantic to the Pacific. Furthermore, his family was prepared to establish the colony at its own expense if allowed to become the proprietors. It was an offer difficult to refuse and in September 1763 amateur Frigate-Captain Bougainville, with professional Fireship-Captain Duclos-Guyot as his second-in-command, sailed with two ships to take possession.

Bougainville was not the only one who could see merit in the strategic placement of colonies and profit in proprietorship of them. In December of the same year John Perceval, Earl of Egmont, asked George III for the grant of St John's Island in the Gulf of St Lawrence. The colonists he proposed to plant there would hold their land by virtue of liability for military service. The scheme was too feudal to be accepted, but Egmont also happened to be First Lord of the Admiralty, and when the British got wind of what the French might be about he and Anson sent for Foulweather Jack. Twenty years after last wetting his feet in the South Seas, Jack Byron was chosen to take the frigates *Dolphin* and *Tamar* on the Royal Navy's first commissioned voyage of southern discovery since Dampier.

The motivation was strategic and the objective was to forestall Bougainville, but that was not all. Byron's Instructions, which reflected Egmont's wider conceptions, referred specifically to the Falklands and an elusive Pepys Island, but set them in the context of 'lands and islands of great extent hitherto unvisited by any European Power' and believed to lie 'in the Atlantic Ocean between the Cape of Good Hope and the Magellanic Streight, within the latitudes convenient for navigation, and in climates adapted to the produce of commodities useful in commerce'.[22] In spite of his South Sea experience, Byron, a conventional naval officer, was probably not the man for a project of such wide scope.

He was directed to the Cape of Good Hope, thence westwards between 33–53°S, but if circumstance dictated otherwise he could start from Rio, searching the indicated latitudes west to east for 300 leagues. Byron, whose inclination seemed to be to take the shortest route that his instructions permitted, found nothing there and quickly moved on to his second objective. He rediscovered and claimed the Falklands and proceeded to the Pacific. Here he was expected to look for a route to Hudson's Bay in the vicinity of Drake's New Albion and return via this North-West Passage, but again he invoked an escape clause in his instructions. If provisions were short, he could cross the Pacific and return via the Indies.

Taking the hint, he struck out across the ocean hoping to find Davis Land or the Solomon Islands. Like all of his predecessors, he found a westerly course hard to maintain and headed north to find the trade wind. Not until he reached 26°S was he able to push WNW. By then he was in a well-worn track and as a result found only a few new islands before reaching the Marianas. Like Schouten, however, he noted that the mountainous swell that usually persisted from the south was not in evidence when among the islands. He was sure that land lay in that direction and would have hauled away southward 'and attempted the discovery' had not scurvy been playing havoc among his men. All of the islands seen were well inhabited, which Byron could only account for 'by supposing a chain of islands reaching to a continent'. But the sickness of his crews put it beyond his reach.[23]

On return to London he was congratulated for the fastest circumnavigation to date, 22 months. Stories about the 'giants' of Patagonia titillated public interest but as an exploration his voyage added little. He had even failed to find Bougainville's Falklands settlement, though his ship had encountered the Frenchman's in Magellan's strait. When, three years later, Bougainville was forced to give up his colony, it was the result of Spanish insistence rather than British pressure. He was compensated for his expenses and he and Duclos-Guyot were sent back to South America to hand over to the Spanish, but that was not the end of the affair. Five years earlier he had unsuccessfully proposed exploration and colonisation of the South Seas along the lines proposed by de Brosses. Now, Louis XV endorsed his plan for the first French circumnavigation, instructing him to

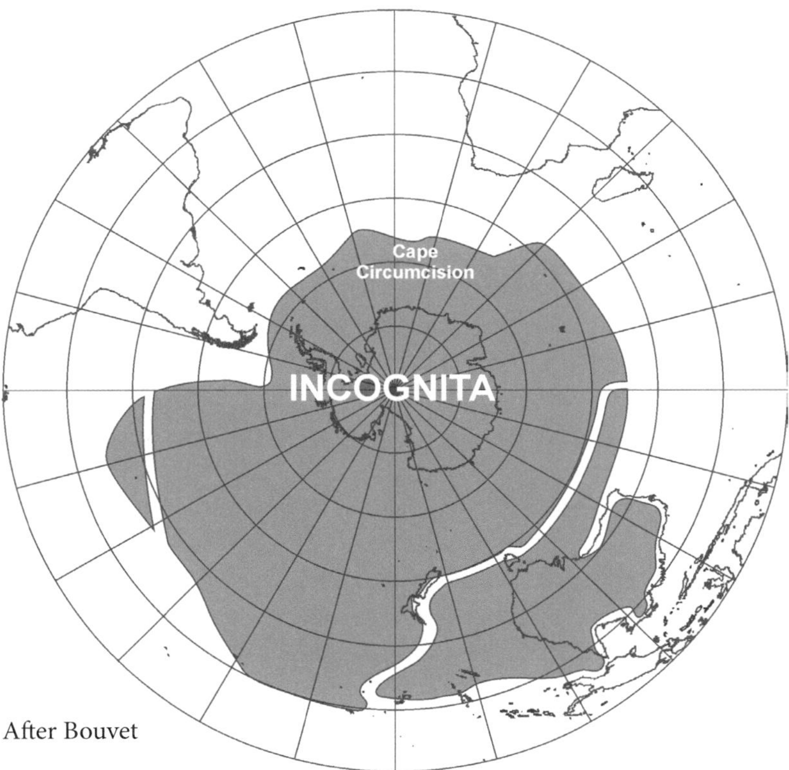

After Bouvet

> … examine in the Pacific Ocean as many as possible and as best he can the lands lying between the Indies and the western shores of America of which several were sighted by navigators and called Diemen Land, New Holland, Carpentaria, Land of

> the Holy Spirit, New Guinea etc. Knowledge of these islands or continent being very slight, it is of interest to improve it … it can only be in France's interest to survey them and take possession of them should they offer items useful to her trade and her navigation … the area that M. de Bougainville must concentrate on examining is especially the one stretching from the fortieth degrees of southern latitude towards the north, surveying what may lie between the two tropics … It is in those climates that one finds rich metals and spices.[24]

The trade of most interest to France was that with China. A Pacific route, defended by a settlement in Australasia, would outflank the Dutch and, what was even more to be desired, pre-empt the British.

The philosophy of natural man

The fable is always made for the moral, not the moral for the fable. – Daniel Defoe

In the considered opinion of Jean-Jacques Rousseau, *Robinson Crusoe* was the only reading suitable for a young person up to the age of fifteen years. The philosopher had not become an over-enthusiastic reviewer of juvenile literature – he was commending the book's message, not its amusement value.[25] Its focus on the basics of human life and, by inference, condemnation of the artificiality and constraints of civilisation, fitted neatly with his advocacy of the natural man who, he would later famously declare, was born free but everywhere in chains. Rousseau considered that natural inequality was of no significance; what distinguished social man from natural man was property, to which he attributed – following Locke – most of the wars, murders, misfortunes and horrors of the human species. Without this fell concept, for 'infant man' …

> The productions of the earth yielded him all the assistance he required, instinct prompted him to make use of them. Among the various appetites, which made him at different times experience different modes of existence, there was one that excited him to perpetuate his species; and this blind propensity, quite void of anything like pure love or affection, produced nothing but an act that was merely animal. The

> present heat once allayed, the sexes took no further notice of each other …

But then there arose Difficulties. Physical obstacles to gathering subsistence and competition from other animals and other men put an end to this idyllic state. From consciousness of man's superiority over other animals, it was only a short step to consciousness of superiority over some of his own kind. Furthermore, the Instruments created to establish that superiority also made Leisure that could be employed to create Conveniences. These softened both body and mind until they no longer pleased and even became Wants, at which time the loss of them 'became far more intolerable than the Possession of them had been agreeable; to lose them was a Misfortune, to posses them no Happiness'. Nonetheless, at this time there was a balance between the indolence of the natural state and 'the petulant activity of self-love' that was probably the happiest human condition that has ever existed. Most savages had been found in this condition, the real youth of the world, and everything since, apparently leading towards individual perfection, had in fact been towards decrepitude of the species. The chief culprits were metallurgy and agriculture.[26]

Rousseau believed that the savages had much to teach Europeans about happiness, but complained that he could find out little about them. He deplored the inability of Europeans to report foreign cultures in a way free of the prejudices of their own. This had been the work of sailors, merchants, soldiers and missionaries. The first three were subject to the limitations of their professions and, as to the last, the talents for studying man did not always fall even to saints. Europe was the poorer for their myopia. To understand oneself, it was necessary first to understand why others were different. What was required was first-hand experience by a savant like Montesquieu, who would be capable of observing and describing the natives of all savage countries, including Terra Magellanica. A new world would issue from their pens, and Europeans would thus learn to judge their own.[27]

Swift, of course, would have protested that he had done precisely that by using his imagination to describe European behaviour as it might appear to South Sea islanders. Moreover, Rousseau did not seem to regard his own ignorance of the savage state as an impediment when it came to theorising about man in society. To the contrary, he had already made up his mind about what might be learned from the savages of Terra Magellanica and elsewhere.

> A celebrated author, by calculating the goods and evils of human life and comparing the two sums, found that the last greatly exceeded the first, and that every thing considered life to man was no such valuable present. I am not surprised at his conclusions; he drew all his arguments from the constitution of man in a civilized state. Had he looked back to man in a state of nature … the result of his enquiries would have been very different; that man would have appeared to him subject to very few evils but those of his own making, and that he would have acquitted nature. It has cost us something to make ourselves so miserable.[28]

To Bougainville this was a blueprint for castles built on air. He had some claim to be regarded as a savant himself, having published a treatise on integral calculus at the age of 22. Five years later he had been elected to the Royal Society. He was particularly offended about Rousseau's armchair criticism of soldier-sailor voyaging, but he was also highly sceptical of the claims made on behalf of the Noble Savage. He noted that the Patagonians squatted to urinate, and queried if this should be emulated by Rousseau – whose own plumbing was reported to be in disrepair – as the most natural method. As to whether their miserable way of life had any redeeming features …

> To be frank, when one sees these savages, however one would like to philosophise, one could not express any preference for man in the state of nature over civilized man … Being in a condition that challenges the greed of other men and the anger of the gods, they have reached the most difficult point of all; being beyond even the need to express any wishes.[29]

But, as he would learn, the miserable Patagonian was not the only pattern of natural man.

8
Venus and Other Transients

On 9 May 1766 Jack Byron completed his circumnavigation by bringing the *Dolphin* to anchor in the Downs. In less than three months she was again ready for sea under a new commander, Samuel Wallis. The objective was unchanged, but the 'lands and islands of great extent hitherto unvisited' were no longer to be sought in the South Atlantic. Why the change of direction and why the hurry? Byron had raised the possibility that there was land south of his Pacific track and his speculation coincided with the publication of an English translation of de Brosses' work under the title *Terra Australis Cognita*. Its editor was an unapologetic plagiarist by the name of John Callander, who frequently praised 'the French Writer, from whom we have drawn many helps in our present undertaking', for promoting settlement of the South Pacific. Callander was sure that the ideas would find more fertile soil in Britain.[1]

Wallis was directed to search in the southern hemisphere between Cape Horn and New Zealand. His instructions made light of the roaring forties; he should sail about 100–120 degrees of longitude westwards from Cape Horn 'losing as little southing as possible'. Return also should be by Cape Horn, standing as far to the south as possible, this being 'the most probable method of discovering the Continent or land before mentioned'. If the winds carried him too far northwards in the Pacific, however, Wallis could come home via the East Indies.[2]

Philip Carteret, who had been Byron's first lieutenant, was given command of the *Dolphin*'s consort, a 30-year-old sloop named the

Swallow. He could not believe that the two ships were intended for the same duty; in his estimation the *Swallow* would be hard pressed to make it as far as the Falklands. He sought equipment, and was refused; he asked for stores, and was told that they had been provided. In Magellan's strait he told Wallis that the sloop was of little use to the expedition and suggested that she should be dismissed. Wallis replied that, as the Admiralty had tasked the *Swallow* to accompany the *Dolphin*, she must do so for as long as possible. He promised to 'wait her time' and assist should disaster strike but when, three weeks later, the sloop could not keep up as the ships emerged from the Strait, he sailed on. In his later account of the incident, he pleaded a coming fog and a rising sea.

Wallis found that he could no more hold due west than any of his predecessors, but he kept as hard south as he could, passing within 60 miles or so of the supposed location of Davis Land. The course carried him through the Tuamoto Archipelago to his most significant landfall. On 18 June 1767 he 'discovered' King George the Third's Island but, oblivious to the irony, noted that to its inhabitants it was Otaheite. Majestic as the island was, sailing master George Robertson believed that he could see the tops of even more mountains twenty leagues further south. 'We now supposed we saw the long-wished-for Southern Continent, which has often been talked of, but never before seen by Europeans'.[3] The Tahitians were initially hostile but once the power of firearms had been demonstrated a sex-starved seaman's idea of paradise could be had for the gift of a nail.

Wallis was ill for much of the time that the *Dolphin* spent at the island. He did his best to respond personally to native courtesies but strenuous activity was out of the question. Massage by four young girls somewhat restored him. The only exploring party that penetrated any distance inland found the view over the sea to the south blocked by Tahiti's formidable peaks. Wallis and his purser-cum-mathematician John Harrison fixed the island's longitude by measuring the apparent distance between the sun and the moon and working the data through the tables in Dr. Maskelyne's nautical almanac. Their result, accurate to within half a degree, was the more meritorious for being achieved using a method 'which we did not understand'.[4]

Wallis was not given to speculation. His descriptions of what he saw in the month he spent on the island are prosaic, but even he could not avoid using the word 'happy' when writing of the inhabitants. He was entreated to extend his visit, particularly by the queenly Oberea whose gracious hospitality would have shamed many a European monarch.

Their final parting was attended with such tenderness 'as filled both my heart and my eyes'.[5] Sailing on, he discovered or rediscovered other islands further west, but once he had crossed Tasman's track there was no prospect of finding the unknown southland. He made for the Ladrones, Java and home.

Egmont, though no longer in office, naturally wanted to know if the southern continent had been found. Wallis was evasive and Egmont found it hard to piece the story together. He concluded that he was dealing with concealment as well as failure; Wallis, with 'the continent … actually in view', had decided that he could not risk coasting it with just one ship (so it was all Carteret's fault for separating) 'and afterwards thought most prudent on … return, not to take notice that they had ever seen it at all'.[6]

Another interested party was rather more scathing. Alexander Dalrymple, a young Scot formerly in the service of the British East India Company at Madras, had privately researched the Spanish and Dutch voyages of discovery. Among his finds was a manuscript, captured at Manila from Spain during the Seven Years' War, which showed Torres' discoveries south of New Guinea. Some years afterwards Dalrymple had sailed the Malay Archipelago in the *Cuddalore*, a schooner commanded by George Baker, exploring commercial possibilities on behalf of his employers. He claimed that almost from infancy discovery had been 'the fond object of his attention', and in later years he had dreamed of matching the exploits of Columbus and Magellan by discovering a southern continent. 'Every young man enters life with a passion to emulate those characters which have gained his admiration. In most men the rubs of life soon blunt this passion; in some it prevails over all difficulties'.[7]

By 1765, when he returned to England, he was a seasoned navigator and a skilled hydrographer. He had an introduction to Egmont, which recommended him as an expert on South Pacific exploration, but he played no part in the planning of the Wallis expedition. He was disqualified because he was not a naval officer, and it was both misery and vindication for him to watch uniformed incompetents, as he saw them, fumble the great opportunity that by merit should have been his. Before Wallis returned Dalrymple had printed, but had not published, *An Account of the Discoveries made in the South Pacifick Ocean*. In the preface he candidly admitted that it was a job application, and thoughtfully drafted a job description to go with it. He did not specify the employer he had in mind, but the Royal Navy and the East India

Company were not the only institutions interested in the South Seas. Dalrymple was pinning his hopes on the Royal Society, and he told it what sort of person it needed in terms reminiscent of those used by de Brosses.

> Intrepidity, joined to every naval accomplishment, is not adequate to this task. To execute it effectually, not only a knowledge of what has been done, and a retrospect to whatever is worthy [of] imitation, or blameable in past discoverers, are requisite; but also a philosophick idea of winds and seasons; a freedom from prejudice; attention to the temper and disposition of men in their uncultivated state; and, perhaps not less than all, a consideration of the rights and value of man's life, to secure a patient abstinence from the use of firearms against the native Indians, who must be ignorant of the intentions and language of the discoverer.[8]

The long way home

As Carteret had watched the *Dolphin* recede from view he had given up all hope of seeing her again that side of England, 'no plan of operation having been settled, nor any place of rendezvous appointed'.[9] The *Swallow*'s hull was so badly encrusted that she could not tack unless the boat pulled her head across the wind. He had no goods to trade for refreshments, and no forge or iron to make good any equipment failure. The only alternative to going forward was to go back, but Carteret had already decided that the western end of Magellan's strait was too dangerous a navigation to revisit; they would have to go on. The *Swallow* headed north from Masafuero to find a breeze that she could run before. In 25°S it became possible to head west and Carteret went looking for Davis Land. He failed to find it, and declared that he had either sailed over it or would at least have seen it 'if there had been any such place'. He sailed 40 degrees westwards in 28°S, the highest latitude the wind would permit, and so missed Easter Island in 27°S, although he believed that it might lie to the north of his track, as would the 'supposed continent' of Davis Land, if it existed.

Carteret, his ill-sailing ship and scurvy-ravaged crew notwithstanding, was now holding west on a more southerly track than any predecessor and on 2 July 1767 he discovered uninhabited Pitcairn Island. He bore up through the southern Tuamotos, finding several small islands but no indication of a continent. By 22 July the ship was in 18°S and Carteret considered his options. Despite his best endeavours he could not maintain a high southern latitude. Preservation of ship and crew had to be given priority. He headed northward, seeking the mildness of the trade wind. If the charts were accurate, there he might find an island where he could refresh and repair in preparation for another push to the south when the season permitted. 'And if I should discover a continent, and procure a sufficient supply of provisions', it was his intention to follow its coast southward until the equinox, at which time he would get into a high southern latitude and go west about to the Cape of Good Hope or return eastward via the Falkland Islands.[10]

Carteret's plan failed at the first obstacle. The south-east trades did not arrive until the ship was in 16ºS, and then blew so briskly that there was no alternative but to run before them to 10ºS. As that was the reported latitude of the southernmost Solomon Islands, Carteret decided to make the best of a bad job by making west to find them. When five degrees beyond their position he concluded that, if they existed, they were incorrectly charted. His assessment was sound and when land was seen nine days later, in the same latitude, he did not change his mind. The islands he called Queen Charlotte's were in fact Mendaña's Santa Cruz, undisturbed for 172 years. The islands proved to be as fatal to his hopes of southern discovery as they had been to Mendaña's. The sailing master of the *Swallow*, sent to reconnoitre, provoked the natives by cutting down a coconut palm and in reprisal they attacked his boat. Seven men were wounded, four fatally. Among the mortally wounded was the master, a particularly serious loss as he was one of only three navigators on the ship.

With no prospect of refreshment there, Carteret had no choice but to haul off for somewhere he was confident that he could find – Dampier's New Britain. Sailing north-west, the ship passed several small islands. Names were bestowed, because Carteret believed they 'had never been seen by any European navigator before'. He was wrong. He had rediscovered the Solomon Islands, well to the west of the longitude indicated by Mendaña. As they afforded him only a few coconuts he could not tarry. It was late August, and if he were not well to the west by the time the monsoon arrived it would bar him from the Indies.

New Britain provided relief for his crew with the fleshy crown of the cabbage tree palm, which the captain praised as among the most powerful anti-scorbutics known. Wind and current conspired to deny Carteret passage to the east along Dampier's track but made amends by forcing him into St George's Bay, which he found to be a channel that divided New Britain east and west. He named the eastern portion

New Ireland, and had to make a further subdivision when its northern extremity turned out to be a third island. The name Nova Scotia had been bestowed elsewhere so Carteret resorted to the name of his monarch's fourth realm – the island became New Hanover. By November he was in the Celebes, but the 'shifting season' had commenced and Batavia was too far to windward.

It was May 1768 before he reached that port, and another four months before the *Swallow* was in any condition to face the Indian and Atlantic Oceans. In all, Carteret lost nearly a year in the Indies. What that meant, even in such a slow-moving age, was brought home to him as the *Swallow* struggled across the equator in the Atlantic. On 19 February 1769 a ship was seen to leeward. She hoisted French colours and on the following day tacked to come up to the *Swallow*. Carteret was surprised to hear his ship and himself hailed by name, and to be told that after the return of the *Dolphin* it had been supposed in Europe that they had been wrecked in the Strait of Magellan. He asked, in turn, who it was that was so well acquainted with his proceedings?

Overtaken

It was Bougainville. After handing over the Falklands to Spain he had followed Wallis and Carteret into the Pacific. Trailing them by nine months, he had looked for Davis Land in vain and then struck west along Quiros' track between 15–20°S. He had encountered tiny islands and speculated how they had come to be inhabited. He briefly headed south to look for a continent, found nothing, and mildly chided the geographers who he thought had made far too much of what Quiros had been told by the natives.

> I agree, that it is difficult to conceive such a number of low islands, and almost drowned lands, without supposing a continent near it. But geography is a science of facts; in studying it, authors must by no means give way to any system, formed in their studies, unless they would run the risk of being subject to very great errors, which can be rectified only at the expense of navigators.[11]

Bougainville had himself fallen into the error of generalising from the particular. When he reached Tahiti, the alleged joys of the natural state that he had criticised as a great error in respect of the Patagonians seemed here to be no less than the truth. His anchorage was sufficiently removed from that of Wallis for him not to hear of the Englishman's visit. Where Wallis had drily noted that sexual license prevailed, Bougainville rhapsodised. He called the island Cythera, the birthplace of Venus, and she smiled on the French even more than on the British. Wallis' recent demonstration of European firepower had ensured that the daughters of Venus would embrace French seamen without the need for armed foreplay. Here, said Bougainville, is the finest climate in the world, embellished with the most attractive scenery, enriched with all of nature's gifts and filled with handsome, tall and well-built inhabitants. Nature dictated their laws, which they followed in peace to make up possibly the happiest society on the globe.

Property, however, seemed foreign to their way of thinking, if the way they made off with French possessions was any guide. There appeared to be little illness, although the surgeon reported traces of smallpox. Bougainville was determined that his men should not pass on what he referred to as the other pox; seamen without a clean bill of health were not allowed ashore. Rousseau was absolved. Indeed, he was accused of understatement: 'lawyers and philosophers, come and see here all that your imagination has not been able even to dream up'. There was much more in the same vein but then, while contemplating the prospects of a pearl fishery, a shadow crossed Bougainville's mind.

> … it is to be wished for the sake of the inhabitants that Nature had refused them items that attract the cupidity of Europeans. All they need are the fruits which the soil liberally grants them without any cultivation, anything else, which would attract us, would bring upon them all the evils of the iron age. Farewell happy and wise people, may you always remain what you are. I shall never recall without a sense of delight the brief time I spent among you and, as long as I live, I shall celebrate the happy island of Cythera. It is the true Utopia.[12]

In a visit of ten days it was only to be expected that many facets of Tahitian society would be overlooked or misunderstood, but what surprises is that Bougainville, having finally found a substantial Pacific island with a large and sophisticated community, did not enquire after or look for a continent in its vicinity. His attention remained fixed on Quiros' Austrialia, which he continued to seek along the fifteenth parallel. When, a month after leaving Tahiti, seamen began manifesting souvenirs of the visit, Bougainville inserted a 'warning to travellers' in his journal. He noted that several venereal diseases, indeed all of the types known in Europe, had appeared. Aotouru, a Tahitian who had joined the expedition, was examined and found 'riddled'. In spite of his unconcern, he was treated anyway. How had the Tahitians become infected? Columbus' men had carried syphilis from America to Europe, but Tahiti was an island in a vast sea. The consensus aboard the ship was that the disease must be nature's penalty for promiscuity. Lock up four healthy men with one healthy woman and the result would be the same.[13]

On 22 May 1768 the ships came within sight of an island that Quiros had named La Margaritana, 100 kilometres east of Santo. After 162 years the Spaniard's claims were about to be tested, but it would first be necessary for Bougainville to realise where he was. Five days later, having threaded his way past a number of large islands, he was still unsure.

> We see no land ahead of us and I am beginning to believe that this is not the Bay of St James and St Philip, although the aspects are similar to the description given by Quiros and we are exactly in the latitude and longitude indicated in the extract from his relation given in [de Brosses'] history of navigations to the austral lands. The doubts will clear as we continue on a W course.[14]

He had in fact passed south of Santo – unwittingly confirming Diego Prado's contention that it was only another island – and thereby missed Quiros' bay, which was on its north side. Furthermore, his doubts could not be resolved because he had cleared the islands and was facing the wide ocean once more. Behind, he could see a chain of mountains, their heads in the clouds, marching up the western coast of Santo. He thought that between 12 and 14° they might form a fine bay, and wondered if Quiros had deliberately concealed its position by giving false coordinates. 'I have named the archipelago we have sailed through the Great Cyclades ... Now Quiros's longitude and latitude are left behind. Where then is his great land?'[15]

Still ahead, according to the Bellin chart, which showed it attached to New Holland. So he pressed on, confident that by sticking to the fifteenth parallel he would prove or disprove the existence of the lands of Quiros and Bellin; longitude might be problematical, but no navigator worth his salt would get latitude badly wrong. On the night of 4 June, the lookout reported that there were breakers half a league to the south. Bougainville hove to and continued at daylight. On the following day there was a good deal of wood floating alongside and the swell had moderated. Bougainville was sure that there was land to the SSE and the next day more breakers were seen, with some of the people thinking that they could see low land south-west of them. Yet more breakers were seen that afternoon. By now Bougainville was convinced that the Land of the Holy Ghost was none other than the Great Cyclades and that Quiros had failed in either his discoveries or his account of them.

And Bellin? His chart placed the Land of the Holy Ghost further east, in 148°, but according to Bougainville's own reckoning he was already beyond that longitude and the succession of breakers warned him against seeking Quiros's southern continent here. He complained that 'these approaches do not bear any resemblance to indications given by that navigator', but noted that they were like those given by another. Did not extensive breakers announce a low coast, like that encountered by Dampier in this latitude on the west coast of New Holland? These must be outliers of its east coast, which, Bougainville believed, would be no better than the waterless west. He was inclined to think, with Dampier, that the whole of New Holland was nothing more than 'a mass of islands and banks'.

Bougainville Reef, as the third set of the Frenchman's breakers is known today, lies 200 kilometres due east of Endeavour River on the lush tropical coast of Queensland. Between the two lies the navigational nightmare that is the Great Barrier Reef. Had he persisted in following the fifteenth parallel, Bougainville would have come up against the reef within sight of where James Cook came to grief on it two years later. His concept of the lie of the land ahead, as opposed to its nature, was prescient. He believed that it trended south-east to north-west, as it does. Having decided that he was closing on an unknown coast likely to be most unfriendly to navigation and, Vaugondy's strait notwithstanding, likely to embay him, Bougainville turned away.

> I therefore beg M. Bellin's forgiveness, but I shall not verify whether he is right or wrong. I shall be satisfied with the fairly justifiable belief that we are very close to land, that this land is not that of the Holy Ghost, [and that] judging from its approaches it offers no promise of any facilities for the settlement of a colony that would be useful to its mother country.[16]

With this last sentence Bougainville and France relinquished the Known Southland, sight unseen. A northerly course took him to the chain of islands that extends east from New Guinea. These he named the Louisade Archipelago. Unconvinced about the strait shown to the west on Vaugondy's map, Bougainville sought to escape the 'gulf of tribulations' in which he now feared he was enclosed by tacking south-east into the trade wind. Rounding 'Cape Deliverance', Bougainville was surprised to find more and larger islands in his path.

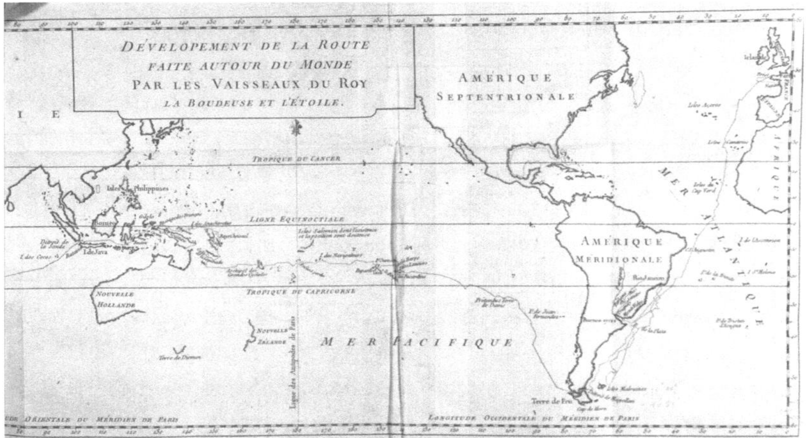

Fearing embayment on the coast of New Holland, Bougainville beats out of the Louisade Gulf and foregoes the opportunity to make a major discovery

He knew that he was too far south to have already reached New Britain, but here was a coast that extended fully 250 kilometres north-west to the very latitude of Dampier's discovery. What was this immense island? It was the one that today bears Bougainville's name. Without realising it, he had rediscovered Mendaña's Solomon Islands. Crossing to New Britain, Bougainville came to a sheltered harbour. Lying by the shore was a fragment of lead plate bearing the inscription:

> HORD HERE
> ICK MAJESTYS

Bougainville had 'followed' Wallis to Tahiti and now, in an even more unlikely juncture, he was following Carteret. Until destroyed by the natives, the plate had displayed the captain's name, the name of his Britannick Majesty's ship, dates of anchoring and departure, and the name given to the cove, Gower's Harbour.

Bougainville estimated that the Englishmen, whoever they were, had been there about three months previously.[17] He had his astronomer, Véron, make celestial observations to establish the longitude. The result, independent of their timekeeper, was 149° 44'15" east of Paris, which is correct to within a degree. Even Bougainville's deduced reckoning, deliberately uncorrected by astronomical observation since entering the Pacific, was only three degrees short. An eclipse of the sun enabled them to determine that their timekeeper was 5'10" fast, making it little more than one degree in error for navigational purposes. Bougainville was delighted that they would at last be able to determine the width of the Pacific. The era of longitudinal uncertainty was drawing to a close.

Bougainville made his way up the east coast of New Ireland and thence west and south to Batavia. There the Dutch told him that the Englishman ahead of him was Carteret, who had sailed only twelve days earlier. At the Cape of Good Hope Carteret was not nearly so far ahead and Bougainville became intent on catching him. At Ascension Island in the Atlantic, a message in the bottle that served as a visitors' book told him that the gap was down to three days. It should have been a proud moment for France later that month when the sails of the *Swallow* appeared above the horizon. Carteret was taken aback to hear himself and his ship hailed by name. Who was asking and what was their business? Bougainville identified himself, but claimed to be from Sumatra and Mauritius in the service of the French East India Company. He sent across a young officer, sans uniform, ostensibly to receive French mail that Carteret had accepted at the Cape. The officer's real task was to find out as much as he could about the British circumnavigation – in particular how far south *Swallow* had been in the Pacific – without disclosing the French one.

Carteret was suspicious of the story about a trading voyage to the Indies and showed his irritation at being questioned, so the officer left with no more than a souvenir arrow for his captain. Carteret's displeasure grew when he learnt that the French officer's boat crew, speaking sailor-to-sailor over the taffrail, had been much franker about where their voyage had taken them.

> After having received this information from my Lieutenant, I could easily account for M. Bougainville's having made a tack to speak to me, and for the conversation and behaviour of my visitor; but I was now more displeased at the questions he had asked me than before, for if it was improper for him to communicate an account of his voyage to me, it was equally improper for me to communicate an account of my voyage to him; and I thought an artful attempt to draw me into a breach of my obligation to secrecy, while he imposed on me by a fiction that he might not violate his own, was neither liberal nor just.[18]

On 16 March 1769 Bougainville put into St Malo, certain that the French still had a great future in the east if only they would stir themselves. The English do not go to the Indies for a change of air, he told his countrymen. Wake up, France, Neptune has not deserted you! He would assist the favorites of Venus, 'but it is only by assiduous devotion that one obtains the sympathy of the gods'.[19] To the harassed officials of the finance ministry it was just another call on an exhausted exchequer. To the merchants of St Malo, however, it was confirmation that the demise of the French East India Company's monopoly had created an opportunity. Four days later, Carteret anchored at Spithead. He was told that Wallis had returned safely with news of a most convenient island in the South Seas and that a vessel was already on its way there with a party of scientific gentlemen. It had something to do with Venus.

The planet of love

In the late 1760s an entire generation of astronomers was nervously contemplating a last-chance opportunity. Venus had passed across the face of the sun in 1761, as predicted by Edmond Halley, and would again in 1769. These paired events had not occurred since the previous century and would not recur until the next. The duration of the transit, if it could be timed to within a couple of seconds, could be used to refine important astronomical data – the diameter of the sun, the distance between the Earth and the sun, and the size of the solar system. One desideratum was to have widely separated observation points at the limits what Halley had called the 'cone of visibility'; another was clear skies. Both had been problematical in 1761 and the results had been disappointing.[20]

The gentlemen of the Royal Society were advised that only a relatively small part of the Pacific, between 4–21°S and 130–190°W, would be suitable for the southern observations in 1769, and that the location of islands within it was uncertain because of the longitude problem. They nonetheless asked the King to fund an expedition, which he was pleased to do, and then used his approval to manoeuvre the Admiralty into providing a ship. They were still pondering where the expedition should be directed when Wallis returned with news of Tahiti – big island, right area, location well fixed. The Astronomer Royal, Nevil Maskelyne, recommended Alexander Dalrymple as 'a proper person to send to the South Seas, having a particular turn for Discoveries and being an able Navigator and well skilled in observation'.[21]

For Dalrymple, observation of the transit of Venus was no more than a means to an end. His personal ambition was to find the Unknown Southland promised by theory and seen by so many navigators. Indeed, in Dalrymple's view it was no longer possible to talk of discovery of another southern continent, it having been seen already by Juan Fernandez on the east and Tasman on the west. As for geographical theory, Dalrymple accepted that there must be another southern continent to counterpoise the landmasses of the northern hemisphere 'and to maintain the equilibrium necessary for the earth's motion'. He argued that from the Tropic of Cancer to 50°N the proportions of land and water were nearly equal, whereas the land so far discovered between the same latitudes in the southern hemisphere was less than one-eighth of the whole area. Moreover, as Halley and Bouvet had reduced the unexplored area between those latitudes in the South Atlantic to 180 square degrees, the balance must be looked for in the South Pacific. The land there probably extended for 100° of longitude in 40°S, 'a greater extent than the whole civilised part of Asia, from Turkey eastwards to the extremity of China'.[22]

The Royal Society selected Dalrymple as an observer but he insisted, after his experience with Baker during their explorations in the *Cuddalore*, that he must also have sole command of the ship. That was a matter for the Admiralty but the President of the Society so recommended. There were precedents, but they belonged to the age of privateering and both the Halley and the Dampier voyages had been uncomfortable experiences for the Royal Navy. While he waited, Dalrymple was sufficiently confident to cast his eye over the collier *Earl of Pembroke* as a likely vessel for the voyage.[23]

For three months the Admiralty deliberated and in April 1768 advised the Society that the appointment would be 'entirely repugnant to the regulations of the Navy'.[24] Egmont's successor, Sir Edward Hawke, was reported to have said that he would cut off his right hand before he would commission another Halley. The Society was still keen to have Dalrymple go as an observer, with custody of the instructions and the captain ordered to follow his 'opinion'.[25] He declined, but disappointment did not dim his interest in the voyage. He provided Joseph Banks, a member of the Royal Society who had obtained permission to take along a number of scientific gentlemen, with a copy of the *Account*. Its chart of the South Pacific Ocean showed Torres' track south of New Guinea – which was sound information – and New Britain as the Solomon Islands – which was not. The chart is suggestive of vast scope for discovery. Dotted along an immense arc from New Zealand to the Tropic of Capricorn and on to South America are tiny sightings of land, real and imagined, by all of the explorers prior to 1764.

If Dalrymple was not to command, then who? For once the Admiralty did not insist that a commissioned officer could do any kind of sea duty with equal distinction. It looked for a specialist and found one in James Cook. Manifest merit had raised him from able seaman to warrant officer – sailing master – and self-taught science had seen him entrusted with a long-term survey of the Newfoundland coast. In 1764 Egmont had discussed with him its implications for the Newfoundland fishery, a mark of singular regard; First Lords of the Admiralty did not usually seek the advice of warrant officers. The Royal Society was disarmed, for here was a naval person who had the combination of experience that Dalymple had advocated, and in greater depth than Dalrymple himself. Neither Cook nor the *Pembroke*, renamed *Endeavour*, needed the King's commission for a task like the one to hand, but by insisting on it the navy was able to bring them both within the ambit of regulations that precluded civilian command.

The President of the Royal Society, the Earl of Morton, offered hints about conduct of the voyage and suggested that after observing Venus other matters could be attended to, particularly the discovery of a continent. The search should be made in low temperate latitudes because a continent in high latitudes or rigorous climate would be of little or no use.[26] That hint became an order in the supposedly secret additional Instructions given Cook by the Admiralty on 30 July 1768.[27] After Tahiti,

> You are to proceed to the southward in order to make discovery of the Continent above-mentioned until you arrive in the Latitude of 40°, unless you sooner fall in with it. But not having discover'd it or any Evident signs of it in that Run, you are to proceed in search of it to the Westward between the Latitude before mentioned and the Latitude of 35° until you discover it, or fall in with the Eastern side of the land discover'd by Tasman and now called New Zeland.[28]

Later that same day HM Bark *Endeavour* weighed from Galleon's Reach off Deptford and proceeded to sea. For a third time in the space of five years a British expedition was Pacific bound. The ship reached Cape Horn in January 1769. The Admiralty's instructions were most specific. Cook was to stand well to the south of the Cape so as to make a good westing, but no better than would permit him to reach the latitude of Tahiti at least 120 leagues to the east of the island. Even if Wallis' longitude for the island proved to be inaccurate, by running west Cook could not fail to find it.

Cook did as he was told, in the process eliminating several of Dalrymple's supposed headlands by sailing west and south of them. The land reported by the Dutch ship *Orange* in 1624, Juan Fernandez's continent, Roggeveen's 'signs' near Easter Island – all were relegated to the status of islands at best. On 24 March smooth seas and a floating log led some to think that land was nearby. Cook did not regard himself 'at liberty to spend time in searching for what I was not sure to find', even though he thought he was not far from some of Quiros' island discoveries.[29] Banks believed that they had converted enough square degrees of land into water to upset Dalrymple's theory of hemispherical balance.[30]

The *Endeavour* reached Tahiti in good time for the transit of Venus. Saturday 3 June 1769 dawned cloudless and clear. Hopes were high. Disappointingly, Venus chose to make her appearance veiled in a 'dusky shade' that made it difficult to time the exact moments when the planet's rim crossed each side of the sun's disc. Readings made by the various observers differed more than had been expected, in part because the natives had stolen the quadrant and damaged it. Cook also made a circuit of the island by boat and on foot and recorded that it was about 30 leagues in circumference. He then struck out for the southern continent. In mid-winter the *Endeavour* pressed south, westerlies abeam. In 40°22'S, with gales, rain and cold and not 'the least visible signs of land', Cook decided to backtrack to a more temperate latitude from which to make course for New Zealand.[31]

His instructions specified a crossing in 35–40°S. It was typical of the man that, although he had to retreat north almost as far as the tropic, by the time New Zealand was sighted on 7 October 1769 he had worked back south almost to 39°. Banks believed that their landfall was the unknown southland, as did master's mate Pickersgill, who entitled his survey of the coast *A Chart of Part of the So(uthern) Continent.*

Cook was non-committal but sailed south along the coast to 40°S as instructed, and a degree beyond. Like Torres, he knew that the way to avoid subsequent criticism was to do more than one's duty. Finding no suitable harbour or prospect of 'valuable discovery', he named the nearest cape Turnagain and reversed course, expecting a 'greater probability of success'. But as he sailed north along that coast, which he knew had never before been seen by a European, Cook could not have imagined how closely contested his priority would be. On 10 December 1769 he saw North Cape, the tip of the north island, and was then blown from the coast. By the time he regained it, on 17 December, a French ship coming from the west had doubled that same cape and was even then retracing Cook's route south. The ships missed each other by half a day. This time it was not Bougainville, but his spirit was abroad.

On 26 December Cook identified Tasman's Three Kings Islands. He was now in the Dutchman's territory but closer to the coast, so that when he entered Zeehan's Bight and crossed to Queen Charlotte's Sound he could see, from Arapawa Island, indications of the passage that Visscher had suspected lay there. This discovery of Cook Strait provoked an on-board debate. After the *Endeavour* had passed through, some of the officers continued to speculate that the north island, now behind them, might yet be part of a continent that extended to the south-east from the 12–15 leagues of its land they had not seen. Cook, although in no doubt that there was open sea east of Arapawa, took advantage of a south-westerly to sail within sight of Cape Turnagain. 'I then called the officers upon deck and asked them if they were now satisfied that this land was an Island to which they answered in the affirmative and we hauled our wind to the eastward'.[32]

He had been at pains to satisfy the question rather than dismiss it on the strength of his own knowledge, and a week later he repeated the exercise. When Lieutenant Gore insisted that he had seen land to the SSE, Cook, although sure it was cloud, dutifully went looking for it. He was resolved, according to Banks, that nobody should say he had left land unsought behind him. Again there was no land, but Banks was not discouraged. When they regained the New Zealand coast, the great height of the mountains led him to hope that it might 'absolutely be part of the southern continent.' He had read somewhere that the Dutch had sent other ships to follow-up Tasman's voyage, and that these had followed the land as far as 64°S. Still Cook reserved judgement, and although the coast continued to lead them south, Banks recorded that the enthusiasm of the continental theorists had waned.

> We were now on board two parties one who wishd that the land in sight might, the other that it might not be a continent; myself have always been most firm for the former tho sorry I am to say that in the ship my party is so small that I firmly

> believe that there are no more heartily of it than myself & one poor midshipman, the rest begin to sigh for roast beef [in England].[33]

Banks thereby places Cook among the 'No Continents', as he called them. On 5 March 1770, as the ship rounded what appeared to be the southernmost point of the south island, the captain wrote that he hoped it would prove to be so. Banks took temporary comfort when Stewart Island, further south, appeared out of the haze, but four days later even he had to concede that the island appeared to end in a point, to the regret of his 'Continent mongers'. On the following day they rounded this South Cape 'to the total demolition of our aerial fabrick calld continent'.[34]

By the end of March circumnavigation of the south island was complete. Cook finally delivered his judgement. New Zealand was two large islands divided by a strait four or five leagues broad; it was not part of 'the imaginary southern continent'.[35] He reviewed Dalrymple's evidence but found it hard to reconcile much of what he read. In particular, he believed that Dalrymple had misrepresented Quiros as saying that hanging clouds and a thick horizon seen in 146°W were signs of a continent. Cook could find no reference to this in other accounts of the voyage, his own experience was to the contrary, and he did not believe that Quiros himself looked upon such things as known signs of land. If so, he would have stood on to satisfy himself, 'for no man seems to have had discoveries more at heart than he had'. Cook's own voyage had left little space north of 40°S where the 'grand Object' could be, but what lay south of that latitude he could not say. In giving this as his opinion, he was not trying to discourage future attempts to find the southern continent. To the contrary,

> I think it would be a great pitty that this thing which at times has been the object of many ages and Nations should not now be wholly clear'd up, which might very easily be done in one Voyage without either much trouble or danger or fear of miscarrying as the Navigator would know where to go to look for it ...[36]

Even if it were not found, the voyage would not be wasted for there was a multitude of islands still awaiting discovery in the tropics south of the line. Cook here speaks with two voices. One chides those who allow imagination to subvert judgement; the other contemplates further employment to disabuse them. And so, in a few lines, he foreshadows the remainder of his life's work – opening unexplored seas to the gaze of the world.

The east coast of New Holland

He had fulfilled the Admiralty's instructions to the last black letter, including having enough stores in reserve at this point to carry him to a known port where he could refresh for return to England 'either round the Cape of Good Hope, or Cape Horn, as from circumstance you may judge the Most Eligible ...'[37] The shackles that had bound him to specified courses, latitudes, lands and duties were at a stroke removed. He high-mindedly declared that he wanted to follow 'such a rout as might conduce most to the service I am upon', and declared a wish to return by Cape Horn.[38] Bearing in mind that the Admiralty's objective for the latter part of the voyage was discovery of the unknown southern continent, and that it had recommended return via Cape Horn to Wallis as the best way of finding it, it might be expected that an easterly route in high southern latitudes would have been the outcome. It would, however, have made a second voyage less necessary.

Cook's power of decision was absolute, but he followed his usual practice and consulted with his officers. The Cape Horn option was discarded on the grounds that the ship was in no condition for such an undertaking. For the same reason direct passage to the Cape of Good Hope was rejected, 'especially as no discovery of any moment could be hoped for in that rout'. That left passage via the East Indies, to be reached by falling in with 'the East Coast of New Holland' and following it northward, or whatever other direction it might take, 'untill we arrive at its northern extremity, and if this should be found impractical then to endeavour to fall in with the land or Islands discover'd by Quiros'.[39] In this we can read the power of images. In addition to Banks' copy of Dalrymple, the ship carried de Brosse's *Histoire*, with the Vaugondy map that showed Austrialia attached to New Holland. The northern extremity of New Holland might be unattainable because Austrialia was part of it.

The New Holland option was adopted. Even without benefit of hindsight the choice seems hardly less hazardous than a Cape Horn transit, which would have taken place before the worst of the winter storms and with favourable winds. We can be certain that had Dalrymple been there, with Cook under instruction to follow his 'opinion', there would have been the mother of all debates in which Cook, ever respectful of their Lordships' wishes, would eventually have had to give way, for the Scot would have been adamant for the Horn at any cost, sure that somewhere along the way – admittedly south of his great arc of navigators' headlands – he would find the elusive continent.[40] Instead, Cook chose to boldly go where all before him, from Gallego to Bougainville, had faltered and turned away. He deliberately committed his ship to a near-certain lee shore from about 30°S northwards. If Vaugondy were right, they would be embayed and perhaps wrecked off Austrialia. Disproving Quiros was a high stakes game.

Banks was regretful at having to forego the unknown southern continent. He firmly believed in its existence, but confessed that his reasons were weak and his 'prepossession in favour of the fact' hard to account for. He had been impressed by navigators' accounts of the immense ice masses that had been seen from time to time off Cape Horn and, subscribing to the view that they were fresh water, could only think that they came from land to the southward, Tierra del Fuego being insufficiently cold to give rise to them. Furthermore, their motherland must lie well to the westward, in the Pacific, from whence the prevailing westerlies carried them to the Horn.

> The Body of this land must however be situated in very high latitudes: a part of it may indeed come to the Northward, within our track; but as we never saw any signs of land … it must be prodigiously smaller in extent than the theoretical continent makers have supposd it to be. We have by our track provd the falsity of above three fourths of their positions, and after that the rema[in]ing part cannot be much rely'd upon.[41]

As for Dalrymple's theory of a balanced earth ('which always appeard to me to be a most childish argument'), so much of the counterbalance had been shorn off as to make the South Pole already much too light. For all that, Banks still believed in the southern continent and, probably prompted by Cook's musings, turned his mind to designing a voyage that would prove or disprove its nonexistence once and for all.

Cook fetched the east coast of New Holland in 38°S and surveyed it northwards. He found that from 25° it trended north-west, reducing the likelihood of a lee shore, but one hazard to navigation was replaced by another. A great barrier line of reefs appeared to seaward, running parallel to the coast. To sail outside the reefs would compromise the coastal survey; to continue inside was to run the risk of entrapment. For the next 360 leagues Cook had a leadsman sounding whenever the *Endeavour* was under way. It was a trial that he dared say 'never happen'd to any ship before, and yet here it was absolutely necessary'.

On 11 June the ship was in the latitude of Quiros' Austrialia 'which some Geographers, for what reason I know not, have thought proper to tack to this land' and Cook, seeing islands and rocks ahead to the north, decided to stretch off east for the night in hopes of finding the Spanish discovery. A few minutes before 11 o'clock, in clear moonlit, the leadsman called 11 fathoms. Before he could cast again the *Endeavour* was aground, pierced by a coral outcrop. The following day she was lightened and dragged off, the leak slowed by a piece of coral that had broken off and lodged among the broken timbers. They got her back to a river mouth on the mainland and effected repairs as best they could. Nearly two months passed at Endeavour River before the ship was again ready for sea. Cook, concerned that he might be locked within the reef, sought and found a way out to the blue water beyond. He was reluctant to quit the coast, whose northern extremity he was sure could not be far, 'for I firmly believe that it doth not join to New Guinea, however this I hope yet to clear up being resolved to get in with the land again as soon as I can do it with safety'.[42]

He noted that bamboo, coconuts and pumice – none of them native to New Holland – had been seen on the strandlines at Endeavour River. The trade winds must have carried them from a country to the east. Most charts (for which read Bellin and Vaugondy) might place Austrialia as far west as New Holland, but Cook was 'morally certain' that Quiros had never seen its coast. His own assessment placed Quiros' discoveries 22° further east.[43] In spite of the now-obvious inaccuracy of Vaugondy maps in respect of Austrialia, Cook was still prepared to credit his depiction, and Dalrymple's, of a passage between New Holland and New Guinea. What he continued to doubt at the time was Dalrymple's contention, supported by Banks, that Torres had sailed through the passage.

One day after escaping northwards from the tangle of reefs that Cook had named The Labyrinth, he was looking for a way back to the coast, 'being fearfull of over shooting the passage supposeing there to be one'. On the night of 16–17 August the ship was becalmed. At 4am breakers were heard. Daylight revealed that the reef was less than a mile away, dashed by great waves that were carrying the ship towards it. The boats were put out to tow but by 6am the ship was 'a dismal Vally the breadth of one wave' from destruction, with no bottom at 120 fathoms. Occasional breaths of wind kept them off until a narrow passage came into sight. The ebbing tide denied them use of it but at least carried the ship away from immediate danger. At turn of the tide the ship was left embayed in a curve of the reef. Another passage was seen and a boat went to examine it while the ship grimly held off against the flood tide. Lieutenant Hicks reported that the gap was narrow and dangerous but navigable. The *Endeavour* was surrendered to the tide, which dragged her through as though down a mill race. This Providential Channel readmitted them to the shoals they had left with relief only two days earlier. Cook summed up his dilemma.

> The world will hardly admit of an excuse for a man leaving a Coast unexplored he has once discover'd, if dangers are his excuse he is than charged with Timorousness and want of Perseverance and at once pronounced the unfitest man in the world to be employ'd as a discoverer: if on the other hand he boldly incounters all the dangers and obstacles he meets and is unfortunate enough not to succeed he is than charged with Temerity and want of conduct. The former of these aspersins cannot with Justice be laid to my charge and if I am fortunate enough to surmount all the dangers we may meet the latter will never be brought in question. I must own I have ingaged more among the Islands and shoals upon this coast than may be thought with prudence I ought to have done with a single Ship and every other thing considered, but if I had not we should not have been able to give any better account of the one half of it than if we had never seen it, that is we should not have been able to say whether it consisted of main land or Islands ... [44]

Inside the reef once more, Cook resumed his running survey until 22 August, when, satisfied that he had reached the northern extremity of the coast, he went ashore on Possession Island to claim for his sovereign, as 'New South Wales', the east coast of New Holland. It was clear that New Guinea was not part of the Known Southland and that Austrialia, if it existed, lay elsewhere. The strait, that opened to the west, Cook named for his ship. The epic voyage was effectively at an end, as Cook did not think he could add to the Dutch discoveries further west, but it was a subdued moment. He had settled a centuries-old question, but the answer was no more than Vaugondy and Dalrymple had led him to expect.

> ... I allways understood before I had a sight of these Maps that it was unknown whether or no New-Holland and New-

> Guinea was not one continued land, and so it is said in the very History of Voyages these maps are bound up in: however, we have now put this wholy out of dispute, but as I beleive it was known before tho' not publickly I clame no other merit than the clearing up of a doubtfull point.[45]

The word 'publickly' is probably a veiled reference to Dalrymple's unpublished pamphlet, but as an acknowledgement it was both slighting and unjust. Dalrymple's chart showed Torres' track as his authority for the Strait. True, neither Torres nor Dalrymple had attached the Spaniard's name to it, but it was an obvious acknowledgement that Cook could have made. We might speculate that Endeavour Strait is so named because Cook was still unconvinced that Torres had passed that way, even after Banks had pointed out the reference in Dalrymple's pamphlet. As for the Yahoos of New South Wales, briefly encountered in two places, Cook saw in them Rousseau's natural men, and repudiated Dampier. Far from being wretched, they were happier than Europeans because they had no knowledge of the 'necessary conveniences' so sought by civilised peoples. Unlike the Tahitians, they seemed to want nothing more of Europeans than to be left alone.

> They live in a Tranquillity which is not disturb'd by the Inequality of Condition: the Earth and sea of their own accord furnishes them with all things necessary for life … they live in a fine and warm Climate … so that they have very little need of Clothing and this they seem to be fully sencible of, for many to whome we gave Cloth etc., left it carelessly upon the Sea beach and in the woods as a thing they had no manner of use for. In short they seem'd to set no Value upon any thing we gave them, nor would they ever part with anything of their own for any one article we could offer them.[46]

This echo of Swift's doctrine that autonomy is a precondition for human happiness reveals Cook's sensitivity to the impact that Europeans would have on the peoples of the Pacific. Manufactured demand for necessary conveniences could be as destructive of their culture as colonisation would be of their society.

At Batavia Cook was informed that Bougainville had crossed the Pacific. At the Cape of Good Hope he was told that the French intended to settle Tahiti. He feared that on the way they would also find the east coast of New Zealand. He could not know that the French ship so nearly encountered off North Cape had already done so, and that its voyage had the potential to derail his own developing plans.

Surville's unhappy venture

The *St Jean-Baptiste* had sailed from India, as recommended a decade earlier by de Brosses, but without official sanction. It was seeking opportunities for France in the Pacific, as advocated by Bougainville, but the object of the voyage was only incidentally imperialistic. This was a private trading venture inspired by vague reports of Wallis' discovery of Tahiti, as one of the principal partners, the governor of Chandernagore, explained to the Minister of Marine.

> This island, according to reports, must be situated in approximately 102° west of the Paris meridian. We suspect that it may be the one seen by the Englishman [Davis] in 1686 which is marked on the French chart. However, the English say that it is not shown on any of theirs. Whatever it is, the adventure is worth attempting and its success could become too important for our nation for me not to be in honour bound to sacrifice everything to make it succeed.[47]

If it failed, the cargo could be sold in Manila. Association of the discovery with Davis Land may have originated in seamen's gossip at the Cape of Good Hope about a continent seen by Wallis, but unexplored, south of Tahiti. It is otherwise hard to account for such commercial and patriotic interest in a mere island. The expedition was commanded by Jean-François-Marie de Surville, senior investor and a veteran of the French East India Company and the French navy.

The expedition sailed from Chandernagore on 3 March 1769, and made slow progress for one being sent to pre-empt the British. Not until August did Surville round Luzon and enter the Philippine Sea. Sailing south-east he came to the Solomon Islands but, like Bougainville failing to recognise them as Mendaña's discovery, he wondered if they might not be a continent. Unsure of his longitude and badly in need of a place to refresh his scurvy-stricken crew, he decided to make for New Zealand and struck south-west to ensure that he was not already to the east of it. The course took him to within perhaps a hundred miles of the coast of New Holland in 33°S before he was satisfied that he could safely turn east. He made landfall on the west coast of New Zealand's north island near Hokianga. After unknowingly passing Cook off North Cape, he proceeded to the east coast anchorage so recently vacated by the *Endeavour* at Doubtless Bay. By then he had lost a third of his men and, what was more dangerous, four anchors. Relations with the Maori were strained by his reprisals for theft of a boat and the anchorage proved to be unsafe.

Surville consulted his officers. He told them that the original plan was to cross the Pacific and double back to the Philippines. They agreed that it was now beyond the endurance of ship and crew, both of which needed time in a port with European facilities as soon as possible. Lima was suggested. Surville chose for the first time to disclose part of his instructions. They forbade any call at Spanish American settlements. He made all of those present sign the record of their collective decision. Forbidden or not, Lima it would have to be, exploring as they went.

On New Year's Day 1770 the ship began her Pacific crossing, holding steadily east between 34 and 40°S. No islands were seen because there were none to see. In late February Surville shared another snippet from his instructions. They were approaching the reported position of Davis Land, and were expected to look for it. For a week Surville persevered, making north towards its supposed latitude, but nothing disturbed the horizon. On 6 March he again called the officers together. They represented that water, wood and food were all in short supply and that scurvy was again wreaking havoc; it was imperative that they make for South America without delay. Surville agreed that they could no longer 'amuse' themselves looking for Davis Land. On 24 March they passed Juan Fernandez. By the time the mainland was seen Lima was beyond reach and Surville sought assistance at the small port of Chilca. He attempted to land in a small boat that capsized on the bar, drowning all aboard. The ship was arrested and detained for three years.[48]

When the voyage became known, it was dismissed as a failure and a disaster. Only later was it realised that Surville had rediscovered the Solomon Islands, but in the story of Terra Australis his search for Davis Land is at least as significant. Between the two of them, he and Cook had cut all but one of Dalrymple's Pacific headlands adrift from the supposed southland, leaving no room for a continental landmass in the Pacific between the Equator and 40°S. As for further south, there was a dubious report dated 1622 that Dutch navigator Dirk Gerritz had seen land in 64°S near Cape Horn in 1599, but even Dalrymple had expressed little interest in what might be found beyond 50°, as the climate was 'probably too severe for such countries to be of much value'.[49] Spice would be out of the question, and the only elephants likely to be encountered would be Anson's sea lions.

Unfinished business

The *Endeavour* anchored in the Downs on 13 July 1771. The last words in Cook's journal are not about the voyage just finished; they propose another. Sail for New Zealand via the Cape of Good Hope and refresh at Queen Charlotte's Sound. Leave via Cook Strait no later than early October and run with the west winds 'in as high a latitude as you please'. If there is no land you will round the Horn before summer is out, or haul northward to find the trade wind back to islands already discovered, and beyond them to others mentioned by the natives; 'thus the discoveries in the South Sea would be compleat'.[50]

While Cook had been away Bougainville had published his voyage. The literati admired its style and the philosophers were enthralled by the sexual mores of Tahiti, but Alexander Dalrymple was not interested in such trivia. What seems to have caught his eye was an anonymous French newsletter published four months after Bougainville's return. It presumed that New Cythera was more extensive than France, 'although the crews of the two ships were able to explore only about one hundred leagues of the interior'.[51] This vast province lay somewhere between the Strait of Magellan and Batavia. Its precise location had been supressed by M. de Bougainville. Dalrymple was convinced that the French had discovered his continent and rushed into print a long-planned collection of historical voyages to support the arguments of his earlier pamphlet. [52] He also escalated his rhetoric.

> The number of inhabitants in the Southern Continent is probably more than 50 millions, considering the extent, from the eastern part discovered by Juan Fernandez, to the western coast seen by Tasman, is about 100° of longitude … There is at present no trade from Europe thither, though the scraps from this table would be sufficient to maintain the power, dominion and sovereignty of Britain, by employing all its manufacturers and ships.[53]

Furthermore, he claimed, it was from this continent that the first Inca had introduced civilisation to Peru. The book began with a mock dedication to Byron, Wallis and Bougainville for their sins of omission. Commendation was reserved for one who was yet to come.

> The man who, emulous of MAGALHANES and the Heroes of Former Times, Undeterr'd by Difficulties, And Unseduc'd by Pleasure, Shall persist through every Obstacle, And Not by Chance,

> But By Virtue and Good-Conduct Succeed in establishing an Intercourse with A SOUTHERN CONTINENT[54]

This is not, as may appear, a dedication to Cook – who was yet to return – nor indeed to any previous explorer. As with his earlier pamphlet, Dalrymple was inventing a new role and he was inventing it for himself. When Cook did return, with only New Zealand and New South Wales to show for his voyage,[55] it was added to Dalrymple's list of naval failures. The Admiralty-commissioned account of the Byron, Wallis, Carteret and Cook voyages, written by John Hawkesworth, provoked him to furious pamphleteering. One thing that rankled was Cook's decision on 24 March 1769 not to follow up signs of Quiros' islands. In Dalrymple's opinion, not seeking what one was not sure to find was 'almost' enough to place Cook beneath further notice.[56] No matter that Cook had shown New Zealand to be islands, and had pushed Juan Fernandez's continent into a corner not large enough to accommodate more than one of those islands. He had neglected to investigate south of 40°, and had only sailed that parallel across a few degrees of longitude. For all Cook knew, 40 to 50°S could be solid land the breadth of the Pacific, with a headland much further north, somewhere south and east of Tahiti.[57] Hawkesworth understood why Dalrymple's attack was so intemperate.

> I am very sorry for the discontented state of this good Gentleman's mind, and most sincerely wish that a southern continent may be found, as I am confident nothing else can make him happy and good humoured.[58]

The yellow line

Cook's plan for a second voyage was well received in Whitehall. On 25 September 1771 the Admiralty issued orders for the purchase of two ships for service in 'remote parts'. Cook selected two barks by the Whitby yard that had built the *Endeavour*. Their names were to be *Drake* and *Raleigh* until it dawned that the Spanish might take offence, so they became *Resolution* and *Adventure*. Tobias Furneaux, who had circumnavigated with Wallis, was given command of the latter. Cook also caught up on his reading and found that the ever-busy Dalrymple was suggesting that the Atlantic too might hide a southern continent. Confusingly, he had called it Australia, 'comprehending the discoveries at a distance from America to the eastward', and represented it as 'another head of partition' to add to de Brosse's Magellanica, Polynesia and Australasia.[59]

On *A Chart of the Ocean between South America and Africa* Dalrymple had revived the Ortelius/Mercator Gulf of San Sebastian and Bouvet's Cape Circumcision as possible headlands of this continent. The South Atlantic had not figured in Cook's original plan. He now varied it and appended a chart that showed in yellow the track he proposed to follow. If land intervened the track would be altered accordingly, 'but the general rout must be pursued otherwise some part of the Southern Ocean will remain unexplored'.[60] The yellow line followed the sixtieth parallel around the southern hemisphere. Banks, publicly acclaimed as the eminent person of the *Endeavour* voyage, was optimistic that he and Cook (for that is how he saw their relative importance) would attain the South Pole, where he might set his heel and rotate 360° in a second.[61]

By following the yellow track, Cook's plans to avoid revisiting the discoveries of others unless it is necessary to resolve doubtful points like the Gulf of San Sebastian and Cape Circumcision

If that had been the extent of his ambition a second successful collaboration might have been possible, but Banks assembled a scientific party of seventeen and insisted that the ships be altered to accommodate it. Cook surrendered the great cabin of the *Resolution* to the scientific gentlemen without demur and had a round house built above it for his own use. The round house, and other alterations made to meet Banks' requirements, rendered the ship so unseaworthy that they had to be removed, but that was the least of it. Banks sought power of direction over Cook as to time of sailing from places touched during the voyage. The Earl of Sandwich, First Lord of the Admiralty, was prepared to mandate consultation but he drew the line at requiring obedience. Cook could not be expected to do anything that, in a captain's opinion, was inconsistent with the safety of the ship or the success of the expedition. Banks also sought power of promotion over the officers, so that he might influence them. Sandwich rejected the proposal outright as 'another attempt on [Banks'] part to get possession of the command'.[62]

The divided command that Dalrymple had foreseen and rejected five years earlier was threatening to become a reality, but it was avoided when Banks withdrew from the expedition, unable to accept that mere seamen knew better than he what sort of ships would be suitable and what the proper seasons for sailing might be. On 13 July 1772, a year to the day after *Endeavour*'s return, Cook sailed from Plymouth for the Cape of Good Hope, directed thereafter to the eastern parts of the far south Atlantic.

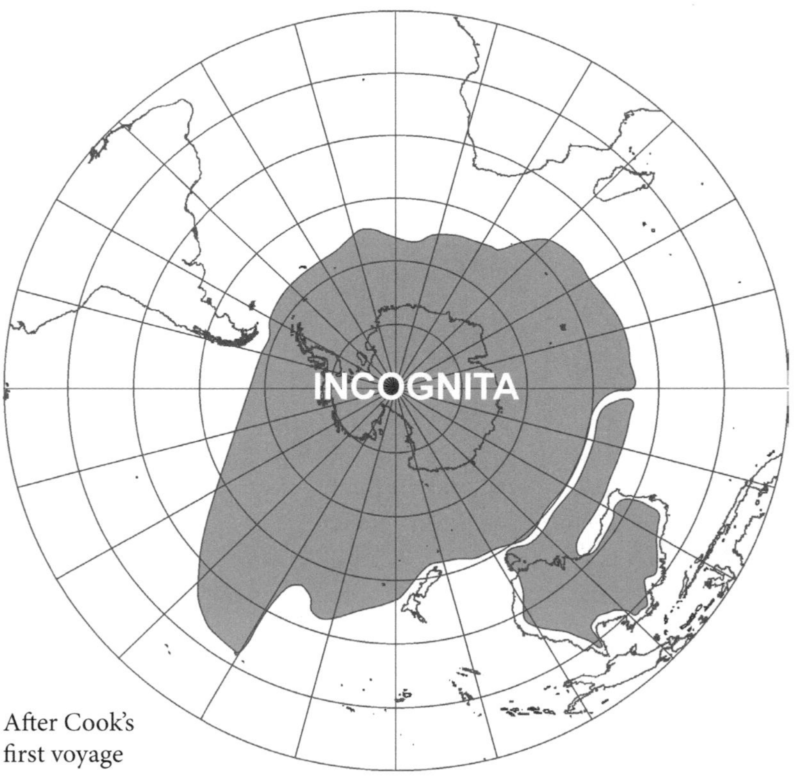

After Cook's first voyage

The constitution of Isla Grande

Opportunity is the great bawd. – Benjamin Franklin

Alexander Dalrymple had belittled the work of Cook's first voyage but immediately sought to exploit it. If New Zealand were used to establish intercourse with the Pacific it could also function as a base from which to search for the southern continent. Within seven weeks of Cook's return Dalrymple had enlisted the support of Benjamin Franklin, still one of His Majesty's more-or-less loyal American subjects, for a scheme to convey the blessings of European commerce to the Maori. It could not be a trading voyage – New Zealand lay within the area of monopoly of the East India Company – and there was no mention of exploration, but the proposed arrangements look familiar. Dalrymple would command a bark of 350 tons, taken up from the coal trade, on a three-year voyage that was *not* commercial in character. No profit was expected, but should any arise it would be ploughed back into future voyages of a similar character.

Franklin was persuaded that this was an exercise in enlightened self-interest. The object was not to cheat, rob, dispossess or enslave, but to do good. On the other hand, civilising the Maori would be to the advantage of a commercial nation, as trade with people enjoying the 'arts and conveniences of life' was always more extensive than that with naked savages. In this way Britain would be served even as the country discharged its moral obligation to those who, as Franklin saw it, 'however distant from us, are in truth related to us, and whose interests do, in some degree, concern every one who can say, *Homo sum*'. Not for him the doubts of Cook; he simply assumed that the Maori would welcome admission to the brotherhood of man. The scheme required twenty subscribers at £100 each. They were not forthcoming.[63]

Dalrymple soon developed another scheme, but Cook was already five days at sea on his second voyage before it was ready for presentation to the Prime Minister, Lord North. The proposal was now for a trading voyage, but well outside the area of the East India Company's monopoly. It was in fact an attempt to beat the *Resolution* to the western part of the supposed Atlantic continent, which Cook, circumnavigating eastwards, would not reach for a year or more. Dalrymple proposed to sail from England before October 1772 to find

Isla Grande, the mid-Atlantic island in 45°S that had been reported by la Roché in 1675. There he and his fellow venturers would recoup the expense of the voyage by hunting whales, seals and sea elephants. By February it would be possible to detach a schooner to look south of the tracks of Halley and Bouvet for la Roché's other reported discovery (probably South Georgia) where, 'if there is any Continent in a lower Latitude than 50°S, the most Northern part of that Continent must lie'.[64] If it were there, it would be found in a fortnight. The whole expedition could be back in England by June 1773.

All that Dalrymple asked of the government in return was the grant of as many unoccupied lands south of the Equator from 0–60°W (one-twelfth of the globe) as he could find over the next five years. By comparison, the rights claimed by Columbus for his American discoveries look modest. Lord North did not respond, and as the deadline for departure approached Dalrymple's requests for a meeting became increasingly urgent. When they did meet, on 13 August, North was more interested in discussing other matters, and thereby passed up an opportunity. Dalrymple had wanted to lay before him the details of his plan, which included a constitution for his new Australian colony in the South Atlantic.

Dalrymple's constitution provided for the original venturers to become an hereditary aristocracy: The Barons. They would form the upper chamber of the legislature, with voting rights in proportion to their land holdings. Most of the provisions were about land and taxation but the spirit of enlightenment was diffused throughout; female suffrage, freedom of religion, limited capital punishment, no imprisonment for debt, decimal accounting – all had a place. Other provisions unfortunately ranged from the self-serving to the bizarre. At one end of the scale The Governor (presumably Dalrymple) would hold office for life, subject only to removal by The People, in which case his salary would nevertheless continue for life; at the other end, owners of mad dogs would be disqualified from holding public office.

One of Dalrymple's friends, 'no enemy to public liberty' (possibly Franklin), described it as a very good model of the worst of all governments – a pure republic. It was certainly not Plato's idea of a republic, much less a utopia, but some of Dalrymple's prescriptions for political reform were flags in the wind. They would have been offensive to Lord North, but they were the future. Colonial notions of liberty, personal and collective, were increasingly at odds with British social and constitutional conservatism. In a few short years Franklin and his countrymen would decide that their situation was intolerable, and their revolt would destroy Lord North's administration.

As to Dalrymple's proposal, North was non-commital; he would have to consult his colleagues. It was the last that Dalrymple heard from him. Anyhow, it was now too late. By next season, the man who had displaced him on the *Endeavour* voyage would most likely have found Australia in the south-west Atlantic as well.

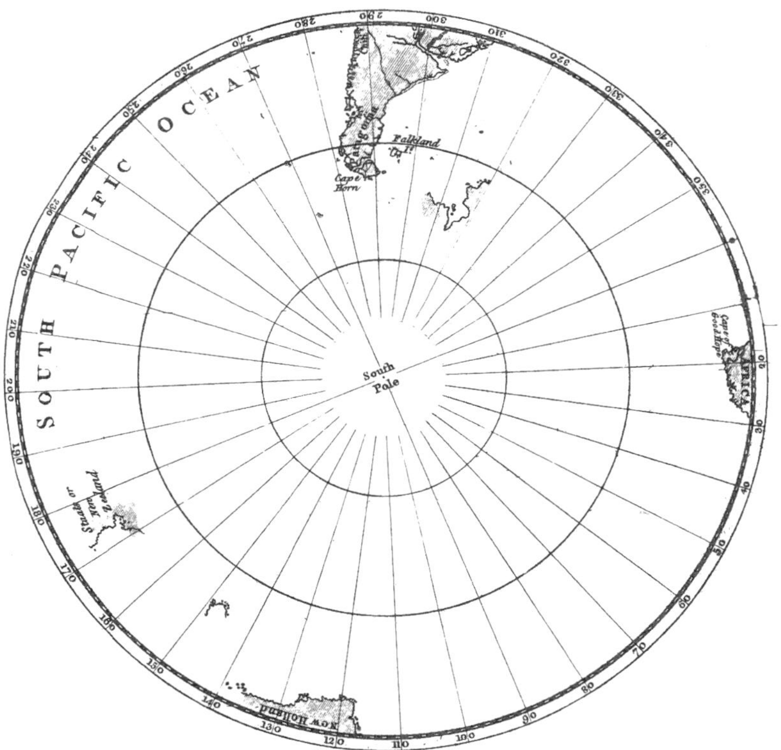

Isla Grande, east of South America, the headland of Dalrymple's Atlantic Australia

9

Sandwich Land

James Cook's secret instructions, based largely on his own plan, sent him to effect 'farther discoveries towards the South Pole'. He was first to seek Cape Circumcision in about 54°S and 11°20'W. If he found it, he was to 'satisfy [himself] whether it is part of the Southern Continent which has so much engaged the attention of Geographers & former Navigators, or Part of an Island'. If it was only an island, or could not be found, Cook was to stand southward for as long as he judged it likely that he might fall in with the Continent and then proceed eastward in latitudes as high as possible around the globe until the supposed location of Cape Circumcision was reached again. In the course of this cruise he could 'retire to some known place to the Northward' to refresh and refit, but was required to resume the southern circuit as soon as the season would permit.[1]

In contrast to the uniformed straitjacket of the *Endeavour* instructions, this was a comfortable, loose-fitting garment of his own design. Its ample dimensions were also highly suitable for field-testing the most advanced navigational instrument of the day, John Harrison's marine chronometer. If it were reliable enough, Cook would be able to fix his longitude by comparing the local time of astronomical events with the predicted time of their observation at Greenwich. Commissioned to go further than any explorer before him, he was better equipped than any of them to calculate how far that would be. On arrival at the Cape of Good Hope at the end of October he was told that he had competition, of sorts. Two French expeditions had passed that way in recent months. From the little he could find out, Cook was unable to determine whether these were 'real or pretended' voyages of discovery.[2]

He was told that Marc-Joseph Marion-Dufresne, formerly an officer of the French East India Company, had been tasked with repatriating Aotourou, the Tahitian who had been taken to France by Bougainville. The islander died of small pox in Madagascar but Marion had put it about at the Cape of Good Hope that he and his second-in-command, Julien Marie Crozet, would nonetheless continue the voyage via Brazil and Cape Horn. At about the same time two other French ships, the *Fortune* and the *Gros Ventre*, had sailed from Mauritius under Yves-Joseph de Kerguélen de Trémarec, a naval officer and hydrographer, and François Alesne de St Allouarn. All Cook could learn was that they had claimed a discovery of land in 48½°S and 57–8°E. The ships had sailed 40 miles along it to a bay that they tried to enter. A gale had driven them off, the ships had separated, and on return to Mauritius Kerguélen had reported the *Gros Ventre* lost.

The lost ship had since returned to Mauritius from Batavia with a cargo of arrack, which persuaded Cook that trade, not discovery, had been the chief object of the voyage. He would have been less comfortable had he been told that along the way St Allouarn had landed in Dampier's Shark Bay, and had there claimed possession of New Holland for France.

Cook's search for Cape Circumcision was methodical and thorough. Having reached the indicated latitude 'as it is laid down in Mr Dalrymple's chart' he sailed east along it, encountering vast ice islands that prompted more than one report of land. Then he doubled back, several degrees further south. Still nothing. By 3 January 1773 he was satisfied that Bouvet too had mistaken ice for land. He decided to waste no more time in searching for an 'imaginary land' but, impressed by the quantity of ice seen and noting the received opinion that ice only formed in the vicinity of land, he held it probable that there was land to the south or west. If so it could wait, as Cook had 'a greater desire to proceed to the east in Search of the land said to have been lately discovered' by Kerguélen.[3]

Never one to retrace a course when there was an unexplored alternative, Cook tracked south and east to well below his planned mean latitude of 60°S. On 17 January 1773 the *Resolution* crossed the Antarctic Circle, 'undoubtedly the first and only Ship' to do so. Cook had good reason to be proud of the achievement, but it was ungenerous of him not to acknowledge his escorts, Furneaux and the *Adventure*. The sea was clear but on the following day, in 67°15'S, massive ice from west to south-east barred the way. From the masthead Cook could not see the least sign of a break. A flat-topped field of ice 16–18 feet high, 'of such extend that I could see no end to it', showed to the south-east. He was looking in the direction of what later became known as the Prince Olav coast of the Antarctic mainland, about 75 miles distant. Cook decided that with the summer half gone he could not spare the time to get around the ice even if it were practicable, which he doubted. He turned north to look for Kerguélen's discovery.

When nothing was found in the indicated location, Cook struck east again. Although unwilling to dismiss the land as a fiction, he believed that it could only be a small island unless it lay further west. Lieutenant Clerke was less charitable, believing that the only discovery here was the disagreeable one 'that our friends the French were only amusing the good folks at the Cape with a little of the marvellous'.[4] Two days later a thick fog cloaked the ships from each other although they were little more than a mile apart. After half an hour the *Resolution* fired a gun but there was no reply, nor to others fired at regular intervals therafter. Cook was perplexed at how *Adventure* could have got beyond hearing in so short a time. He returned to the point of last sighting, the appointed rendezvous in the event of separation, and waited for two days (although he had stipulated three). He then gave up hope of seeing her again before the winter rendezvous in New Zealand. In the course of the next few days both ships passed south of Kerguelen's land, which in fact lay well to the east of its supposed location, and so unwittingly extinguished the possibility that it might be a headland of the southern continent.

It was Cook's intention to penetrate the Antarctic Circle a second time but summer was waning. Increasing ice and darker nights warned him off. On 23 February he again turned north and east, having on this push reached 61°52'S, within 200 miles of what is today called the Shackleton Ice Shelf. After tracking along his preferred parallel of 60° for another three weeks, Cook put the ice behind him and made the best of his way for New Holland or New Zealand. His motive for wishing to visit the former, if the wind would permit, was to satisfy himself whether Van Diemen's Land was 'a part of that continent'.

The wind did not favour Cook but when *Resolution* and *Adventure* came together again in New Zealand Furneaux reported that he had sailed northwards along the east coast of Van Diemen's Land until it swung west, where there was open water with islands. In Furneaux's opinion it was not a strait but a deep bay. Not all of his officers agreed (it was in reality Bass Strait) but Cook gave Furneaux benefit of the doubt, deciding that he had 'in a great degree cleared up this point', and that it was sufficiently well established that the whole was 'one continued land'. There was therefore no longer a need for Cook to visit it. The winter could be better spent in unexplored seas to the east and north of New Zealand.[5]

Cook was perturbed at the degraded behaviour of the Maoris at Queen Charlotte's Sound. He blamed his previous visit. Formerly the women had been relatively chaste; now their menfolk would prostitute them, willing or not, for a nail or anything else the men valued. Wants, diseases and an end to tranquility – these were the fruits of commerce with Europeans, and 'if any one denies the truth of this assertion let him tell me what the natives of the whole extent of America have gained …'. It was a far cry from Dalrymple's civilising mission and more in keeping with Swift's vision of the future than Defoe's. The crew, who had fondly imagined some idle months in New Zealand with more degradation in prospect, were unhappy to leave until told that Tahiti would be the next refreshment stop. There was, however, the small matter of how the captain proposed to get there.

> It may be thought by some an extraordinary step in me to proceed on discoveries as far South as 46° in the very depth of Winter for it must be own'd that this is a season by no means favourable for discoveries. It nevertheless appear'd to me necessary that something must be done in it, in order to lessen the work I am upon … [6]

And east across the Pacific, cold and wet they went, generally about five degrees south of Surville's track. Had Cook known of that voyage he would certainly have made a more southerly track, not because Surville had failed to find a continent but because he had reduced the amount of ocean large enough to hide one. Cook was not expecting to find land; the more emptiness that had been traversed by others, the less work there was for him. As it was, he turned north in the longitude of Carteret's Pitcairn Island and, unable to find it, made for Tahiti.

> As I have now in this and my former Voyage crossed this Ocean from 40°S and upwards it will hardly be denied but what I have formed some judgement concerning the

> great object of my researches (viz) the Southern Continent. Circumstances seem to point out to us that there is none but this is too important a point to be left to conjector, facts must determine it and these can only be had by visiting the remaining unexplored parts of this Sea which must be the work of the Insuing summer … [7]

After visiting Tahiti, the Cook Islands and Tonga, in October 1773 the ships headed for Queen Charlotte's Sound to prepare for a second summer in the ice. Off the coast of New Zealand, the ships again became separated. Cook waited in the Sound for three weeks before setting off alone. He cannot be blamed for being impatient about losing precious weeks of good weather but the note that he left behind, which was found by Furneaux a week after Cook's departure, was unhelpful to a fault. Cook wrote that he had no hopes that his subordinate would ever read the note and so 'would not take upon him' to name a rendezvous. For what it was worth, he might be at Easter Island in March next year, or Tahiti, or one of the other Society Islands, or not, depending 'so much upon circumstances that nothing with any degree of certainty can be depended upon'.[8]

This strange lack of precision, unusual for Cook, was the outcome of earlier onboard debates. To Furneaux's way of thinking, Cook's judgement that there was no southern continent in the Pacific had fulfilled one part of their instructions. The next requirement was to continue along the sixtieth parallel across the Atlantic. Cook, arguing against a document that he had drafted himself, held that the next winter, like this one, would be more profitably spent in the Pacific. He thought that he had talked Furneaux around but his note contained no orders. Cook merely recorded in his journal that he supposed Furneaux would head across the Atlantic to the Cape of Good Hope. He was unperturbed at having halved the strength of his expedition, unconcerned about what might have happened to the *Adventure*, and content to expose the *Resolution* to all the hazards of single-ship navigation in unknown waters. The voyage of course came first, but was it the Admiralty's voyage or was it James Cook's?

In the evening of 7 December the officers drank to their friends in London, from whom they were now 'as far removed … as possible'. William Wales, the astronomer, recorded that 'the good People of that City may now rest perfectly satisfied that they have no Antipodes besides Pengwins and Peteralls, unless Seals can be admitted as such

…' Five days later they saw their first ice island of the season, 11½° further south than its counterpart the previous year. When the ship was almost on the Antarctic Circle the officer on watch imprudently got *Resolution* to windward of one of these giants, which was twice as high as the masthead, and in trying to dodge around it found himself sailing down on another. Cook, startled from dinner by the shout for all hands, ordered that the ship be made ready to fend off. Everyone knew that it would be futile. The ship entered the back surge at the base of the berg. Able Seaman Elliot braced himself. 'The first stroke would have sent all our Masts overboard, and the next would have knocked the ship to pieces, and drown'd us all', but Providence smiled and the stern missed the ice by a ship's length or two. Even Cook was chastened. A miss was as good as a mile, 'but our situation requires more misses than we can expect'.[9]

If there was land to the south, which seemed improbable, it would be impossible to explore in the presence of the ice. Cook hauled to the north, but not for long. Six days later the ship crossed the Antarctic Circle for a second time, making east. By 24 December, with the sails as hard as boards and the sheaves frozen fast in their blocks, Cook was despairing of finding land or getting further south. Additionally, he was now concerned that having come so far south he had left fully 24° of latitude unexplored to his north. He steered towards the track he had taken in 1769 until he thought it improbable that the intervening 200 leagues would yield a discovery, and then zig-zagged south again. To crewmen hoping that a change of course might signal a start for home these were cruel disappointments, exacerbated by the captain's silence about where they were going.

As *Resolution* threaded her way through ice islands numbered in hundreds, every bird, seal, scrap of weed and long swell was read for evidence of land, but the auguries were always ambiguous. On 26 January 1774, as they crossed the Antarctic Circle for a third time, there was an appearance of land that soon disappeared in the haze. Four days later, in 71°10'S, Cook met his match. Unbroken ice ran east to west. Its compacted northern edge was impenetrable. Inside, flat field ice was studded with ice islands that seemed to rise, ridge beyond ridge, until lost in the clouds. Wales thought that the last ridge was a fog bank illuminated by ice blink, and unlikely to be ice or snow 'unless land was under it, of which we had no other signs'. His tentative supposition was correct but the land was 120 miles to the south-west, well beyond visual range. Cook made the best of the setback.

> I who had Ambition not only to go farther than any one had done before, but as far as it was possible for man to go, was not sorry at meeting with this interruption as it in some measure relieved us, at least shortened the dangers and hardships inseparable with the Navigation of the Southern Polar Rigions; Sence therefore, we could not proceed one Inch farther to the South, no other reason need be assigned for my Tacking and Standing back to the north … [10]

But why not east, as instructed? Cook had a ready answer. It would take him what was left of summer even to reach the supposed locations of the Gulf of San Sebastian or Bouvet's Cape Circumcision. If they did not exist the search for the southern continent would be over by April (and the expedition at an end). If they did exist, six or seven months would have to be passed in winter idleness before exploration could begin. Such a waste! His ship was sound, his crew healthy and the stores and provisions sufficient.

> For me at this time to have quited this South Pacifick Ocean … would have been betraying not only a want of persererence, but judgement, in supposeing the … Ocean to have been so well explored that nothing remained to be done in it, which however was not my opinion at this time; for although I had proved there was no Continent, there remained nevertheless room for very large Islands in places wholy unexplored and many of those which where formerly discovered, are but imperfectly explored and there Situations as imperfectly known.[11]

He set out a comprehensive itinerary. It took in Juan Fernandez's continent, Easter Island ('or Davis's land'), Tahiti ('where it was necessary I should touch to look for the *Adventure*') and Quiros' Land ('which Bougainville has neither confirm'd nor refuted') before heading east between 50–60° for Cape Horn, aiming to arrive in November. The best part of the following summer could then be devoted to the South Atlantic. When he informed the officers, who had assumed that they would be going to the Cape of Good Hope, he was pleased to record that they all 'heartily concur'd'. More improbably, the men 'were so far from wishing the Voyage at an end that they rejoiced at the Prospect of its being prolonged a nother year …'[12] Overstatement though this may be, it is undeniable that at this point of his career Cook's seamanship and leadership were held in the highest regard by those who sailed with him.

Cook made exhaustive search for the continent of Juan Fernandez in the most commonly given latitude and the range of longitudes suggested by various authorities, particularly Dalrymple. He compared his own tracks with those of Wallis and Bougainville and concluded that if the land was not a fiction it could be no more than a small island.[13] Easter Island was found without difficulty and from the east it seemed to match Wafer's description of Davis' Land. Cook wanted to look for Wafer's low, sandy, offshore island, which would have confirmed the identification but, unable to water at Easter Island, decided that he could not delay. If Davis' Land existed, and Easter Island was not it, it had to lie closer to South America because the same latitude further west was well explored.

Cook then struck north for the Marquesas Islands of Mendaña. His purpose was to fix their location as a reference point for all that navigator's subsequent discoveries. He found that they lay half a degree further south than charted, perhaps 'owing to the Instruments use'd in them days'. Spanish longitudes were, of course, far more suspect than their latitudes, and Cook again made for Tahiti so that Wales would have opportunity 'to know the error of the Watch from the known longitude of this place and to determine a fresh her rate of going'.[14] The astronomer determined that in the five months since leaving Queen Charlotte's Sound the watch had lost eight and a half minutes, a longitudinal error of slightly more than two degrees.

At Raiatea, another of the Society Islands, natives told a story of two ships, commanded by men named Banks and Furneaux, anchored nearby at Huaheine. The descriptions of the two commanders were so accurate that Cook considered sending a boat to search for them, but the informant disappeared. Clerke was sent to the other side of the island to enquire but returned none the wiser. Cook was anxious to be away: 'whether the report proves true or false it appeared now too ill founded to authorise me to send a boat over or to wait any longer here and therefore on'.[15] Given that he had nominated the Society Islands as somewhere Furneaux might find him, and had given that as the reason for his visit, it all seems very casual. Fortunately, no harm was done; Furneaux was already nearing home and Banks, after failing to get an East India Company ship for a Pacific voyage, had opted for Iceland instead.

With a re-rated watch Cook was ready to search for the discoveries of Quiros. From Tonga he steered north-west to 15°S, the latitude indicated by the Spaniard, and on 17 July 1774 sighted what he was sure must be 'Australia Del Espiritu Santo'. After following the islands to their southern extremity he doubled back to the northernmost and entered the big bay of Santo, becoming the first European to do so since 1606. Some doubted that this could be the Bay of St Philip and St James because its port of Vera Cruz was so ill-defined. Clerke blamed the uncertainty on Quiros' 'pompous description' but Cook was less judgemental; Quiros was a great navigator and had reason to suppose Santo to be part of the Southern Continent, 'which at that time and until very lately was supposed to exist'.[16] Bougainville had seen only a few of these islands that he called the Great Cyclades. Cook had surveyed the entire group. On that basis he claimed the right to name it the New Hebrides, thus reducing the Frenchman's work to a Preface to the Voyage of Cook.

The end of the survey coincided with the advent of spring, and like a migratory bird Cook heeded the call. It was time to revisit Queen Charlotte's Sound and prepare for a third season in the ice. New Caledonia and Norfolk Island were unexpected discoveries along the way. At the Sound, there was evidence of a visit and the note left for Furneaux had gone. There was also a native rumour of shipwreck and massacre but no reliable information was forthcoming. On 11 November the ship again set out across the Pacific, it being Cook's intention 'to pass over those parts which were left unexplored last summer'. That summer he had zig-zagged north and south from the 47th to the 71st parallel and back, so the most efficient and effective course would be to head east somewhere between those latitudes. Cook opted for a crossing in 54–5°S which, if there were no continent in the way, would take him directly to the Strait of Magellan.

On 27 November, half way across, he gave up all hopes of finding any more land. Three weeks later he reached the Strait. He complained that never before had he made a passage with so few interesting occurrences. 'I have done with the southern pacific ocean, and flatter my self that no one will think that I have left it unexplor'd, or that more could have been done in one voyage …'[17] Dalrymple had argued that the entire space between New Zealand and the Horn must be solid land. Cook had found nothing and nor would anyone else, because from 30°S to the Antarctic Circle the Pacific displays the largest extent of blank ocean on the face of the planet, unblemished by the slightest island, sandbank or shoal. Without irony, Mendaña had called it the Gulf of Conception. Dalrymple's Void would be equally appropriate.

After surveying the southern coast of Tierra del Fuego, and leaving a note at the Straits of Le Maire for Furneaux 'in case he was behind us', Cook entered the Atlantic to look for Dalrymple's Gulf of St Sebastian. He doubted the existence of the Gulf but made for its western point so that, if it did exist, the remainder would lie ahead. At its supposed location there was nothing and Cook went north-west to 54–5°S in search of another Dalrymple charting, the big island reported by la Roché in 1675 and by the *León* as recently as 1756. Again nothing, but Cook held east in the indicated latitude for ten days and on 16 January 1775 his patience was rewarded. High and snow capped mountains reared from the sea. From a distance, they so resembled the ice islands seen when furthest south in the Indian and Pacific oceans that Wales began to think that the latter might also have been land.

For three days Cook followed the rugged coast south-east. The mighty accumulations of glacier ice that he saw led him to a paradoxical conclusion: large as they were, they could not account for the ten-thousandth part of the ice seen in the open ocean. 'Either there must be more land or else ice is formed without it'. For the first time in the voyage he entertained a hope that this might be 'an extensive tract', perhaps even a continent. A few hours later the coast was seen to be trending more to the south and then west. Cook followed it until he could again see the point first sighted, proving 'that this land that we had taken to be part of a great Continent was no more than an Island of 70 leagues in Circuit'.

The island was South Georgia. Although he called its southernmost point Cape Disappointment, Cook claimed to be unperturbed about not finding an adjacent continent, 'for to judge of the bulk by the sample it would not be worth the discovery'. The sight of snow-covered land in 54° at the height of summer also caused Cook to reconsider his earlier dismissal of Bouvet's discovery: 'I no longer doubted the existence of Cape Circumcision, and did not doubt that I would find more land than I had time to explore.'[18]

More land was seen to the south-east on the 19 January and although it was found to be no more than 'a few stragling rocks' it was with renewed hope that Cook stood east again to seek Cape Circumcision. As to the Gulf of St Sebastian, Cook was now confident that it did not exist. He also doubted from the longitudes that la Roché or the *León* had seen South Georgia, although Dalrymple's latitude for the place was only half a degree out. For all that he would 'allow them the merit of leading me to the discovery' as otherwise he would probably have passed to the south of the island.

And south again he went, adhering to the strategy that he had employed in the Pacific. If any of these charted lands were continental in size, he would come across them in high southern latitudes; if he did not find them, the only place they could exist was further north, where there was insufficient space to hide a continent. Working south and east, on 31 January 1775 the ship fell in with more massed ice in 59°13'30"S, identifiable as land only by exposed cliff faces. Cook's first reaction was to call it Snowland. His more classically-minded naturalist, Johann Reinhold Forster, suggested Southern Thule to acknowledge that it was further south than any land hitherto discovered.

With the wind at west Cook closed to investigate and got to leeward. Unable to double back against a great westerly swell, he prudently decided to reach to the north, a decision prompted by the sight of open sea in that direction. When more land was seen, Cook was uncertain whether he was looking at a succession of islands or promontories with unseen land behind. Whichever, there was not the least sign of an anchorage. The issue was complicated by the presence of large tabular bergs throughout. He gave this 'most horrible Coast in the World' the collective name of Sandwich Land. It was either a group of islands or

> … a point of the Continent, for I firmly believe that there is a tract of land near the Pole, which is the source of most of the ice which is spread over this vast Southern Ocean … the greatest part of this Southern Continent (supposeing there is one) must lay within the Polar Circile where the sea is so pestered with ice, that the land is thereby inaccessible. The risk one runs in exploreing a coast in these unknown and Icy Seas, is so very great, that I can be bold to say, that no man will ever venture further than I have done and the lands which may lie to the south will never be explored.[19]

The question would have been resolved, at least as far as Sandwich Land was concerned, if Cook had been able to follow his usual practice of passing to the south. Three years earlier he might have chanced waiting for the wind to change, but summer was half gone and the ship was no longer in a condition 'to undertake great things'. Cook was conscious of the great corpus of knowledge that he had accumulated over three years, and how irresponsible it would be to risk losing it in exploring a coast to 'no end whatever, or … the least use to Navigation or geography or indeed any other Science'. There was also still the matter of Bouvet's discovery. Rounding what he took to be the north point of Sandwich Land, Cook first put the ship east on the 58th parallel but, after crossing the Greenwich meridian, on 15 February hauled north-east to make the supposed latitude of Cape Circumcision. The great swell coming from the south assured him that the Cape could only be an island, so passing south of it would be to no purpose, but if he held east in 54° he would find it no matter how little it extended north-south.

Such was his reasoning, and it was sound. What he could not know was that Bouvet's longitude was more than usually suspect. Cook was past the Cape's true longitude of 3°15'E even before he altered course to search for it. There was an appearance of land but it was only a fog bank. When within 2° longitude of *Resolution*'s outbound route of 1773, Cook briefly deviated south to demonstrate to his officers that what they had seen then could only have been ice. Then he made for the Cape of Good Hope, satisfied that he had put an end to the search for a Southern Continent, 'which has at times ingrossed the attention of some of the Maritime Powers for near two centuries past and the Geographers of all ages. That there may be a continent or large tract of land near the Pole, I will not deny, on the contrary I am of opinion there is, and it is probable that we have seen a part of it'.[20]

But this would be a polar continent, not a Southern Continent. Cook believed that the polar land projected furthest north into the Atlantic and Indian Oceans, which seems to indicate that he had Sandwich Land in mind. Thomas Perry, able seaman and the *Resolution*'s poet, certainly thought so.

> It is now my brave lads we are clear of the Sea
> And keep a good heart if you'll take my advice
> We are out of the cold my brave Boys do not fear
> For the Cape of Good Hope with good hearts we do steer
>
> Thank God we have ranged the Globe all around
> And we have likewise the south Continent found
> But it being too late in the year as they say
> We could stay there no longer the land to survey ...[21]

The man who had demolished so many headlands imagined by others had created one of his own, the same one that Dalrymple had hoped to find. Both men were mistaken. If Cook had been able to weather Southern Thule he would have found that it was just another small island dashed by a relentless swell from the south, the same swell that he had always considered incompatible with nearby landmasses.

At the Cape of Good Hope there was a letter left for him by Furneaux a year earlier. The Charlotte Sound rumour had been true. Furneaux had lost ten of his best men and a boat in a Maori ambush. A seaman's initials tattooed on a severed hand, a Negro servant's head and other grisly remains indicated that they had been eaten. On that account and because of damaged provisions Furneaux had excused himself from following the route that Cook had proposed. He had however tracked across the Atlantic in the latitude of Cape Circumcision and sailed over its supposed location.

A French Indiaman, bound for Pondicherry, was also at anchor in Table Bay. Her captain was Julien Marie Crozet, who embraced Cook as a kindred spirit and willingly spoke about the Marion and Kerguélen voyages and others shown on the most recent Vaugondy chart. He and Marion had not gone west to Tahiti as advertised but east to explore the trading possibilities of New Zealand and the supposed southern continent. While crossing the Indian Ocean in December 1771 they had seen two islands, the larger of which they named Terre de l'Espérance in hopes that it was an outlier of the southern continent. Further on they came across another group. From Van Diemen's Land they had sailed to New Zealand, where Marion's imprudent relations with the Maori had led to the massacre of 24 crewmen and loss of his own life. Crozet had looked in vain through his dead commander's papers for the voyage plan. In his own view there was no southern continent. At the South Pole there would be nothing but islands, occupied by people 'absolutely similar to New Zealanders'.[22]

He had abandoned the voyage and taken what remained of the expedition to the Philippines. As for Kerguélen, said Crozet, he had found 'a long but very narrow island extending East and West'. Cook was puzzled to see it marked on the Vaugondy chart exactly where he had unsuccessfully searched for it. Crozet also informed him of Surville's voyage. Cook learned that the Frenchman had passed to the west of New Caledonia before nearly meeting him in New Zealand. Clearly he had been wrong to suppose that shoals filled the whole space between New Caledonia and New Holland. He conceded that 'these voyages of the French, tho' undertaken by private Adventurers, have been productive of some usefull discoveries, as well as contributing in exploaring the Southern Ocean'.[23]

Crozet was able to show Cook the most recent French discoveries in the Southern Ocean on Vaugondy's 1773 *Hemisphere Australe ou Antarctique*

By the time *Resolution* anchored at Spithead, on 30 July 1775, Cook had been away on southern voyages for all but one of the preceding seven years. During his most recent absence the Royal Society had urged on the government another attempt to discover the western entrance of the fabled North-West Passage, which was believed to be a sea route between the Pacific and Atlantic oceans. No-one had the temerity to suggest that Cook should undertake it. He had more than earned a respite from sea duty; indeed, an honourable sinecure as Fourth Captain at Greenwich naval hospital was in prospect. But even as he applied for the post, as the Admiralty informally urged him to do, he hedged to the extent of asking to be allowed to give it up in the event that more active service offered. The Admiralty conspired to make something of his request. Lord Sandwich invited Cook to dine with a number of senior Admiralty figures. Discussion naturally turned to the *Resolution*'s new expedition, and Cook's recommendation of a replacement for the *Adventure*. The enthusiasm of the Admiralty men was infectious, and before the evening was out Cook had volunteered.

The expedition's initial task was similar to that of Marion; Omai, a Tahitian who had sailed to England as Furneaux's passenger, had to be taken home. Cook took the opportunity to add another preliminary: Marion's Land of Hope and Kerguélen's South France could only lie between Tasman's track and his own, but those tracks did leave room for 'a long and very narrow island extending east and west' between 45–50°S and 35–120°E that could be nearly as large as New Holland.[24] Might Dalrymple's southern continent exist after all, but in the Indian Ocean rather than the Pacific, as the French seemed to suppose?

Dalrymple – he who had so trenchantly criticised Hawkesworth about the first voyage – seemed satisfied with the thoroughness, if not the result, of the second. Cook was not; he would not have it said that the southern continent might exist because James Cook had failed to eliminate a possibility. He sailed from Plymouth on 12 July 1776, four years to the day after commencing his second voyage. Lieutenant King took it for a prosperous omen. The Sound had been crowded with the ships of a large troop convoy bound for America. Six days before *Resolution* and *Discovery* sailed, Franklin and his compatriots had declared their independence. Now they would have to fight for it.

At Tenerife Cook encountered the French frigate *Boussole* and from her pilot, who had been with Kerguélen, he obtained a good position for South France. From the Cape of Good Hope he made for the Marion/Crozet landfalls. He found that the Land of Hope was no continent but two small islands and, in the absence of a name on Crozet's chart, called them Prince Edward's Islands. He did not even bother to visit the second group but named it Marion's and Crozet's Islands.[25] By 24 December the ships were in thick fog in the vicinity of South France, feeling their way ahead, not altogether confident of the French pilot's information. The ships tentatively approached the land from the north-west, as Kerguélen had done. The party that went ashore found an inscription with the dates 1772 and 1773. Cook was understandably confused.

He was not to know that Kerguélen had made two voyages, both with the same objective. For years this naval officer and hydrographer had urged on successive Ministers for Marine 'a campaign of discovery in the Antarctic seas'. The instructions for his first voyage, largely his own work, had directed him to 'a very large continent' south of the islands of St Paul and Amsterdam, which 'to all appearances' extended from

45ºS to the neighbourhood of the South Pole. It was consistent with the one that Gonneville had visited for six months.[26] When land loomed out of the fog in February 1772 he convinced himself that he had found Gonneville's Terre Australe. Its latitude was similar to that of Paris and so it would be agriculturally productive as well as rich in minerals and all the other good things traditionally associated with Terra Australis. Extreme conditions prevented him landing, although one of the *Gros Ventre*'s boats got ashore. Kerguélen saw only the north and west coasts, and no inhabitants, but these minor setbacks were not prominent in the glowing report that he took back to France.

So persuasive was his advocacy that he was sent again, this time to colonise his discovery with 180 settlers, including 50 of Bougainville's Acadians. He had arrived in December 1773 – ten months after Cook's second voyage had proved that his land could not extend to the pole – and found that in his absence Gonneville's fertile, verdant, inhabited continent had somehow degenerated into a miserable, sterile collection of snow-capped rocks on which settlement seemed to be neither desireable nor possible. Kerguélen saved the only thing he could from the ruin of his ambition; he named the land after himself and sailed away. His masters were unimpressed. They had him imprisoned and court-martialled.

Cook had learned from Crozet that Kerguélen's voyaging had ended in disgrace, but he did not know the detail of it. As for this miserable island to which the French had directed him, he followed its north-east coast to the extremity, concluded that it was of no great size, and sailed for Tahiti and the North Pacific. In the absence of a name on the French chart he called it the Island of Desolation.[27] His journal entry – the last words he wrote about Terra Australis – is in the third person, as a valediction should be.

> The first discoveries (sic) with some reason imagined it to be a Cape of a Southern Continent, [but] the English have sence proved that no such Continent exists …[28]

Two years later, after initially being welcomed by the Hawaiians as an incarnation of their god of peace Lono, Cook caused consternation when he inauspiciously returned at the time of his rival, the god of war, Ku. In an atmosphere of confusion and foreboding he was attacked and killed. It was an undeserved fate for this most peaceable man of war, who in all his dealings with the peoples of the Pacific had been at pains to conciliate. Most of the tributes published when news of Cook's death reached Europe spoke of what he had contributed to science and what science had contributed to his success, but the anonymous testimonial published in the book of his last voyage went further. It brought together the three great traditions that had been at play in the search for Terra Australis – the supernatural, the speculative and the scientific.

> Traveller! Contemplate, admire, revere, and emulate this great master in his profession; whose skill and labours have enlarged natural philosophy; have extended science; and have disclosed the long-concealed and admirable arrangements of the Almighty in the formation of this globe, and, at the same time, the arrogance of mortals, in presuming to account, by their speculations, for the laws by which he was pleased to create it. It is now discovered, beyond all doubt, that the same Great Being who created the universe by his fiat, by the same ordained our earth to keep a just poise, without a corresponding Southern continent – and it does so! 'He stretches out the North over the empty place, and hangeth the earth upon nothing.' Job 26:7.[29]

This reconciliation of science and revelation recalls Pope's intended epitaph for Isaac Newton,[30] but it offered no comfort to a 'speculator' like Dalrymple. Typically, the Scot had added Sandwich Land to his catalogue of southern headlands – claiming that Cook had only found Mercator's Gulf of St Sebastian a few degrees further east than expected – but there was no talk of another Dalrymple expedition. Perhaps he had done his sums and come to the conclusion that even if everywhere south of the Antarctic Circle was solid ice and/or land, as Cook seemed to have demonstrated, it would still be insufficient to make up the deficit of land in the southern hemisphere required by the theory of equipoise. Perhaps he thought Cook already had more recognition than he was entitled to.

Two decades after Cook's death Dalrymple uncovered the so-called Dauphin map, one of the Dieppe corpus, in Sir Joseph Banks' collection. He was quick to draw attention to the similarity between some of the names on the east coast of Java La Grande and those bestowed by Cook on New South Wales, uncritically accepting them as evidence that Cook had not been the first navigator to sail that coast. Whatever Dalrymple's motive – and innocent or not the comparison prompted French allegations that Cook had both used and plagiarised the Dauphin map – he was at least being consistent in his reliance on the unreliable. The work of his later years, as hydrographer at first for the East India Company and then for the Admiralty, involved updating the southern charts by replacing information from old navigators' tales with accurate data provided by Cook and his successors. He must have hoped that some day he would receive a report confirming one of the old sightings of Terra Australis, but it never came.

When Kerguélen, in disgrace, read Cook's third voyage he acknowledged that the Englishman had reduced his discovery to an island, 'neither continent nor great land', but he still believed it to be 200 leagues in circumference in spite of the evidence. He also reconsidered Gonneville's voyage and came to the conclusion that as the Indians were totally naked they could not have been living anywhere south of 35° and certainly not on Kerguélen's Island, which in the opinion of its discoverer had a climate worse than that of Iceland. Kerguélen decided that Gonneville's Terre Australe had to be Madagascar; something less than a southern continent but at least a worthwhile French discovery.[31]

Appropriation and assimilation

Cook had geographically connected the east coast of New Holland to the Dutch-mapped west and north coasts, but were the Dutch maps reliable (after all, they showed New Holland connected to New Guinea) and was Van Diemen's Land definitely part of New Holland? These questions remained open for a generation, and their resolution was more the result of individual initiative than official impetus. The main protagonist was Matthew Flinders, a Lincolnshire lad 'induced to go to sea against the wishes of my friends, from reading Robinson Crusoe'.[32] He was born in the year that Cook declared *Ne Plus Ultra* and by the omen should have been the man to push beyond the Antarctic Circle. Instead, his short life was devoted to completing Cook's work on the Known Southland. He went with Bligh of the *Bounty* – who had sailed with Cook – on the second breadfruit voyage to Tahiti.

In 1795 Flinders was a midshipman on HMS *Reliance* when she sailed to the British colony that had been founded seven years earlier in New South Wales. With the ship's surgeon, George Bass, he there undertook a series of small-boat voyages in the course of which they disproved Furneaux's contention that Van Diemen's Land and the mainland were connected. On the strength of this precocious achievement – he was then 24 – he put it to Joseph Banks, by then the most influential patron of southern exploration and settlement, that if the Admiralty could be persuaded to give him a ship he would complete the charting of New

Holland. Banks got him a ship, HMS *Investigator*, and instructions to do just that. Dalrymple supplied him with charts and with all parts of his works pertinent to the voyage.

Flinders conclusively demonstrated that New Holland and New South Wales were a single landmass. It was the largest island or, if one preferred, the smallest continent on the globe, undivided by any north-south sea or other channel of the kind conjectured by Visscher and Dampier. Flinders respectfully preserved and restored names bestowed on coastal features by the original navigators, but on his own account he sought a name for the whole. On the way home in 1803 his ship became so unseaworthy that he had to put into Mauritius. Britain and France were again at war and he was detained on the island until 1810. By the time he was released his health had been permanently undermined and he lived just long enough to see his *Voyage to Terra Australis* through the press. The first copy was placed beside him as he lay unconscious on his deathbed. He expired the following day, 19 July 1814, aged 40. A fortnight earlier he had asked to be enrolled among the subscribers for a new edition of the book that had first induced him to go to sea. He had often said that 'if the plan of a discovery voyage were read over his grave, he should rise up.'[33]

But what of his own book, a voyage not to New Holland but to the Unknown Southland that Cook had shown did not exist? Just so, Flinders had reasoned; if the Unknown Southland did not exist the Known Southland was the only candidate for the title Terra Australis. Sandwich Land he disregarded.

> There is no probability, that any other detached body of land, of nearly equal extent, will ever be found in a more southern latitude; the name Terra Australis will, therefore, remain descriptive of the geographical importance importance of this country, and of its situation on the globe: it has antiquity to recommend it; and, having no reference to either of the two claiming nations [unlike New Holland and New South Wales], appears to be less objectionable than any other which could have been selected.

He went further, adopting a name that he had read in Dalrymple.

> Had I permitted myself any innovation upon the original term, it would have been to convert it into AUSTRALIA; as being more agreeable to the ear, and an assimilation to the names of the other great portions of the earth.[34]

That label, too, was available. Cook had eliminated both of Dalrymple's southern continents. There was no Terra Australis in the temperate South Pacific, nor an Australia in the Atlantic. Transferring the names to New Holland was tidy and economical, perhaps conceived by Flinders as homage to hydrographer and explorer alike. In 1817 the governor of New South Wales, Lachlan Macquarie, endorsed the use of Australia in place of New Holland, the 'very erroneous and misapplied name hitherto given it'.[35] Three years later a Russian explorer, Thaddeus Bellingshausen, called in at Sydney. He had come from Sandwich Land which, he could attest, was only a long chain of islands. Flinders' case for applying the names Terra Australis and Australia to New Holland – that no land of nearly equal extent could exist further south – seemed complete.

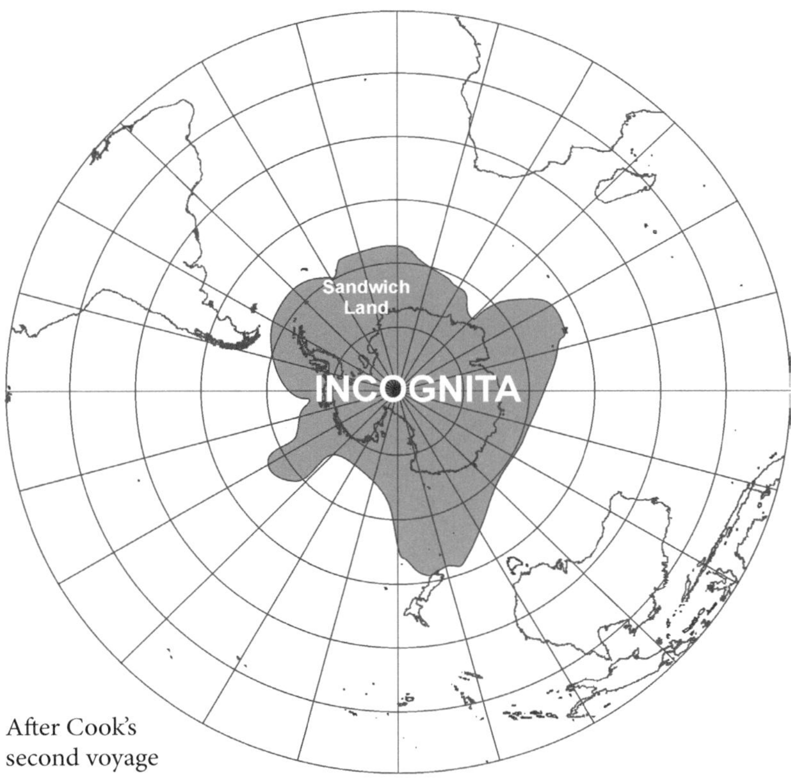

After Cook's second voyage

The theory of Symzonia

Geography is a science of facts. – Bougainville

Matthew Flinders had been educated in the James Cook school of methodical and sceptical exploration. John Cleves Symmes junior, by contrast, was the ultimate armchair geographer, a theorist pure and simple. He had an inspiration, and in 1818 he shared it with the world. The retired captain of infantry, alone with his thoughts at the edge of civilisation – St Louis, Missouri – conceived that our planet is but a shell.

> I declare that the earth is hollow, habitable within; containing a number of solid concentric spheres; one within the other, and that it is open at the pole twelve or sixteen degrees. I pledge my life in support of this truth, and am ready to explore the hollow if the world will support and aid me in the undertaking.[36]

This declaration was circulated as far around the world as 500 copies would take it, accompanied by certification as to the author's sanity. Symmes' followers hailed him as the 'Newton of the West'. He had studied the science of his day and could show how the polar regions were warmer than commonly believed (instance the tanned complexions of the Inuit), how the interior of the earth could be lit by the sun (refraction), and how polar explorers had been misled by their compasses to think that they were going north when they were going south, and vice versa.

It has been suggested that he got the idea of a hollow earth from Cotton Mather's *The Christian Philosopher*, in which that formidable New England divine had picked up Halley's ruminations about why the magnetic poles wandered.[37] Congress was petitioned, influential men spoke in support, and a book appeared. *Symzonia: A Voyage of Discovery* was presented to the world as the work of Adam Seaborn, a sea captain who had sailed beyond Sandwich Land in search of seals. In the book he passes 'the verge' and sails to the concave underside of the outer sphere, where he encounters a utopia whose people are so disgusted with what he tells them of his world that they insist he return to it.

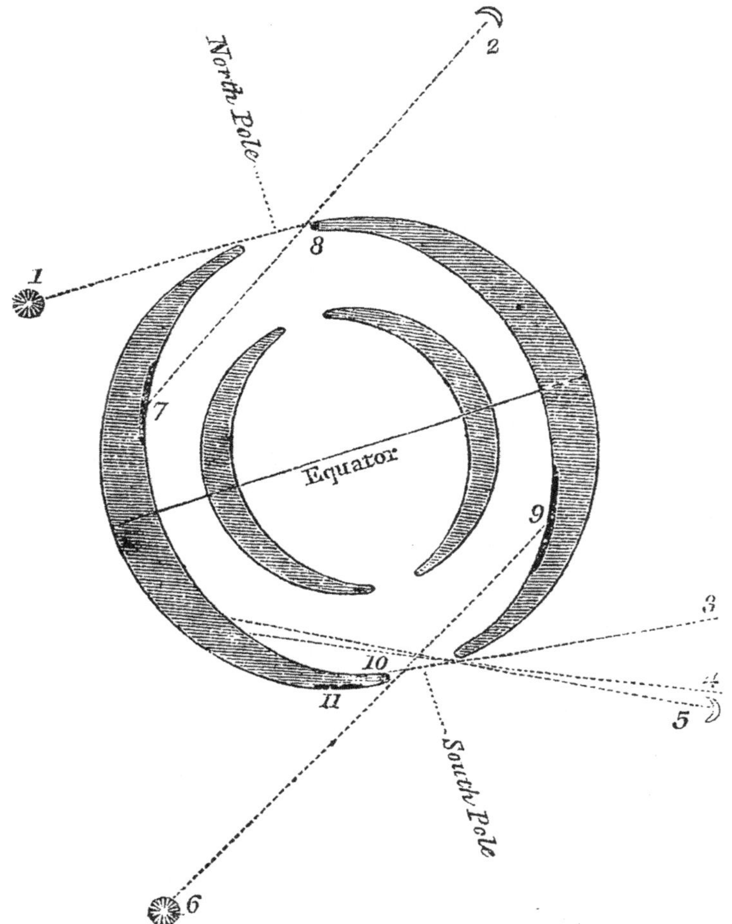

Symmes' hollow Earth was open at both poles, with concentric spheres within

The satire has little literary merit, but the little it has puts it beyond the reach of Symmes, all of whose acknowledged works are deadly earnest and mercifully short. Indeed, the prophet was so reluctant a writer that for a full exposition of his views one had to consult *Symmes' Theory of Concentric Spheres*, written by millionaire James McBride, but it was just this ability to attract talented and influential advocates to the cause that sustained it. The most significant of Symmes' acolytes was Jeremiah N. Reynolds, an Ohio lawyer and newspaper editor who organised a speaking tour for the prophet, defended McBride's book and, most important, knew how to put a Congressional lobby together. How far Reynolds actually believed in the theory it is hard to know. The closer he got to his objective of an Antarctic expedition the less a hollow earth featured in his arguments, but this was in part due to a falling-out with Symmes, who was more interested in the North Pole than the south. Conversely, reports of land being found amidst the ice south of Cook's tracks gave Reynolds a talking point less esoteric and more compelling than any geographical theory. Sub-antarctic land meant fur seals, and fur seals meant money to the shipowners of New England.

Cook's southern islands, from South Georgia and the Crozets to Kerguélen and New Zealand, had long been frequented by sealers. American and British parties had fought over the seals of Bass Strait. Another large breeding colony had been found in 1810 on Macquarie Island, south of Van Diemens's Land. The sealers took every last pelt they could find. There was no thought of leaving females to reproduce next season and no point to sparing the pups because without their mothers they would starve anyway. Few seal colonies lasted more than a season or two, which led owners to urge their captains further south in search of new grounds.

In 1819 word began to circulate in Buenos Aires of a discovery south of Cape Horn. A British trader with experience as a Greenland whaler, William Smith, had been contending with westerlies while on a voyage from Buenos Aires to Valparaiso. He sailed south in search of a favourable wind and found land in 62°17'S. Before he could return to claim this New South Shetland for Britain the islands' seal colonies were already being plundered. Smith persuaded the Royal Navy to charter his ship and explore the discovery further with him as pilot. On 30 January 1820 he and Edward Bransfield, the master in command, saw an extensive coast they named Trinity Land.[38] Smith reported 'a continent or numerous islands' with coasts extending two or three hundred miles. The *Gentleman's Magazine* heralded 'the great discovery' as a 'new southern continent', described by Smith as similar in appearance to the coast of Norway.[39] Smith saw only the north coast of his discovery. He could be only half-sure and he was only half-right; Trinity Land was part of the Antarctic mainland, but was that mainland a continent?

Later in 1820 an American fleet from Stonington under the command of Benjamin Pendleton ranged through the islands, with Nathaniel Palmer doing the scouting for harbours and seal beaches. On 7 February 1821 John Davis, captain of the Connecticut sealer *Huron*, recorded in her log that he had landed the boat from his tender *Cecilia* on a large body of land. Davis was slightly more definite than Smith: 'I think this Southern Land to be a Continent'.[40] *Cecilia*'s boat crew were probably the first human beings to set foot on the Unknown Southland, in what is now Hughes Bay on the Antarctic Peninsula. In the following year Nathanial Palmer met up with George Powell, an English sealer, and together they discovered the breeding beaches of the South Orkney Islands. This was a far more important find than Davis' Southern Land. Terra Australis, continent or not, was of no interest unless there were beaches that offered the seals ice-free access to the sea for a number of months. The beaches of any coasts and islands much further south than the new Orkneys and Shetlands were unlikely to be suitable for pup-rearing. Their ice-free season would be too brief.

Nevertheless, Cook's was no longer the last word. There was accessible land near the Antarctic Circle, and who was to say what might not be found in 74 or 78°S. Perhaps even a Symzonia.

10

Terra Australis Ultima

The voyage of circumnavigation that had taken Thaddeus Bellingshausen to Sydney was a personal initiative of that most erratic of autocrats, Tsar Alexander I. Its apparent objective was to improve on Cook. The imperial instructions directed Bellingshausen to survey South Georgia (because Cook had not sailed its southern coast) and pass down the eastern shore of Sandwich Land (because Cook, with only the west side in view, had suggested that it might be the headland of a southern continent). Thereafter, he was to steer south to the highest latitude he could reach (beyond Cook), making every effort to approach as closely as possible to the South Pole, 'searching for as yet unknown land, and only abandoning the undertaking in the face of insurmountable obstacles'.[1]

All of this was far removed from areas of Russian strategic or geopolitical interest, unlike the expedition that the tsar was simultaneously sending to find the Northwest Passage. In Alexander I, Enlightenment man met Russian mystic and their relationship was always uneasy. He was a sometime freemason, and before the expedition sailed a rumour did the rounds in St Petersburg that its real mission was to look for Roché's Isla Grande, where the Book of Life would be found in a cave guarded by evil spirits.[2]

As a young officer Bellingshausen had rounded Cape Horn during an earlier Russian circumnavigation and had some idea of the conditions his ships *Vostok* and *Mirnyi* would encounter. From the South Sandwich Islands he proceeded south, crossing the Antarctic Circle on 15 January

1820 (Old Style).[3] On the following day icebergs came into view, looking like white clouds through the falling snow. Ahead was a solid stretch of ice running east-west, covered with ice hillocks. The ships turned west in search of a way around. Thick weather denied them. The sighting was probably of land ice attached to what is now called the Princess Astrid Coast, less than 20 miles distant; in clear weather they would certainly have seen it.

Four days later, in 69°25'S, they again encountered the east-west stretch of ice and were unable to see its lateral limits, nor the coastline that lay 30 miles beyond it. The wind drove the ships from the line of ice but by 5 February Bellingshausen had again established contact, and here the ice was different. The now-familiar tabular bergs were stationary against a novel ice formation, the edge of which was perpendicular and formed into little coves, 'whilst the surface sloped upwards towards the south to a distance so far that its end was out of sight even from the masthead'.[4]

Bellingshausen, as cautious as Cook, did not speculate. On the following day he had a view of its eastern continuation and added an observation that in the far distance there were ice hills. The position of the ships was recorded as 69°06'S and 15°52'E, which would have placed them about 50 miles from Princess Ragnhild Coast. The detailed description of the ice edge indicates that they were somewhat closer. The Russians were almost certainly looking at the ice ramp that gradually ascends to the polar plateau in this sector of Greater Antarctica.

An attempt to get further south than Cook in 40°E failed, although Bellingshausen had for a third time crossed the Antarctic Circle and had come within 100 miles of the Prince Olav Coast. Through the next 30° of longitude he deliberately held to a course that kept him south of Cook's diversion to Kerguélen, but was then content to make directly for Sydney. There he prepared for a cruise to the Tuamoto archipelago, with which he occupied the winter months. By 9 September 1820 the ships were back in Sydney, where Bellingshausen found a letter waiting for him. It was from the Russian Minister at the Portuguese court in Rio, reporting the discovery of South Shetland. The captain of an East Indiaman at anchor in Sydney confirmed it. Bellingshausen factored the information into his plans.

The ships made their way south to Macquarie Island, where the Russian observed that after ten years of exploitation there was not one seal left and the sealers had turned to killing sea elephants for oil and hides. His plan of campaign was to get south of Cook's track as soon as he could, find the edge of the ice and track east along it as best as fog, icebergs and the wind would permit. His success may be judged by the fact that between the meridians of New Zealand and Cape Horn, a third of the circumference of the earth, he was south of Cook's latitudes for three-quarters of the distance.

Persistence brought its reward on 10 January 1821. In 69°22'S and 92°38'W a black patch showed through the haze. It was a rock face too steep for snow to cling to. Bellingshausen named his discovery, the first land seen south of the Antarctic Circle, for the founder of the Russian navy, Peter the Great. He reasoned there should be more, 'because the existence of only one island in that vast extent of water seemed to us impossible'. When his second-in-command, Lazarev, confirmed that the find was too small to be part of a continent, Bellingshausen pressed on east, parallel to the ice. Citing the South Sandwich Islands, he argued that it was quite improbable that there were not more islands nearby. A week later his optimism was justified by another, larger discovery. This time the ice allowed no closer an approach than 40 miles, but visibility was excellent and Bellingshausen could see that Alexander Land extended through half a degree of latitude. 'I call this discovery "land" because its southern extent disappeared beyond the extent of our vision'.

The 30 miles of coast that he could see would have persuaded many a predecessor that this was the headland of a continent, but Bellingshausen did not overclaim. In the fullness of time his caution was endorsed: a narrow sound, more than 200 miles long, separates his discovery from the Antarctic mainland. The good visibility did not last. By the following day it was down to two miles and the topsails had to be close-reefed to contend with violent squalls. Bellingshausen set a course to approach the South Shetlands from the south 'in order to ascertain whether this recently discovered land belongs to the supposed Southern Continent'.[5]

One difficulty he faced was that the latitudes provided by his two informants differed by a degree. He followed the advice of his Rio correspondent and as a result came to South Shetland from the west rather than the south. Had he instead accepted the information of the East Indiaman's captain, Bellingshausen would have found it necessary to steer a few degrees further east. There he would have discovered a continuous chain of islands leading north-east and, near the South Shetlands, a continental coast. As it was, he was busy surveying the uncharted south shores of the South

Shetlands when one of several sealing vessels in the vicinity came near. Bellingshausen sent across his boat. It returned with Nathaniel Palmer, and what passed between the Russian and the young American on that occasion is one of the most contentious issues in Antarctic history. Palmer later stated that Bellingshausen was surprised to be told that there was land further south, declared that it should be named for Palmer, and decided that there was nothing further for him to discover.

In Bellingshausen's version, their conversation was limited to the success of the sealers and the dangers to the sealing fleet. It is inherently improbable that Bellingshausen would have been surprised about land to the south – after all, he had recently found some himself – but a few days later he did ignore an appearance of land south of the islands.[6] It was a mistaken sighting but Bellingshausen had no way of knowing without further investigation and that he declined to do. He pleaded thick weather and 'left it to some future navigator to determine'. Abdication was therefore his last act of Antarctic exploration, but the Russian had one further matter to attend to. To give the return journey 'some geographical value', he altered course to pass where Isla Grande was shown on John Purdy's chart.[7]

The ships arrived at the point indicated on the chart in moderately clear weather. Anything within 25 miles in any direction would have been seen by the lookouts. Bellingshausen was confident enough to declare that Isla Grande did not exist, but was also careful to quote the original publisher of Roché's voyage, who had noted that on the coast of Patagonia in the nominated latitude there is a cape with the appearance of an island. Duty done, the ships reached their home port of Kronstadt in July 1821. In the following year Alexander suppressed freemasonry throughout Russia. Bellingshausen was rewarded for his efforts – he had done everything officially asked of him – but his narrative was not published until 1831, well into the following reign, and then in a derisory edition of 600 copies. There is no proof that these subsequent developments were related to Bellingshausen's failure to find the Book of Life, but that is unlikely to have inhibited the gossips of St Petersburg.

The South Sea Fur Company

At South Shetland, Bellingshausen had realised that in such crowded waters there was little prospect of further discovery. Moreover, if the ice did encase substantial land it would be as useless as Cook had foretold. The sealers' stories were also bad news for John Symmes and Jeremiah Reynolds, because it seemed that the south polar region might after all be inaccessible to ships. James Weddell, a British sealer, changed all that. In 1823 he sailed between the South Orkney and South Sandwich islands and improbably found himself in an open sea. Cook's furthest south was surpassed without a particle of ice being seen. On 17 February, in 74°34'S and 30°12'W, there were a few icebergs in sight but the sea ahead was clear enough for Weddell to surmise that it might extend all the way to the South Pole. His crews urged him on, but his ships were short of provisions and a long way from anywhere they could refresh. Weddell turned back, two days sail from what was later named Coats Land on the Antarctic mainland.

Reynolds had no difficulty reconciling the generality of sealing experience with the report of Weddell. According to Symmes' theory, the ice was a 'hoop' that extended around the Pole in 70–80°S. Beyond it lay an ice-free sea. Weddell seemed to have found a way in, and Reynolds was determined to follow him. Part of Reynolds' propaganda campaign involved keeping members of Congress fully informed about the enterprise and discoveries of American sealers and whalers. This particularly recommended him to Edmund Fanning, the doyen of sealers, who had unsuccessfully urged Antarctic exploration on previous administrations. Symmes died in 1829 but by then Reynolds had almost persuaded Congress to authorise an exploring expedition. The measure failed to pass the Senate before it adjourned for the 1828 elections and when Congress returned the new administration was unsympathetic.

President Andrew Jackson's backwoods constituency would have no truck with government expenditure on projects for the benefit of eastern shipowners. The expedition was shelved. Undeterred, Reynolds and Fanning created a South Sea Fur Company and Exploring Expedition that outfitted three sealing vessels and engaged the services of Benjamin Pendleton and Nathaniel Palmer. The expedition, funded partly from the proceeds of Reynolds' lectures, sailed for the south in October 1829 provisioned for a twelve months' cruise. Exploration was hostage to commerce: the crew would be paid nothing unless seals were found. A small 'scientific' group was included and Reynolds also went, nominally as historiographer, but in reality to live the adventure of his *alter ego*, Captain Seaborn. He would not see the United States again for four years.

The quest resumed

British sealing firms were also active in the search for new grounds, and none more than the Enderbys. Three generations of the family had prospered in the skin and oil business of the southern seas. In 1830 the firm dispatched John Biscoe with the *Tula* and her tender *Lively* 'to make discoveries in a high southern latitude'. Biscoe started from Sandwich Land, where field-ice prevented him from going south to investigate what he thought were signs of land. Trying again further east, the ships reached 65°57'S and 47°20'E on 27 January 1831. From there Biscoe distinctly saw land of a considerable extent. For three weeks he attempted to close with it but ice and weather kept him 20–30 miles distant. By the time the *Tula* reached Hobart, Biscoe had with him only two officers, one man and a boy fit enough to work her. He named their discovery Enderby's Land.

At the beginning of the following season he sealed in New Zealand waters with little success before resuming an easterly course along the Antarctic Circle. In 71°48'W, half the world around from Enderby's Land, Biscoe again saw an Antarctic coast. His landfall was Adelaide Island, north of Alexander Land, but, unlike Bellingshausen, Biscoe tracked north-east through the islands off the Antarctic Peninsula and was able to land on one of them. East of the islands he could see 'a high continuous land', subsequently named Graham Land. There were ideal seal beaches, with water so still and deep that skins could have been loaded directly on to the ships – but no seals. Biscoe was aggrieved at their lack of co-operation: '… the sun was so warm that the snow was melted off all the rocks from the waterline, which made it more extraordinary that they should be so utterly deserted'. From a commercial perspective the voyage was a failure – two years effort for 30 skins – but, like Reynolds' venture, the voyage was not entirely commercial. Charles Enderby, the firm's most active partner, was also a founding member of the Royal Geographical Society, to which he immediately reported Biscoe's discoveries. The editor of the Society's journal was enthusiastic.

> Two distinct discoveries have been made, at a great distance the one from the other; and each in the highest southern latitude, with very few exceptions, which has yet been attained, or in which land has yet been discovered. The probability seems thus to be revived of the existence of a great Southern Land, yet to be brought upon our charts, and possibly made subservient to the prosperity of our fisheries.[8]

The quest for Terra Australis could resume. Not only had Biscoe put the Unknown Southland back on the map, but he had discovered how it could best be explored by sailing ships. The Roaring Forties, the Furious Fifties and the Shrieking Sixties were all westerly winds, but along the edge of the ice he had found more tolerable easterlies. Antarctic explorers could hold further south by sailing east to west. What Biscoe could not tell them was how much of the solid Antarctic was ice and how much was land. There was also the mystery of Weddell's penetration, which suggested that the ice/land might not be circumpolar and/or that it might be divided into a number of masses.

Whichever, it was almost certainly uninhabited and uninhabitable. Biscoe had seen no signs of animal life except birds. There might be whales in the adjacent waters, but only so-far undiscovered minerals could offer any prospect of wealth ashore and extraction would be difficult, as the Russians had found on their Arctic islands. The place was of no strategic interest to any power, not even the Russians. What was the point of going there?

Ex ex

In the course of a decade Jeremiah Reynolds had developed a whole suite of answers to that question, but none of them had cut ice with the men of the South Seas Fur Company. When he returned to the United States in 1832 it was not with the expedition but as the captain's secretary on USS *Potomac*, which he had joined in Peru. The Fanning venture had collapsed within a few months of departure. Thwarted in an attempt to follow Weddell's route, the ships had wandered west through the long-deserted sealing grounds. It soon became apparent to the crews that they would get no seals in Antarctic waters and the captains agreed to try off Chile. Reynolds was unwilling to waste time and decided to explore ashore.

For two years he wandered in Chile, building a close relationship with the Araucanian Indians in regions the Spanish feared to enter. On his return to Washington, Reynolds found that the Jackson administration had mellowed. What had been dismissed out of hand four years previously now seemed more acceptable to some, including the President. Jackson's second inaugural address had even contained a reference to 'diffusion of knowledge'. Reynolds renewed his agitation, dressing his argument to suit the new climate of opinion. Edgar Allan Poe became an unofficial publicist when he included Symmes' verge in *The Narrative of Arthur Gordon Pym*, which leaves its American whaleman hero poised on the edge of a chasm at 84°S in the Weddell Sea. Some readers refused to believe that the story was fiction.

When Reynolds rose to speak, by invitation, in the hall of the House of Representatives on 3 April 1836, his discourse was of national prestige, safety of navigation, scientific enquiry and the protection of American interests. The South Pole was almost an afterthought, and a dubious one at that. Reynolds was still unsure what might be found at the Pole, and his rhetoric betrayed it: 'yea, to cast anchor on that point where all the meridians terminate, where our eagle and star-spangled banner may be unfurled and planted, and left to wave on the axis of the earth itself!'[9]

Mahlon Dickerson, Secretary of the Navy, who was being asked to make room for the enterprise in his budget, was an unrepentant sceptic and Reynolds had played right into his hands. He drily observed that it would be difficult to leave a flag in the middle of the ocean unless the Pole turned out to be a flagstaff, but he was relieved to learn that his ships would not now have to sail into a hole. Dickerson's opposition was not restricted to sniping. He put every obstacle he could conceive in the way of an expedition, so successfully that by 1838 his arrangements, or lack of them, had become a joke and a scandal. Finally Van Buren, Jackson's successor, took the matter out of his hands. The United States Exploring Expedition, six ships strong, sailed on 18 August, but not before Dickerson had engineered one petty, mean triumph; Jeremiah Reynolds, lauded by Poe as the 'originater of the expedition', its tireless advocate and aspiring historian, was not aboard.

The Ex Ex, as it was popularly known, had promotion of commerce and navigation as its primary objects. Science and exploration were secondary but Lieutenant Charles Wilkes, the commander, was instructed to penetrate the Antarctic as deeply as he could at three points. The first two were predictable – Weddell's and Cook's furthest. The third was as yet a blank on the map; south of Van Diemen's Land the Ex Ex should attempt to find Biscoe's icy easterlies and run before them to Enderby's Land. The great mathematician Carl Gauss had predicted that the South Magnetic Pole would be found almost on the meridian of Hobart and just north of the Antarctic Circle. The British were known to be preparing an expedition to locate it, but that was no reason for Americans to defer.

Wilkes arrived too late in the season to penetrate far into the Weddell Sea. The attempt to reach Cook's furthest south, on the other side of the Antarctic Peninsula, also failed. No land was seen. After a winter spent surveying in the Pacific, the Ex Ex refitted in Sydney for a second cruise in the ice. There Wilkes met John Biscoe, no longer with the Enderbys but still in the 'skinning business'. He had personally been no further south than 62° in this quadrant but he knew that a Sydney sealer, the *Venus*, was said to have bettered it by nine degrees in 1831, and he had also heard rumours of land south of Macquarie Island.

Southlands enough for all

Biscoe did not play favourites. He gave the same information to a French expedition visiting Hobart. Its commander, Dumont d'Urville, was even keener than the Americans to pre-empt the British. King Louis Phillipe had given him this, his third Pacific expedition, on condition that he would try to reach the South Pole along Weddell's track. Having failed, like Wilkes, to get beyond the Antarctic Peninsula, d'Urville had renamed some of its features for the royal family but still had no genuine Antarctic discovery with which to humour his sovereign. The magnetic pole would be a poor substitute for the real thing, but according to Gauss' theory it should at least be accessible. The American and French expeditions left their respective Australian ports a week apart. It was an unacknowledged race.

Wilkes sailed for the islands rumoured to lie south of Macquarie. Dumont d'Urville sailed along the magnetic meridian, which was the shortest route to the magnetic pole. Wilkes encountered field ice south of Macquarie Island and sailed west looking for a way through, hoping that the elevations he could see beyond it were land. All attempts to break through to the south failed. Some of the orders that he gave presupposed the existence of Symmes' ice-free polar sea; if this ice-field or icy hoop should close behind them, all ships were to make for Weddell's exit – assuming that it still existed. Dumont d'Urville had better luck with the ice but the magnetic pole was not where Gauss had forecast. Instead, on 20 January 1840 he saw an ice ramp that sloped gently from the sea to a far horizon silhouetted against the setting sun. Not all aboard were convinced that it was land, but on the following day offshore rocks showed amidst the ice. It was enough; a landing was made on one of them and Terre Adélie was claimed for France.

For another ten days d'Urville cruised the ice looking for a way through to the mainland. Instead he came across one of the American ships, USS *Porpoise*. He ignored his competitors but took the hint. If the Americans were already in those parts they might find and – *horreur* – claim his discovery. On the following day the French came upon a continuous ice cliff 30–45 metres high and 60–75 miles in length. D'Urville was convinced that such a mass could not form in the open sea and therefore must be grounded. He called it Côte Clarie and sailed for Hobart to get his discoveries on the public record. Adelie Land, he wrote to his Minister of Marine, was not just an isolated stretch of coast. In his opinion – based on that belief that at least shoals or islands underlay the Clarie Coast ice – land surrounded the greater part of the polar region and would be found almost everywhere that a mariner could penetrate.

On the same day that d'Urville snubbed the *Porpoise* his fears about the Americans had been realised; three degrees to the east Wilkes did indeed see the rocks of Adelie Land. He took the USS *Vincennes* into what he called Piner's Bay. The doubts of the previous weeks were banished. 'Antarctic land discovered beyond cavil', he wrote in his journal, but ice and weather kept it beyond his reach. By 12 February he had tracked along the field ice for a month, naming features visible beyond the ice barrier with increasing confidence. Here at Knox's High Land he decided that 'Antarctic land' inadequately described his discovery: 'The above land I think clearly determines or settles the question of our having discovered the Antarctic continent, for we have traced it now through about 30° of long[itude] – equal to 900 miles'.[10]

It was a bold statement. Wilkes had landed nowhere and had no physical proof that anything he had seen was land, let alone continuous land. To put his claim in context, New Guinea was known to be all of 1,500 miles in length but by universal agreement it was counted as an island, not a continent. Perhaps Wilkes thought that 30° of longitude in the Antarctic counted for more than New Guinea's 20° in the tropics. In later usage he capitalised his discovery as the 'Antarctic Continent', a description rather than a name, but as apt as any since Flinders had appropriated Australia for the Known Southland.[11] Wilkes had demonstrated that the girdle of ice protecting the chastity of the far southland, whatever kind of land it might turn out to be, lay roughly along the Antarctic Circle, prohibiting the presence of winter sun and would-be discoverers alike.

A year passed before the British expedition was ready to follow its French and American rivals into Antarctic waters. James Clark Ross, already famous as the locator of the North Magnetic Pole, had been tasked to find the other. As the expedition was about to sail from England, Charles Enderby came to tell Ross of a new find. One of his captains, John Balleny, had been sealing at Campbell Island, south of New Zealand, when he had come across the ubiquitous John Biscoe. Biscoe had told him – as it seemed he had everyone else – of the rumoured land south of Macquarie Island. Unlike the others Balleny had found it, a series of volcanic specks in 68°S. The doom of the House of Enderby was upon the place, however, and there were no seals. Pushing east in 64°S, Balleny had glimpsed something else that he took for land and named for his tender, *Sabrina*. Ross was not sure whether this was good news or bad. He had hoped to sail to the pole. On the other hand, perhaps this land, midway between Biscoe's discoveries, was the missing piece of a continent-sized puzzle.

At Hobart Ross heard of the French and American discoveries, which the *Hobart Town Advertiser* had already decided were 'merely a continuation of the same continent' discovered by Biscoe.[12] He was confident that his converted bomb ketches *Erebus* and *Terror* were superior ice ships, but why follow in the wake of others, perhaps to be stopped by the same ice his rivals had encountered? He altered his plan. He would try to penetrate the Antarctic further east, where Balleny had seen open water beyond the ice in 69°S. From there he could approach the magnetic pole by sailing west – if Gauss' calculations were to be trusted. The ships tracked south from Campbell Island along the 170th meridian and met pack ice soon after crossing the Circle. Four days of hard bumping saw them through to clear water in 70°S, in what is now the Ross Sea.

Free of the ice, Ross could follow the south end of his compass needle directly towards the magnetic pole. He was brought up short, but by nothing as insignificant as d'Urville's ice ramp. The Transantarctic Mountains stretched north and south across his course as far as the eye could see, a backbone of continental dimensions. After landing on an island to take possession of Victoria Land, Ross sailed south, looking for a way around the mighty obstacle. Three hundred miles on, it was intersected from the east by another. The equally formidable Great Icy Barrier, as Ross called it, was anchored off the mountains by an active volcano, Erebus. The continuous ice face, 60 metres high, presented a front as impenetrable as the cliffs of Dover. After failing to find a way around it, Ross turned north, hoping to outflank the mountains in the opposite direction. At Cape North, in 70°S, the coast appeared to turn south of west. Ross thought that it could be the back passage he was seeking, but pack ice barred the way. The closest he came to the magnetic pole was 160 miles.

Ross had seen a mountain chain five hundred nautical miles long, with many peaks in excess of 3,000 metres high. Surgeon Robert McCormick was sure that it was 'a Southern Continent' but Ross was more circumspect. From Cape North to Balleny's Islands he sailed along the edge of the pack, toying with the idea of returning early next season to see if the Transantarctic Mountains might be nothing more obstructive than a narrow Antarctic peninsula with open water on its western side. In the meantime he found the Balleny Islands without difficulty and went looking for the American discoveries that Wilkes had charted nearby. He found nothing and wrote with quiet satisfaction of sailing over the American's 'mountain range'. And if Wilkes had been mistaken here, he might have been similarly mistaken in his other sightings. For his own part, Ross soberly reported to the Admiralty that he had found 'the great southern land'.

With these words – which as recently as Halley's day he would have written as *terra australis magna* – he brought centuries of speculation to an anti-climax: *incognita* no longer, but not yet worthy to be designated a continent or capitalised as Wilkes would have it. Ross also reported that pack ice filled the entire space westward between Victoria Land and the islands discovered by Balleny in 1839 'and more extensively explored by the American and French expeditions in the following year'.[13] The Hobart correspondent for Lloyd's List was quick to point out the 'extraordinary mistake' of the Americans. Not only had Ross found sea where the American chart showed land, but the closest part of the British discovery was 300 miles further south.[14] Ross could not query the French claims by reference to his own voyage but he did not have to, for there was Balleny's. If the Antarctic Continent and Adelie Land and Clarie Coast existed then so must Sabrina Land, discovered a year earlier in about the same latitude.

What infuriated Wilkes about the French and British claims was that, as he saw it, one party was claiming priority over his discovery and the other was denying its existence. Both had understated their achievements, robbing the Americans by restricting Antarctic land to the smaller parts they had seen. He did not help his own case by failing to acknowledge French precedence at Piner's Bay and he seriously offended Ross by referring to Victoria Land as an extension of 'our Antarctic continent'.[15] D'Urville was killed in a railway accident in 1842, which spared him the ever more acrimonious public debate into which Wilkes and Ross were drawn. Ross insisted that Biscoe, Balleny, d'Urville and Wilkes had seen no more than small patches of land that were likely to be a chain of islands rather than 'a great southern continent'.

Unfortunately for Ross, information that might have settled the matter in his favour did not come to public notice until 1858. In 1850 an Enderby whaler named Tapsell had sailed west from the Balleny Islands in a latitude well to the south of Wilkes' track and saw no land in the vicinity of the American's eastern claims. The Royal Geographical Society mislaid Tapsell's log and his voyage went unreported for nearly a decade. There was some justice in this. It was true that Wilkes had no grounds for claiming that his discoveries and those of Ross were continuous, but Ross had no evidence that they were not, other than in places that he had sailed – likewise Tapsell. Still, no doubt the next explorer would quickly resolve the matter.

The princess of Antarctica

There was not another explorer in those parts for nearly sixty years. Tapsell's had been the last Enderby ice voyage. There were seals at the margins of the ice, but they were in small numbers and not fur seals. Ross had reported whales, but no one was sure that they were the right whales, those whose baleen was so suitable for ladies' corsets and gentlemen's buggy whips. In short, science was the only benefit on offer. To its credit the British government in 1872 made HMS *Challenger* available to transport Royal Society and other scientists on the first global oceanographic expedition. For four years the ship trawled the surface and dredged the depths, but only once did it cross the Antarctic Circle. There, ice-transported gneiss and granite debris found on the sea bottom in the Indian Ocean sector suggested that the Antarctic must conceal an ice-calving continent or great islands. Analogy with deposits elsewhere in the world indicated that a major landmass had to exist no more than 200 miles south of the Circle. The *Challenger* was then near the charted position of Wilkes' westernmost Antarctic landfall, Termination Land, and steamed in search of it. Like Ross at the eastern end thirty years earlier, they found nothing. John Murray, an assistant naturalist on the scientific staff, later made a point of informing a Manchester audience that the expedition had also failed to find any sunken traces of Atlantis in the Atlantic, of Lemuria (after the Madagascan primates) in the Indian Ocean or of a Tertiary continent supposed to lie under the South Pacific.[16] One mystery that Murray did clear up, however, was that of Bathybius.

Standard operating procedure on the *Challenger* stipulated that whenever mud or ooze was brought up from the bottom it should be immediately bottled and the container topped up with spirit. At the conclusion of the voyage these samples were examined and some of the mud was found to have a jelly-like appearance. A few years earlier Thomas Huxley, 'Darwin's bulldog', had suggested that this substance was protoplasm, the simplest form of life and the starting point of evolution. He had named it Bathybius. Murray was puzzled; he had detected no evidence of such a creature in or on the mud. He suspected that the gelatinous substance might have come from seawater in the mud. The expedition's chemist, John Buchanan, confirmed that the jelly was amorphous sulphate of lime, which was precipitated but not crystallised by the action of four parts of wine spirit on one part of seawater.[17] Huxley promptly admitted his 'blunderibus', but the episode became a favorite with creationists keen to discredit evolutionary theory.

The *Challenger*'s Antarctic work prompted public interest in the idea of an attempt to reach the South Pole. The director of the expedition's scientific staff, Sir Wyville Thomson, doubted that the journey would be possible with current 'methods and appliances' and pointed out that although Ross had found a way through the pack ice, he had still been halted by an even more formidable ice barrier 700 miles short of the pole. Conditions were worse than those in the Arctic. The number of lives already lost in the quest for the North Pole would be multiplied a hundred-fold should nations begin to compete in the south.[18] The first historian of the Antarctic, Hugh Mills, described this as the generation of averted interest, but in a way it was the sheer volume of *Challenger* data that presented the single greatest obstacle to further British exploration.

It took the Edinburgh-based *Challenger* Commission two decades to digest the expedition results into fifty volumes of reports. Thomson did not live to see them all but his work was continued by John Murray, who found that the closer he came to completing it the less complete it seemed. With the *Challenger* evidence at his fingertips Murray became a more credible but still Reynolds-like advocate of further Antarctic exploration. He presented the evidence in favour of an Antarctic continent to a British Association meeting in 1885, but it was a sober academic exercise. The following year, when addressing the Scottish Geographical Society, he was bolder, his case supported by a striking visual aid. 'It may be regarded as conclusively proved that there is a great mass of continental land within the Antarctic Circle. Its probable position and extent is indicated on the map'.[19]

The map was the work of John George Bartholomew, foundation secretary of the Society and cartographer of the *Challenger* Reports. It showed a 'Supposed Outline of [the] Antarctic Continent' that embraced the discoveries of Smith, Bellingshausen, Balleny, d'Urville, Wilkes and Ross, but it was not a simple exercise in joining up the dots. Biscoe's Enderby Land was excluded from the continent because in that sector Ross had recorded no bottom at 4,000 fathoms, which indicated to Murray that there could be no large landmass nearby,[20] but even so the whole was larger than Australia. Thus began a long campaign in which Murray solicited letters of support for more Antarctic exploration from many of the most credible figures in international science, but little happened until 1893 when the dynamic Sir Clements Markham, recently-elected President of the Royal Geographical Society, decided to make the project his own.

Markham invited Murray to present the case for a naval and scientific expedition. It was an alliance of convenience. Markham was fixated on the idea of a Royal Navy expedition to the South Pole – *The Times* called it 'naval adventure'; Murray had always emphasised the need for systematic and deliberate scientific exploration rather than a dash for the pole, but with the happy and fruitful partnership of the *Challenger* in mind he had no difficulty with naval command. On 27 November 1893 he addressed the Society in London. He began with an historical review of southern exploration and the science it had made possible, using the adjective Antarctic to denominate ocean and land alike. Then he referred to the 1886 map, since re-engraved by Bartholomew to label the probable landmass 'Antarctica'.[21] In the ensuing discussion all but one of the luminaries present continued to refer to 'the Antarctic', but Alexander Buchan, meteorologist and *Challenger* associate, followed Murray's lead. The name Antarctica, assimilable to those of the other continents – Flinders' desideratum – had taken its first halting steps towards acceptance.[22]

Not unnaturally, Murray declared that the first task of an expedition should be to determine the nature and extent of his hypothetical continent, which in turn would ascertain the distribution of land and water on the planet. The hydrographer of the Navy, Captain Wharton, took exception to a gentle dig by Murray at Dalrymple's unscientific speculation, pointing out that the only difference between the two was that Murray had been exercising 'scientific imagination', but the meeting ended in heated agreement that a new expedition was necessary and that the British government should find the money.[23] The Sixth International Geographical Conference, held in London in 1895, went further, resolving that the learned societies of the world should be encouraged to promote Antarctic expeditions. The delegates had been enthused by the report of Carstens Borchgrevink, a Norwegian-born Australian just returned from the Antarctic. He had been there on a failed whale hunt but had landed on the mainland at Cape Adare, near Ross' Possession Island. Now he volunteered to return and ski to the South Magnetic Pole. Murray was ecstatic. In a kind of delirium he piled up the possibilities.

> … it being in an area of high atmospheric pressure, there may possibly be a greater amount of evaporation than precipitation and possibly, if Mr. Borchgrevink were to penetrate into the interior of this great southern continent he might find, besides plants and animals, a Princess of Antarctica, or the remains of Paleolithic man. It is possible that every year there may be vegetation coming up … [24]

He factored Borchgrevink's recommendation of Cape Adare into the expedition that was forming in his mind. It would be one of two landing sites – the other to be near Bellingshausen's Peter I Island – whence parties would make for the geographic South Pole from both sides of the Transantarctic Mountains while their ship dredged and sounded the ocean sector between. Bartholomew adapted his map of Antarctica to illustrate the routes. He also penned a poem that advertised the name Antarctica and, in its last stanza, urged his countrymen to stop dithering.

> And now spirits bold, as in days of old,
> Would these wonders weird display,
> Antarctica's shores they would fain explore,
> And her unknown realms survey.
> Then let us maintain our country's fame!
> Bold Britons! Lead the way! [25]

In 1898 Murray presented his arguments to the Royal Society in a paper that provoked a discussion of unprecedented duration. It did much to get that august body, the government's principal scientific advisers, to participate in what became a joint venture, but it was not until Markham had raised about half of the estimated cost from private sources that the government was shamed into covering the shortfall. Markham was indignant that a magazine publisher, Sir George Newnes, had chosen to fund a Borchgrevink expedition instead. In 1899, Borchgrevink and nine companions overwintered at Cape Adare. They were unable to penetrate the mountains towards the South Magnetic Pole as planned, but they were able to confirm that the Ross Sea was accessible to a higher latitude than any other known route south. The Transantarctic Mountains were a formidable obstacle, but the region offered tempting bases for expeditions with the geographic or magnetic poles as their objectives. The Ross Sea became the preferred jumping-off point for land expeditions, and the first of these in the new century was the joint venture of the Royal Geographical Society and the Royal Society.

Markham's agitation might well have failed without John Murray's credible and enthusiastic support, but at its president's instigation the Royal Geographical Society focused on the polar journey rather than on the science that it was to facilitate. The Royal Society insisted that research, particularly magnetic research, be given equal importance. The instructions finally given to Robert Falcon Scott, the naval officer hand-picked by Markham to command the expedition, did include a comprehensive scientific program and they directed the expedition to the east coast of Victoria Land rather than the South Pole but, in Markham's own satisfied phrase, 'everything else' was left to Scott's discretion.[26] A wink was as good as a nod to Scott who, when his temporary scientific director disembarked at Cape Town, was left with no-one to query his decision to build winter quarters as conveniently close to the South Pole as he could, at McMurdo Sound in the shadow of Mount Erebus.

In 1902, accompanied by Edward Wilson and Ernest Shackleton, Scott set out for the geographical pole but was unable even to reach the head of the Ross Ice Shelf. In the following year, lacking time for another attempt, he instead climbed the eastern slope of the Transantarctic Mountains onto the polar plateau, altitude 9,000 feet, and trekked west for 200 blank miles. At the outward limit, still at 9,000 feet, he found himself in a shallow hollow, its horizon higher than his head in all directions. He was suddenly seized with an irrational hope that over the rim ahead there might be a long slope downwards, or a mountain range in the distance heralding a western coast for Victoria Land, or indeed anything. There was nothing. Scott wrote of himself that he was a man without imagination, but it took little enough to conceive the vast emptiness ahead. He could only describe it in terms of what it was not: a place without tree or shrub, living thing or inanimate rock, for hundreds or thousands of miles. It had been like this for countless years, he wrote, would be for countless more, 'and we, little human insects, have started to crawl over this awful desert, and are now bent on crawling back again'.[27]

When in 1904 the expedition left the Ross Sea, Scott hoped that steam power would allow him to round Cape North and penetrate further west than his predecessors. Pack ice stopped him west of the Balleny Islands, but not before he was able to eliminate the remainder of Wilkes' eastern discoveries. Having steamed more or less along the Antarctic Circle nearly as far as 155°E, Scott could declare that there was no case for land – at least near the Circle – anywhere eastward of Adelie Land. Wilkes' first sightings were thereby discredited in their entirety but his assertion that Victoria Land was an extension of Adelie Land had been neither proved nor disproved. Indeed, in Scott's opinion the coastline west of Cape North probably ran almost directly to Adelie Land. He also believed that the Transantarctic Mountains extended to the Antarctic Peninsula, and had no reservations about using the term Antarctic Continent.[28] But was it a single landmass?

It was not a question that troubled Ernest Shackleton. Disappointed at not having reached the South Pole in 1902, resentful at having been evacuated with scurvy in 1903 and implacably determined to return, by 1907 he had put together an expedition of his own. His intention was to moor the ship *Nimrod* against the Ross Ice Shelf even closer to the pole than Scott's base and from there to make a bee-line south. So short were the funds and so single-minded was the enterprise that although the South Magnetic Pole was listed as a secondary objective the ship sailed without a trained magnetic observer.

Only when the ship reached New Zealand did the Australian and New Zealand governments agree to contribute. Finally there was enough money for a physicist. Douglas Mawson was a geologist who had hoped to spend a single summer in Antarctica studying glaciers. He was told that neither the position nor the option was available. His former professor, T. W. Edgeworth David, who had already been recruited by Shackleton, recommended him for the magnetic work. A base on the Ice Shelf would be a long way from the magnetic pole, and there were unlikely to be many rocks in the immediate vicinity, but teacher and pupil both knew that it would be the opportunity of a lifetime.

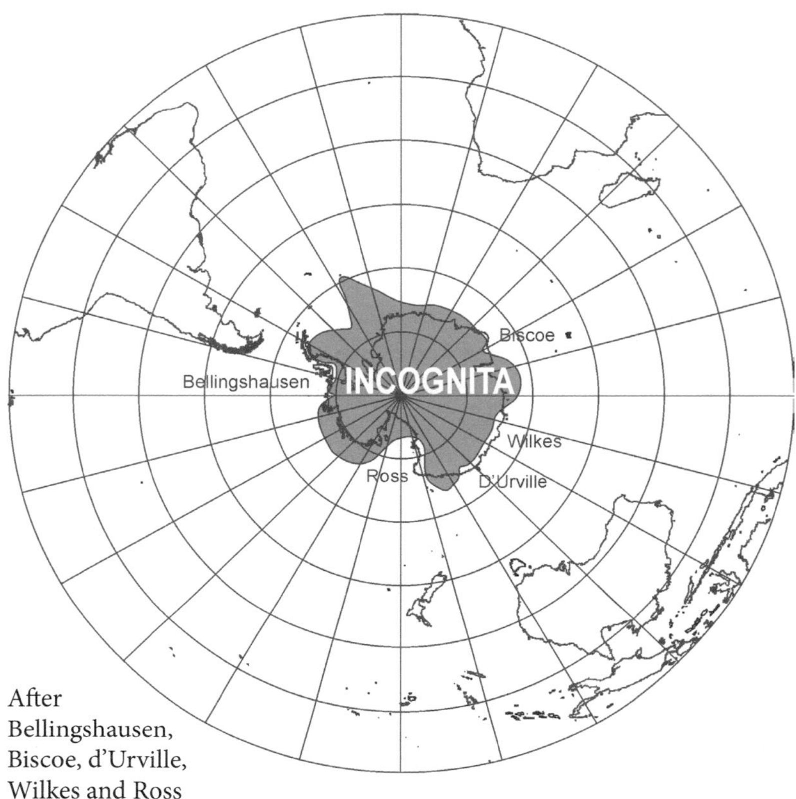

After
Bellingshausen,
Biscoe, d'Urville,
Wilkes and Ross

The dream of Bathybia

From a weird wild clime that lieth, sublime, out of Space,
out of Time. – Edgar Allan Poe

Shackleton could not find a landing place on the Ice Shelf. He was forced to make his base at McMurdo Sound, near Scott's old base. When spring came he would face the prospect of following the same route that had defeated him in 1902, and even if the Ice Shelf were to be conquered this time it would only be the start. Would the mountains beyond be passable? For Mawson and David, on the other hand, the change of base was more positive – it put the South Magnetic Pole within reach.

As the expeditioners waited for the return of the sun, Shackleton had a care to ensure that the blackness outside did not infiltrate the hut. 'The Boss' encouraged home-grown entertainments and demanded contributions for *Aurora Australis*, a collection of original poetry and prose that he edited into what became the first book printed in Antarctica. Mawson was one of the writers. His little story fantasised about the wonders that next summer's trek to the South Pole might reveal. It opened by mischievously suggesting a start along the alternate route that Scott had followed in 1903, up the Ferrar Glacier onto the plateau west of McMurdo. The push south could begin from there. It was less direct, but the additional distance would be offset by certainty of ascent. And it was by this route that Mawson took the expedition to Bathybia.

Two hundred and fifty miles SSW of the Ferrar Glacier (beyond Scott's furthest west), a water sky appeared somewhat to the west of the expeditioners' course. Fog enveloped them and they camped for the night. In the morning the fog had gone, and before them lay what one of them called 'The Bottomless Pit'. A steep slope descended to what appeared to be snow-free undulating plains some 30,000 feet below. As they were at 8,000 feet on the plateau, the plains had to be about 22,000 feet below sea level! On the way down, the atmosphere grew steadily denser and increasing levels of carbon dioxide and water vapour created a greenhouse effect, causing the temperature to rise to 70°F.

The plants and animals that began to appear were exotic, but many seemed to be giant versions of microscopic life forms found on the Antarctic shore. Around the margins of a vast inland sea there was algae that intoxicated and giant fungi that provided logs, decking and rope for a raft. Other algae contained enough oil to be used as torches. Much of the vegetable matter was edible. There were no elephants but there were 30-centimetre mites that looked like ticks and a sort of water bear four times that size, large enough to attack the biologist. A five-metre high toadstool on which the artist perched himself exploded, indiscriminately launching spores and artist into the air.

Mawson speculated that all of these life forms had been brought there in their familiar, tiny forms by the warmer anti-trade winds and had grown great in their age-long isolation. Bathybia itself was volcanic in origin, featuring an active peak that bore a passing resemblance to Mount Erebus. The mountain was the dominant feature in 'a great depression some hundreds of miles across, bound on the East by a great fault face, but with more gently rising boundaries in other

Artist Marston and the exploding mushrooms of Bathybia

directions. In fact it might be likened to a portion, for example, of the basin of the Pacific Ocean from which the water had been removed'.[29]

Mawson's ambitions were more modest than those of Plato, More, Defoe, Swift or Rousseau. He sought to invent a scientifically coherent geography that would more or less fit into Symmes' inherently improbable hollow earth. He also drew on Huxley's mistake, Murray's delirium and Scott's frustration. This was intellectual sport, not mental engineering, but fiction was still a lie and the scientist, more responsible than the polemicists, could not leave his readers misinformed. Hints to the deception would not suffice; *Bathybia* ends with Mawson, woken by the night-watchman, bemused at 'how much can happen in dreamland during a short quarter hour'.

Six months later, Shackleton's party stood on the polar plateau 97 miles short of the South Pole. They had found an accommodating glacier at the head of the Ross Ice Shelf, but the plateau had exhausted them and this was as close as they would get. Shackleton scanned the southern horizon. It was as featureless as the horizon to the east, west and north. There was no reason to expect that the miles ahead would be any different than those behind. Ice and snow, not alcoholic algae and giant ticks, were the realities of Terra Australis Ultima. A week later and more than a thousand miles to the north-west, Mawson and David reached the vicinity of the South Magnetic Pole. The polar plateau there was equally empty, as it is everywhere beyond the Transantarctic Mountains. Surely the dream of warmth and life in the unknown south had to be over.

Epilogue

Douglas Mawson went on to become one of the most successful of all polar explorers. In 1912 three men of his Australasian Antarctic Expedition sledged over the plateau to within 280 kilometres of Mawson's 1909 mark, thus demonstrating that Ross's discoveries had to be continuous with those of Wilkes. The Unknown Southland was indeed a continent, as Murray had foretold, but it was a continent that still held a great secret at its heart. At the point where Mawson had turned back in 1909 the ice sits on land below sea level – not 22,000 feet below, but in a deep depression that covers as much as a fifth of East Antarctica. Bathybia had been literally at his feet.

When Mawson died, in 1958, an International Geophysical Year was in progress. From the coast near Wilkes' Termination Land[1] the Soviet Union sent its hulking Kharkov snow tractors on a seismic traverse nearly 2,000 kilometres into the interior. Their objective was the geomagnetic pole, a mathematical abstraction marked only by the aurora, which plays in an ever-changing halo around it. Near the pole the Soviets built Vostok base, which remains the highest and coldest in Antarctica. In 1974 British scientists conducting an aerial survey with ice-penetrating radar discovered an anomaly under the base. About four kilometres down there was, improbably, a lake.

This Bathybic sea is Lake Vostok, 14,000 square kilometres in area – nearly as large as Lake Ontario – and in places half a kilometre deep. Before the weight of the ice sheet compacted the land beneath it the lake bottom would have been more than 800 metres above sea level. It has been isolated from the world since the Antarctic ice cap formed fifteen million years ago. The Russians began drilling in the 1990s, initially to within 120 metres of the lake surface. The ice cores from that depth turned out to be frozen lake water, with sediments showing 400,000 years of bacterial life – no water bears, but life nonetheless. One of the bacteria is known from other locations to favour temperatures of 50–60°C. Was the lake kept from freezing by Mawson's volcano?

The Russian drillers had paused for fear of contaminating what might be an ecosystem with an independent evolutionary history longer than that of our own species. It was recognised that it would be an irrevocable and potentially disastrous step to break through and sample the water. In H. G. Wells' *War of the Worlds* humankind was rescued from the Martian invaders by a humble terrestrial microbe against which they had no immunity. Would the Vostok bacteria devastate the human invaders? Would the invaders destroy the bacteria? The Russians pressed on and in January 2012 broke through just before the weather again brought a halt. They presented a vial of Lake Vostok water to then Prime Minister Putin. The slight yellowish tinge was unexpected but all four of the types of bacteria detected were or could have been contaminants from drilling oil. In the meantime, British and American expeditions had began exploring two of the many other sub-glacial lakes discovered since Vostok. The journal *Nature* dubbed them Raiders of the Lost Lake[2], perhaps suggesting that the race for priority might be encouraging cowboy geology.

In Lake Whillans, the Americans found clear evidence that living cells were metabolising energy, which they could only have obtained from existing organic material or, more intriguingly, from bedrock minerals and carbon dioxide dissolved in water. Similar activity has been observed near deep sea hydrothermal vents. No doubt drilling and sampling will continue. We can only hope that the expeditioners do not encounter anything so unimagined by their protocols that containment or preservation of the discovery, as necessary, will be beyond them.

John Symmes never did see Earth's polar regions, but through his telescope he could look at those of Mars. The Lowell lines that mark the limit of the red planet's ice sheets in summer were among his 'proofs' that all celestial bodies are hollow at the poles. The discovery that lakes lie under the Antarctic ice has revived scientific speculation that the same conditions might exist on Mars or on Europa and Callisto, the frozen moons that circle Jupiter. NASA is formulating plans to send missions. One would hope that by then we will have learned from Antarctic drilling how to explore without compromising the explored, but history gives little cause for confidence. It is, after all, the challenge that has been faced by every would-be discoverer since Columbus first hailed the inoffensive and unsuspecting Arawak Indians in 1492; how does one transform an unknown into a known without degrading or destroying it in the process? Unsurprisingly, there has also been speculation that sub-glacial water in Antarctica indicates the presence of Atlantis, submerged there 11,400 years ago.[3] This is a failure of the imagination, not a triumph for it. It is received folly, on a par with veneration for the geography of St Augustine. Plato would be appalled – he was trying to make us think.

'All men by nature desire to know', said Aristotle,[4] but it was forbidden and humankind was expelled from the Garden of Eden for sampling the fruit. Genesis records that the landlord was unhappy but the tenants tell a different story. They were not pushed; they walked, answering a call from over the hill and far away. Incognita beckoned, teasing their imaginations, exercising their ingenuity and providing opportunities for mischief – in short, making them human. Besides, they did not like the small print in the lease. Gulliver discovered it when he met the immortal Struldbruggs. He was envious until it dawned on him that to be bored for all eternity, even in paradise, would be hell on Earth.

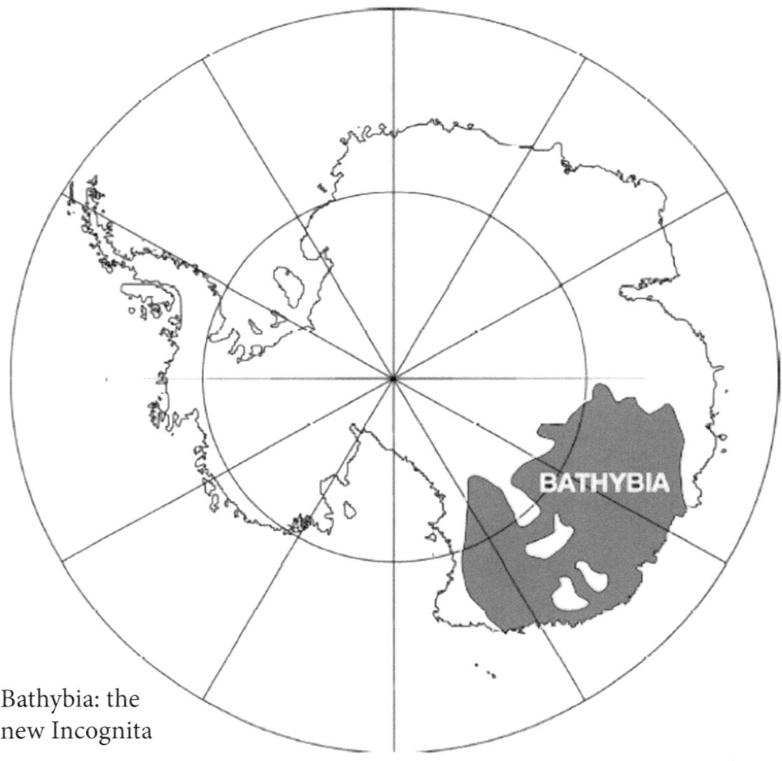

Bathybia: the new Incognita

Notes

Introduction

1 In the context of this book Europe, Asia and Africa are a single landmass.

1 | An Earthly Paradise

1 Later geographers moved it offshore and south of the equator. It reached Terra Australis as Regio Patalis.
2 The statement is made in *On the Heavens*, long attributed to Aristotle but now doubted. Complete Works, J. Barnes (ed.) Princeton University Press, 1984, p.489.
3 Division of the equator into 360° is first recorded in a Babylonian horoscope from 410 BC.
4 The world bulges slightly at the equator, which is thereby longer than the meridians. Syene lies three degrees east of Alexandria.
5 Eratosthenes chief directional points of reference were sunrise, sunset and the pole star. He also had the directional indications of the wind rose.
6 Only fragments of Eratosthenes' *Hermes* survive, the relevant one in a paraphrase by Virgil who tells us that men live in both temperate zones 'to the antipodes'. A. Couat, *La Poésie Alexandrine*, Hachette, Paris, 1882, p. 468.
7 J. O. Thompson, *History of Ancient Geography*, Cambridge University Press, 1948, p. 202.
8 H. L. Jones (trans.), *The Geography of Strabo*, William Heinemann, London, 1942, I. 2. 28.
9 Jones, H. E. (trans.), *The Geography of Strabo*, William Heinemann, London, 1917–32, Book I, pp. 115–7.
10 E. L. Stevenson (ed.), *Claudius Ptolemy: The Geography*, Dover, New York, 1991, p. 160. His source was Crates, via Strabo (*op. cit.*, p. 395). Ptolemy was more circumspect elsewhere, admitting that the regions south of the equator were unexplored 'and what people say about them must be considered guesswork rather than report.' (*Ptolemey's Almagest*, trans. G. J. Toomer, Duckworth, London, 1984, p. 83).
11 Identified by Thompson (*op. cit.*, pp. 316–7) as Java (to the Indians, Java-dvipa = barley island).
12 Stevenson, *op. cit.*, p. 109.
13 This would have had the *oikumene* extending west to east about 167 degrees (the distance between the Canary Islands and Japan, and closer to the mark than Ptolemy), south to seven degrees above the equator (Sri Lanka) and north to seven degrees short of the pole (two degrees further north than the Siberian islands of Severnaja Zemlja).
14 Borneo is 900 miles SSE of Da Nang. Java, much smaller, is 1500 miles from Da Nang, but due south.
15 H.Yule, *Cathay and the Way Thither*, Hakluyt Society, London, 1866, p. 467.

16 Probably the earliest reference to the Southern Cross in Western literature. *Purgatorio*, Canto I, lines 22–7 in E. H. Plumtre's translation of the *Commedia and Canzoniere of Dante Alighieri,* Wm. Ibister, London, 1886.
17 *Inferno*, Canto XXVI, lines 124–9, *ibid.*
18 B. de las Casas, *Historia de las Indias* (ed. A. M. Carlo), Fondo de Cultura Economica, Mexico, 1951, vol. I, p. 157.
19 O. Dunn and J. E. Kelley jnr (eds), *The Diario of Christopher Columbus's First Voyage to America*, University of Oklahoma Press, Norman, 1989, pp. 17–9.
20 From *Bresail*, a Gaelic demigod.
21 F. Armesto-Fernandez, *Columbus*, OUP, 1991, p. 128.
22 C. Jane (ed.), *Select Documents Illustrating the Four Voyages of Columbus*, Hakluyt Society, London, 1933, vol. II, p. 30.
23 The Soderini letter, in M. Waldseemüller, *Cosmographiae Introductio* (1507), Ann Arbor University Microfilms, 1966, p. 87.
24 C. R. Markham, *The Letters of Amerigo Vespucci*, Hakluyt Society, London, 1894, p. 57.
25 The published Medici letter, *ibid.*, pp. 46–7.
26 F. J. Pohl, *Amerigo Vespucci, Pilot Major*, Columbia University Press, New York, 1944, p. 128.
27 It remained received wisdom for nearly three centuries. In his 1766 preface to *Terra Australis Cognita* John Callander held that Terra Australis 'in its Magellanique quarter' had been discovered by Vespucci in 1502 (p. v).
28 Forty years later, Jean Rotz explained that compass directions refer to a course, route or art of wind. *Boke of Idrography*, Roxburghe Club, London, 1981, p. 81.
29 In some editions of the published Lorenzo letter it is printed as an isosceles triangle but others show it, as specified, with the unequal sides of an orthogonal triangle.
30 Markham, *Vespucci, op. cit.*, p. 48.
31 In the Jagellonian University Museum, Krakow.
32 In 1580 Sarmiento de Gamboa saw a 'bow of Iris' for the first time and wrote that he knew of no-one other than Vespucci who had. C. R. Markham, *Narrative of the Voyages of Pedro Sarmiento de Gamboa to the Straits of Magellan*, Hakluyt Society, London, 1895, pp. 162–3.
33 Markham, *Vespucci, op. cit.*, p. 76.
34 Pohl, *op.cit.*, p. 78.
35 *ibid.*, p. 81.
36 T. More, *Utopia*, Penguin, London, 2003, p. 89.
37 *ibid.*, p. 17.
38 R. King, *The Jagellonian Globe, Utopia and Java La Grande*, 11th Symposium of the International Coronelli Society, Venice, September 2007. Dr. King places Utopia in *America noviter reperta*, which he argues is a double of Waldseemüller's America of 1507. The placement of the landmass is suggestive of Vespucci's Antarctic Coast, which would be entitled to the label in its own right.

2 | Magellanica

1 The map compiled in 1524 by his nephew Juan, who succeeded Vespucci as Chief Pilot, shows a *Tera Australe* extending 75° east from the South American coast, with its northernmost limit in 53°S.
2 G. Menzies, *1421:The Year China Discovered the World*, Bantam, London, 2002, pp. 397–8.
3 It was probably the work of Johann Schöner.
4 C. E. Nowell (ed.), *Magellan's Voyage Around the World*, Northwestern UP, Evanston, 1962, pp. 17, 54.
5 Stanley of Alderly, *The First Voyage Round The World*, Hakluyt Society, London, 1874, p. xxix.
6 Nowell, *op. cit.*, p. 118. Pigafetta does not say that a strait was shown on Magellan's own sea-chart before the discovery – merely that Magellan has seen such a map.
7 A. Pigafetta, *First Voyage Around the World*, Filipiniana Book Guild, Manila, 1969, p.15.
8 Septem Cidades, the Isle of Seven Cities, said to have been discovered by the Portuguese in the Atlantic before Columbus.
9 Pigafetta, *op. cit.*, p.21.
10 Translated from the 1525 Paris edition of Pigafetta's *Voyage et navigation faict par les Espaignols es Isles de Mollucques*, p. 13 as reprinted by P. S. Paige in *The Voyage of Magellan*, Prentice-Hall, Englewood Cliffs, 1969.
11 See K. G. McIntyre, *The Secret Discovery of Australia*, Pan, Sydney, 1987, pp. 140–5.
12 Pigafetta, *op. cit.*, p. 68.
13 In his edition of Pigafetta for the Folio Society, R. A. Skelton suggested Enggano off the south-east coast of Sumatra (p. 151).
14 The identity and location of Cattigara have long been debated, exacerbated by a scribe's error that placed it south of the equator. The name could be Kotti-nagara (Sanskrit for Strong City) but Ptolemy describes Cattigara as a *stadio* (roadstead). Most recent scholarly opinion favours Óe Ce, an inland city at 9½°N linked to the Mekong delta by canal, where archeologists have found gold jewelry that imitates Antonine Roman coins. A phonetic alternative (and a roadstead, but well out in latitude) is Kauthara, at 12½°N on the Vietnamese coast.
15 Pigafetta, *op. cit.*, p. 20.
16 The dead end with which Vespucci concealed Magellan Strait had a long subsequent history. Rotated 90° it became Mercator's Gulf of San Sebastian and was still credited by Alexander Dalrymple in the late eighteenth century.
17 A. Galvão, *The Discoveries of the World … to… 1555*, Hakluyt Society, London, 1862, pp. 176–7. Manus Island is approximately 280 leagues from Tidore and straddles 2°S.
18 *ibid.*, p. 204.
19 M. Transylvanus, *De Moluccis Insulis*, Filipiniana Book Guild, Manila, 1969, p.129.
20 Galvão, *op. cit.*, p. 142.
21 J. W. Jones (trans.), *The Travels of Ludvico di Varthema* (1510), Hakluyt Society, London, 1863, pp. 249–50

22 Pigafetta, *op. cit.*, p. 94.
23 Polo's Java Minor.
24 He is also known as Jean Alphonse, the French rendition of his Portuguese birth name.
25 G. Musset (ed.), *La Cosmographie ... par Jean Fonteneau*, E. Leroux, Paris, 1904, pp. 391, 399
26 *ibid.*, pp. 388–9, 399.
27 J. Alfonse, *Voyages avantureux* (c. 1536), Marnef, Poitiers, 1559, f. 68.
28 Quoted in C. Jack-Hinton, *The Search for the Islands of Solomon*, Clarendon Press, Oxford, 1969, p. 19.

3 | Gold, Spice and Elephants

1 The account written by Juan Gaetano, one of Villalobos' pilots, said Retes sailed 650 leagues along the coast from ½°S to 6–7°S, west to east. See G. B. Ramusio, *Navigationi et Viaggi* (1563), Theatrum Orbis Terrarum, Amsterdam, 1970, vol. I, p. 377.
2 S. Clissold, *Conquistador*, Derek Verschoyle, London, 1954, p. 27.
3 Amherst of Hackney and B. Thomson, *The Discovery of the Solomon Islands by Alvaro de Mendana in 1568*, Hakluyt Society, London, 1901, p. 420.
4 Jack-Hinton, *op. cit.*, p. 26. It will be remembered that 15–16° was the latitude of 'mainland' Java according to Alfonse, who also claimed that it extended towards the Strait of Magellan. It is highly unlikely that either of the Spaniards had read Alfonse's manuscript but its compatibility with Sarmiento's theory is striking, including its vagueness about longitude.
5 Amherst and Thompson, *op. cit.*, p. 420. The latitudes are credible and, although the distance is not unless Retes had sailed as far as New Ireland, a more modest 300 leagues would have taken him to a very prominent cape in 8°S known today as Cape Ward Hunt. Note that 500 leagues was Saavedra's length for the north coast of New Guinea, according to Galvão.
6 C. Kelly, *Calendar of Documents*, Franciscan Historical Studies, Madrid, 1965, p. 94.
7 Amherst and Thompson, *op.cit.*, p. 83.
8 *ibid.*, p. 85.
9 *ibid.*, pp. 8–9.
10 *ibid.*, p. 12–13. Gallego's reckoning to that point was 300 leagues in deficit, failing to make allowance for the unsuspected west-setting South Equatorial Current. Had they held course for New Guinea, the current would have compensated for all but 200 of the 600 leagues that comprised Gallego's underestimate of the distance from Lima to New Guinea. The underestimate, some 34°, is similar to that made by Albo on the Magellan voyage.
11 *ibid.*, p. 102.
12 *ibid* , p. 129.
13 *ibid.*, p. 107.
14 *ibid.*, p. 198.
15 *ibid.*, p. 62.
16 *ibid.*, pp. 184–5.
17 *ibid.*, p. 432–4.
18 *ibid.*, p. 64.
19 *ibid.*, p. 66. The land was the Gilbert Islands, 20° east of New Guinea.

20 Galvão, *op. cit.*, pp. 238–9.
21 Amherst and Thomson, *op. cit.*, p. lviii.
22 *ibid.*, p. 94.
23 R. Hakluyt, *Principal Navigations of the English Nation* (1589), Dent, London, 1907, vol. 8, p. 206.
24 P. Sarmiento de Gamboa, *Historia de Los Incas* (1572), Emecé Editores, Buenos Aires, 1942, Dedication to Philip II, p. 21.
25 *Geographical Journal*, January 1930 and *Mariner's Mirror*, April 1930.
26 Francis Fletcher, chaplain of the *Golden Hind*, as reported by Drake's nephew in 1628. J. Hampden (ed.), *Francis Drake, Privateer,* Eyre Methuen, London, 1972, p.155.
27 *ibid.*, p. 159.
28 C. R. Markham (ed.), *Narratives of the voyages of Pedro Sarmiento de Gamboa to the Straits of Magellan*, Hakluyt Society, London, 1895, pp. 32–3.
29 *ibid.*, p. 180.
30 W. Raleigh, *History of the World*, Walter Burre, London, 1614, book II, p. 574.
31 Markham, *Sarmiento*, *op.cit.*, p. 369. From Tomé Hernandez, a survivor taken off by Cavendish.
32 Clissold ,*op. cit.*, p. 200.
33 Jack-Hinton, *op. cit.*, p. 87.
34 C. R. Markham, (ed.), *The Voyages of Pedro Fernandez de Quiros*, Hakluyt Society, London, 1904, p. 70
35 *ibid.*, p. 104–42.
36 *ibid.*, pp. 87–8.
37 The two main islands became known as *Mas a Fuera* (More Seawards) and *Mas a Tierra* (More Landwards).
38 Letter to the Viceroy of Peru, 1575. Quoted by J. T. Medina in *El Piloto Juan Fernandez…*, Gabriela Mistral, Santiago, 1974, pp. 118–9.
39 Markham, *Quiros*, *op. cit.*, pp. 526–7.

4 | Austrialia

1 J. V. Mills, *Eredia's Description of Malaca, Meridional India and Cathay* (1613), Malaysian Branch, Royal Asian Society, Kuala Lumpur, 1997, p. 257.
2 *ibid.*, p. 69.
3 The year of Polo's departure for China and at about the time of Kublai Khan's attempts to exact tribute from Java.
4 M. P. Cox *et al.*, A small cohort of Island Southeast Asia women founded Madagascar, *Proceedings of the Royal Society B*, vol. 279, no. 1739, 22 July 2012.
5 Mills, *op. cit.*, p. 250.
6 *ibid.*, p. 263.
7 Markham, *Quiros*, *op. cit.*, pp. 167–78.
8 His own son was too young to go with the expedition.
9 Markham, *Quiros*, *op. cit.*, p. 177.
10 Kelly, *op. cit.*, p.194.
11 As stated by Prado, possibly indicating that Torres was from the Biscay province of Galicia.

12 Markham, *Quiros*, *op. cit.*, pp. 191–2.
13 Central to Quiros' geography was the then common theory that inhabited islands had to be adjacent to mainlands from which they had been populated. By the nineteenth century it was obvious to Europeans that Polynesian navigators had not subscribed to the idea.
14 Markham, *Quiros*, *op. cit.*, p. 227.
15 *ibid.*, pp. 364–6.
16 H. N. Stevens (ed.), *New Light on the Discovery of Australia*, Henry Stevens, Son and Stiles, London, 1930, p. 125.
17 P. F. de Quiros, *Relacion de un Memorial* (Eighth), Luis Estupian, Seville, 1610.
18 Markham, *Quiros*, *op. cit.*, p. 280.
19 Stevens, *op. cit.*, pp. 195–6.
20 S. Purchas, *Purchas His Pilgrimes*, Henry Fetherstone, London, 1625, part I, p. 385.
21 J. E. Heeres, *The Part Borne by the Dutch in the Discovery of Australia*, Luzac, London, 1899, p. 3.
22 J. Henderson, *Sent Forth A Dove*, UWA Press, Nedlands, 1999, p. 29.
23 In 1618 the VOC stated that he had been sent to discover 'the land of Nova Guinea *and the islands situated east of the same*'. Heeres, *Dutch Discovery*, *op. cit.*, p. 4.
24 Francis Yunkaporta, as told to Henderson, *op. cit.*, pp. 146–7. Cartensz' log from the expedition of 1623 mentions one *Duyfken* man killed on the peninsula coast. Heeres, *Dutch Discovery*, *op. cit.*, p. 42.
25 Purchas, *op. cit.*, p. 385.
26 P. van Solt, *Narrative and Journal of the voyage made from Bantam to the coast of Coromandel and other parts of India*. Heeres, *Dutch Discovery*, *op. cit.*, p. 6.
27 Stevens, *op. cit.*, pp. 129–33.
28 *ibid.*, p. 229.
29 Cornelius de Jode, *Novae Guineae forma & situs*, in *Speculum Orbis Terrae*, Gerard de Jode, Antwerp, 1593
30 Stevens, *op. cit.*, pp. 231–3.
31 On or about 21 September 1606 the ships passed an island that Prado named Our Lady of Montserrat because of its resemblance to the monastery mountain near Barcelona. A similarly twin-peaked hill – Diughabai (Horned Hill) – stands on Narupai (Horn) island, well within visual distance of Cape York Peninsula.
32 Stevens, *op. cit.*, p. 177.
33 The vessel could have been the *Duyfken*, returned from New Guinea. Normally she would have carried much less ordnance, but this was wartime. Jansz had lost as many as nine of his crew in conflict with natives, and replacing them with Dutch seamen would have been difficult. At Bachan, the two earliest European expeditions to see Australian shores, Spanish and Dutch, might have missed each other by days.
34 C. Kelly, *La Austrialia del Espiritu Santo*, Hakluyt Society, Cambridge, 1966, pp. 96–9. Kelly disputes Prado's allegations of mutiny but concedes 'a serious situation … in regard to responsibility for navigation'.
35 J. Hall, *Another World and Yet the Same* (trans. J. M. Wands), Yale University Press, New Haven, 1981, p. 12.
36 *ibid.*, p. 16.

37 That is, non-existent. Satires, VI, line 165.
38 F. Bacon, *The Advancement of Learning and the New Atlantis* (1627), Henry Frowde, London, 1936, p. 273.
39 R. W. Shirley, *The Mapping of the World*, Early World Press, Riverside, 2001, p. 340.

5 | Zyderlants

1 Quiros' Eighth Memorial, published as *Terra Australis incognita*, John Hodgetts, London, 1617, pp. 3–4.
2 Report of the Council of State, 25 September 1608. Stevens, *op. cit.*, p. 211.
3 Markham, *Quiros, op.cit.*, pp. 508–9.
4 Eredia was in Goa at the same time, and some of the information in his maps, including a passage south of New Guinea, appears to have been provided by Prado. Celsus Kelly, *Some Early Maps Relating to the Queirós-Torres Discoveries of 1606*, Congresso Internacional de Historia dos Descobrimentos, Lisbon, 1961, pp. 14 & 18–9.
5 Originally attached to Prado's *Relation*, but since lost.
6 Prado to the King's secretary and to the King, 24–25 December 1613. Stevens, *op. cit.*, pp. 239–41.
7 Council of State to the King, 2 September 1614. Kelly, *Documents, op. cit.*, p. 306.
8 J. van Spilbergen, *The East and West Indian Mirror*, Hakluyt Society, London, 1906, p.188.
9 The debate between Schouten and Le Maire is reconstructed from Alexander Dalrymple's *Historical Collection of Voyages in the South Pacific Ocean* (self-published, London, 1769–71, vol. II, pp. 33–4) in which he published a composite of Schouten's journal (W. Jansz, Amsterdam, 1618) and Le Maire's *Australian Navigation* (M. Colijn, Amsterdam, 1622).
10 *ibid.*, vol. II, p. 57.
11 Although Schouten's account incorporates material from Le Maire's, it is clear that Schouten's references to his colleague are his own work.
12 Spilbergen, *op. cit.*, p. 219.
13 *ibid.*, p. 152.
14 *ibid.*, p. 163.
15 *ibid.*, p. xlvi
16 *Speculum Orientalis Occidentalisque Indiae navigationem*, Nicholaes van Geelkercken, Leyden, 1619, title page.
17 Spilbergen, *op. cit.*, p. 162.
18 Response to advice given to the States of Holland and West Friesland on the Australian Company charter, 2 August 1618. Heeres, *Discovery, op. cit.*, pp. 4–5.
19 E. Duyker, *Mirror of the Australian Navigation by Jacob Le Maire*, Hordern House, Sydney, 1999, p. 26.
20 So named in Tasman's instructions, 1644. Heeres, *Discovery, op. cit.*, p. 6.
21 *ibid.*, p. xiv. It is possible that the unprecedented speed of this voyage gave rise to one of the variants of the Flying Dutchman legend, in which a skipper – sometimes named Hendrik – makes a pact with the devil in return for a fast passage, subsequently forfeiting his life.

22 J. P. Sigmond and L. H. Zuiderbaan, *Dutch Discoveries of Australia*, Batavia Lion, Amsterdam, 1995, p. 33.

23 Not to be confused with Le Maire's ship of the same name.

24 Resolution of the Governor-General and Councillors, 8 October 1616. Heeres, *Discovery*, *op. cit.*, p. 7.

25 *ibid.*, p.12.

26 Dedel to the VOC Managers, 7 October 1619. Heeres, *Discovery*, *op. cit.*, p. 16.

27 GG and Council to Managers, 6 September 1622. Heeres, *Discovery*, *op. cit.*, p. 18.

28 *ibid.*, pp. 19–21.

29 *ibid.*, p. 38.

30 Today's Jardine River.

31 Isaac de Brune to Carpentier. Heeres believed that Carstensz had Jansz's chart. If so, Carstensz was guilty of affixing names to some features that had already been named by Jansz. It is more likely to have been Gerritsz's chart of the Pacific.

32 Heeres, *Discovery*, *op. cit.*, p. 39.

33 *ibid.*, p. 52.

34 He was either remarkably prescient or had learned something unknown to his contemporaries, because Brouwer did not establish the insularity of Staten Land until ten years after Gerritsz's death.

35 T. Keuning, *Hessel Gerritsz*, in *Imago Mundi*, Stockholm, 1949, vol. 6, p. 58. For a contrary view, that Gerritsz rejected Torres Strait, see R. A. Skelton, *Explorers' Maps*, Routledge & Kegan Paul, London, 1958, p. 225. Gerritsz certainly knew of Torres' voyage and might have seen a version of Prado's map.

36 This is the first mention of Speult's Land. To be within the latitudes indicated it would have to be west of Arnhem Land or on the New Guinea coast opposite Torres Strait. Heeres suggested Groote Eylandt, in 14°S. It should not be confused with Van Speult's River near CapeYork.

37 Instructions. Heeres, *Discovery*, *op. cit.*, p. 65.

38 Memoir, 22 January 1642. J. E. Heeres, *Abel Janszoon Tasman: His Life and Labours*, p. 142 in *Abel Janszoon Tasman's Journal*, Frederick Muller, Amsterdam, 1898.

39 *ibid.*

40 Resolution, 1 August 1642, Heeres, *Tasman*, *op. cit.*, pp. 129–30.

41 Council of India to the Managers, 12 December 1642. Heeres, *Tasman*, *op. cit.*, p. 138.

42 *ibid.*, p. 131.

43 Emphasis added. Instructions, Heeres, *Tasman*, *op. cit.*, p. 133.

44 Had Tasman taken this option he would have anticipated James Cook by 128 years.

6 | New Netherlands

1 That is, 147°04' east of Greenwich and accurate to two degrees, a remarkably good result.

2 A. Sharp, *The Voyages of Abel Janszoon Tasman*, Clarendon Press, Oxford, 1968, p. 132.

3 *ibid.*, p. 147.

4 The fringes of the Fiji group.
5 Sharp, *op. cit.*, pp. 178–88.
6 *ibid.*, p. 219.
7 *ibid.*, p. 226.
8 *ibid.*, p. 253.
9 Heeres, *Tasman*, *op. cit.*, pp. 143–45.
10 *ibid.*, p.145.
11 *ibid.*, pp. 149–50.
12 *ibid.*, p. 73??
13 *ibid.*, pp. 153–7.
14 Council of India Resolution, 4 September 1643. Heeres, *Tasman*, *op. cit.*, p. 114n.
15 Managers to Council of India, 9 September 1645. Heeres, *Tasman*, *op. cit.*, p. 115n.
16 The so-called Bonaparte map. M. Destombes, *Cartes Hollandaises*, Saigon, 1941, pp. 77–9.
17 Reproduced in *Abel Janszoon's Journal*, Muller, Amsterdam, 1898.
18 The change of nomenclature appeared earlier on a Blaeu globe c. 1648. It probably originated with the VOC or the Blaeus, who were the Company's hydrographers and mapmakers, following Brouwer's revelation in 1643 that Staten Land was only a small island.
19 J. Callander, *Terra Australis Cognita*, A. Donaldson, Edinburgh, 1766, vol. 1, pp. 63–73.
20 J. P. Purry, *Memoire sur Le Pais des Cafres et La Terre de Nuyts*, Humbert, Amsterdam, 1718, p. 4.
21 Heeres, *Discovery*, *op. cit.*, p. 92.
22 Actually 10°43'S, a discrepancy of only 13 nautical miles.
23 Heeres, *Discovery*, *op. cit.*, p. 94.
24 Shelburne Bay, on the east coast of Cape York Peninsula, lies 1°15' south of Cape York.
25 Gerrit de Haan to Council of India, 30 September 1756, in Heeres, *Discovery*, *op. cit.*, p. 99.
26 W. Dampier in *A Collection of Voyages*, James and John Knapton, London, 7th edition, 1729, vol. I, pp. 86–7.
27 L. Wafer, *A New Voyage and Description of the Isthmus of America*, James Knapton, London, 1699, p. 214.
28 Dampier, *op. cit.*, vol. I, p. 464.
29 *ibid.*, vol. III, pp. 124–5.
30 *ibid* , vol. III, p. 102.
31 *ibid.*, vol. III, pp. 225, 240.
32 W. Rogers, *A Cruising Voyage Round the World*, A. Bell and B. Lintot, London, 1712, pp. 126, 130–1.
33 Defoe regarded gunpowder and the compass – Chinese inventions – as the cornerstones of European technological superiority.
34 [D. Defoe], *The Life and Strange Surprising Adventures of Robinson Crusoe* (1719), Macmillan, London, 1866, p. 66.
35 Isaac Disraeli, Benjamin's father, believed that Will was the model for Friday. In the television series *Lost in Space* the young hero was named Will Robinson.
36 [D. Defoe], *Serious Reflections During the Life And Surprising Adventures of Robinson Crusoe* (1720), Constable, London, 1925, p. ix.

7 | South Sea Bubbles

1 M. Balen, *A Very English Deceit*, Fourth Estate, London, 2002, p. 37.
2 D. Defoe, *An Historical Account of the Voyages and Adventures of Sir Walter Raleigh …* , W. Boreham, London, 1720, title page.
3 D. Defoe, *The Case of Mr Law Truly Stated*, A. Moore, London, 1721, p. 13.
4 A. Sharp (ed.) *The Journal of Jacob Roggeveen*, Clarendon, Oxford, 1970, p. 108.
5 *ibid.*, p. 141–4.
6 D. Defoe, *A New Voyage Round the World by a Course never sailed before*, A. Bettesworth and W. Mears, London, 1725, p. 7.
7 *ibid.*, p. 178.
8 *ibid.*, pp. 120–1.
9 *ibid.*, p. 187.
10 *ibid.*, pp. 175–7.
11 *ibid.*, p. 202. This is hard on Mendaña and Gallego. Quiros is more probably the target and for him it is deserved injustice: he never saw the Solomons.
12 J. Swift, *Gulliver's Travels* (1726), Oxford University Press, 1998, pp. 6, 66. The latitude would place Lilliput, an island, in the Great Victoria Desert of South Australia.
13 *ibid.*, pp. 275–6. The charts would have had to place it more like 30° too far east for Gulliver to have reached it in the time stated. This may be an exaggeration of Dampier's reservations about Tasman's accuracy.
14 *ibid.*, p. 277.
15 *ibid.*, pp. 286–7.
16 R. Walter, *A Voyage Round the World by George Anson*, C. & J. Rivington, London, 1828, p. 131. It was Bougainville who suggested that this animal should be looked upon as 'a kind of marine elephant'.
17 Vespucci's 'land seen'. R.V. Tooley, *The Mapping of Australia and Antarctica*, Holland Press, London, 1985, p. xx.
18 J. Callander, *Terra Australis Cognita*, A. Donaldson, Edinburgh, 1768, vol. III, p. 643.
19 *ibid.*, vol. I, pp. 2–3.
20 C. de Brosses, *Histoire des Navigations aux Terres Australes*, Durand, Paris, 1756, vol. II, p. 383
21 *ibid.*, vol. II, pp. 389–91.
22 J. Hawkesworth, *An Account of the Voyages … for making Discoveries in the Southern Hemisphere*, Strahan and Cadell, London, 1773, vol. I, p. i.
23 *ibid.*, vol. I, p. 108.
24 J. Dunmore (ed.), *The Pacific Journal of Louis-Antoine de Bougainville*, Hakluyt Society, London, 2002, p. xlv.
25 J-J. Rousseau, *Emile, or On Education* (1755), Basic Books, New York, 1979, pp. 184–8.
26 J-J. Rousseau, *A Discourse upon the Origin and Foundation of the Inequality among Mankind* (1754), R. and J. Dodsley, London, 1761, pp. 98–9, 110.
27 *ibid.*, pp. 231–6.
28 *ibid.*, pp. 203–4.
29 Dunmore, *op. cit.*, pp. 12, 25, 28.

8 | Venus and Other Transients

1 Callander, *op. cit.*, vol. I, p.ii.
2 H. Wallis (ed.), *Carteret's Voyage Round The World*, Hakluyt Society, Cambridge, 1965, vol. II, pp. 302–3
3 O. Warner (ed.), *An Account of the Discovery of Tahiti*, Folio Society, London, 1955, p. 19
4 Samuel Wallis' MS journal, 20 August 1766, cited by J. C. Beaglehole, *The Journals of Captain James Cook*, Hakluyt Society, Cambridge, 1968, vol. I, p. 119n.
5 Hawkesworth, *op. cit.*, vol. I, p. 479.
6 H. Wallis, *op. cit.*, vol. II, p. 312.
7 A. Dalrymple, *An Account of the Discoveries made in the South Pacifick Ocean, previous to 1764*, self-published, London, 1767, p. iii.
8 *ibid.*, p. xi.
9 Hawkesworth, *op. cit.*, vol. I, p. 531.
10 *ibid.*, pp. 559, 564.
11 L.-A. de Bougainville, *A Voyage Round the World*, J. Exshaw et al., Dublin, 1772, p. 212.
12 Dunmore, *op. cit.*, pp. 72–4.
13 *ibid.*, p. 88.
14 *ibid.*, p. 95.
15 *ibid.*, p. 96.
16 *ibid.*, pp. 101–2.
17 It was eleven months.
18 Hawkesworth, *op. cit.*, vol. I, pp. 667–8.
19 Dunmore, *op. cit.*, p. 155.
20 A French astronomer noted that 1769 would be the most favorable opportunity until 9 June 2255 for observers on the south coast of New Holland, 'which will without doubt be then better known than it is at present.' Pingré, p. 88.
21 A. S. Cook in the Hordern House edition of Dalrymple's *Account*, Sydney, 1996, essay, p. 30.
22 Dalrymple, *Account, op.cit.*, p. 102.
23 The *Earl of Pembroke* became Cook's *Endeavour*.
24 J. C. Beaglehole, *The Journals of Captain James Cook*, Hakluyt Society, Cambridge, 1968, vol. I, p. 513. Extract from the Royal Society's Council Minute Book; the draft minutes used the words 'contrary to the usage'.
25 Memoirs of Alexander Dalrymple, Esq., *European Magazine and London Review* 42, 1802, p. 325
26 Beaglehole, *Cook, op. cit.*, vol. I, p. 516.
27 They were briefly reported in the *Gazetteer*, London, of 18 August 1768.
28 Beaglehole, *Cook, op. cit.*, vol. I, p. cclxxxii.
29 *ibid.*, vol. I, p. 66.
30 J. C. Beaglehole, *The Journal of Joseph Banks*, Angus & Robertson, Sydney, 1962, vol. I, p. 239.
31 Beaglehole, *Cook, op. cit.*, vol. I, p. 161.
32 *ibid.*, p. 250.
33 Beaglehole, *Banks, op. cit.*, vol. I, p. 470.
34 *ibid.*, pp. 471–2.

35 Beaglehole, *Cook, op. cit.*, vol. I, p. 274.
36 Beaglehole, *Banks, op. cit.*, I, pp. 289–91.
37 Beaglehole, *Cook, op. cit.*, vol. I, cclxxxiii.
38 Beaglehole, *Banks, op. cit*, vol. I, p. 272.
39 *ibid.*, p. 273.
40 '... although four voyages have been made under [Admiralty] auspices ... I would not have come back in ignorance.' *A Letter from Mr. Dalrymple to Dr. Hawkesworth*, J. Nourse et al., London, 1773, p. 32
41 Beaglehole, *Banks, op. cit.*, vol. II, pp. 39–40.
42 *ibid.*, pp. 375–6.
43 Correct to within a degree, attributable to Cook's skill at calculating his own longitude from astronomical observation and better estimates of Quiros' longitude from the published accounts of his voyage.
44 Beaglehole, *Cook, op. cit.*, vol. I, p. 380.
45 *ibid.*, p. 410.
46 *ibid.*, p. 399.
47 J. Dunmore (ed.), *The Expedition of the* St Jean-Baptiste *to the Pacific 1769–1770*, Hakluyt Society, London, 1981, pp. 21–2. The longitude given places the island 99° 40' west of Greenwich; Tahiti is 149° 30' W.
48 *ibid.*, p. 44.
49 Dalrymple, *Account, op.cit.*, p. 92.
50 Beaglehole, *Cook, op. cit.*, vol. I, p. 479.
51 L. D. Hammond (ed.), *News from New Cythera*, University of Minnesota Press, Minneapolis, 1970, p. 26
52 A. Dalrymple, *An Historical Collection of the Several Voyages and Discoveries in the South Pacific Ocean*, self-published, London, 1770, vol. I, p. vii.
53 *ibid.*, pp. xxviii–xxix.
54 *ibid.*, Dedication.
55 He described them to John Walker, his old master in the coal trade, as 'no very great discoveries'. Beaglehole, *Cook, op. cit.*, vol. I, p. 505.
56 Dalrymple, *Letter, op. cit.*, p. 23.
57 Dalrymple did not know that Surville had since eliminated the possibility that Tahiti might be a continental headland.
58 Hawkesworth, *op. cit.*, vol. I, preface to the second edition.
59 Dalrymple, *Collection, op. cit.*, vol . I, p. xv.
60 Beaglehole, *Cook, op. cit.*, vol. II, p. xxi.
61 *ibid.*, p. xxvii.
62 *ibid.*, pp. 713–4.
63 A. Dalrymple, [*Scheme of a voyage to convey the conveniences of life, domestic animals, corn, iron etc., to New Zealand*], self-published, London, 1771, p. 5.
64 A. Dalrymple, *A Collection of Voyages Chiefly in the Southern Atlantick Ocean*, self-published, London, 1775, p. 11.

9 | Sandwich Land

1 Beaglehole, *Cook, op. cit.*, vol. II, pp. clxvii–clxix.
2 Cook knew that Bougainville had misled Carteret and, to add insult to this attempted injury, the first French book about the *Endeavour* voyage had been entitled *Supplément au Voyage de Bougainville*.

3 Beaglehole, *Cook, op. cit.*, vol. II, p. 72.
4 *ibid.*, p. 89.
5 *ibid.*, p. 165.
6 *ibid.*, p. 173–5.
7 *ibid.*, p. 189.
8 *ibid.*, p. 297.
9 *ibid.*, pp. 302–5.
10 *ibid.*, p. 321–3.
11 *ibid.*, p. 327.
12 *ibid.*, p. 328.
13 This should have been conclusive, but in 1785 La Pérouse was instructed to have another look for it.
14 Beaglehole, *Cook, op. cit.*, vol. II, pp. 371, 381.
15 *ibid.*, p, 427.
16 *ibid.*, p. 520.
17 *ibid.*, p. 587.
18 *ibid,*, pp. 625–6.
19 *ibid.*, p. 637–8. 71°10'S became known as Cook's *Ne Plus Ultra* (No Further – the traditional inscription on the Pillars of Hercules) and a challenge.
20 *ibid.*, pp. 638–43.
21 *ibid.*, p. 870.
22 H. L. Roth, *Crozet's Voyage to Tasmania, New Zealand, the Ladrone Islands and the Philippines*, Truslove & Shirley, London, 1891, p. 71.
23 Beaglehole, *Cook*, *op. cit.*, vol. II, p. 657. Cook was still ignorant of the official nature of Kerguelen's voyage.
24 '… which if not a Continent is one of the largest islands in the World'. Beaglehole, *Cook, op. cit.*, vol. III, Pt. 1, p. 56.
25 The larger island in the Prince Edward Group is today called Marion Island, and the second group is named for Crozet alone.
26 Y-J. de Kerguelen de Tremarec, *Relation de Deux Voyages …* , Knapen et Fils, Paris, 1782, pp. 4–5
27 The first editor of Cook's journal reverted to Kerguelen's Island, accepting the name that the discoverer had used in his *Relation* (p. 31).
28 Beaglehole, *Cook, op. cit.*, vol. III, Pt. 1, pp. 42–3.
29 *ibid.*, p. lxxxviii–lxxxix.
30 'Nature and Nature's laws lay hid in night: God said, Let Newton be! and all was light.'
31 Kerguelen, *Relation, op.cit.*, pp. 93–5. Modern research has revealed that Essomericq's name in his native Carijo language was Içа-Mirim, and that Gonneville's landfall was the Ilha de São Francisco off Brazil. See R. J. Howgego, *Encyclopedia of Exploration*, Hordern House, Sydney, vol. I, p. 443.
32 *Naval Chronicle*, vol. 32 (1814), p. 178.
33 *ibid.*, p. 191.
34 M. Flinders, *A Voyage to Terra Australis*, G. & W. Nichol, London, 1814, vol. I, p. iii. In English the name of each continent begins and ends with the same letter.
35 Historical Records of Australia, Commonwealth Parliament, Sydney, 1917, Series I, vol. IX, p. 747 and note 84. The Admiralty adopted the change in 1824.
36 P. Fitting (ed.), *Subterranean Worlds*, Weslyan University Press, Middletown, CT, 2004, p. 95.

37 Mather had mentioned one of Symmes' ancestors in another book. Fitting, *op. cit.*, pp. 19–24.

38 The tip of the Antarctic Peninsula, 64°S and 57°W.

39 *Gentleman's Magazine*, vol. 90, pt. 2, September 1820, pp. 267–8. Dirck Gerritsz was alleged to have made the same apt comparison with respect to his 1599 sighting of land south of Cape Horn, also in 64°. See the account appended to Herrera's *Description des Indies …*, Colijn, Amsterdam, 1622.

40 E.A. Stackpole, *The Voyage of the* Huron *and the* Huntress, Marine Historical Association, Mystic CT, 1955, p. 51.

10 | Terra Australis Ultima

1 F. Debenham (ed.), *The Voyage of Captain Bellingshausen to the Antarctic Seas 1819–21*, Hakluyt Society, London, 1945, vol. I, p. 14.

2 *ibid.*, p. 437n.

3 The Russians dated by the Julian calendar. To align it with the Gregorian calendar, add twelve days.

4 Debenham, *op. cit.*, vol. I, p. 128.

5 *ibid.*, pp. 410–21.

6 Many years later the name Palmer Land did appear on Russian charts, but its first appearance anywhere was in *Woodbridge's School Atlas*, Hartford, Connecticut, 1821.

7 Debenham, *op. cit.*, p. 437. The island is annotated 'position very doubtful' on Purdy's 1815 chart, which also indicated that La Perouse and Vancouver had sought it without success.

8 C. Enderby, Recent Discoveries in the Antarctic Ocean, *Geographical Journal*, London, 1833, vol. 3, pp. 111–2.

9 J. N. Reynolds, *Address on the Subject of a Surveying and Exploring Expedition to the Pacific Ocean and South Seas*, New York, 1836, p. 99.

10 Charles Wilkes' journal, US National Archives and Records Administration, Washington, M 75/8.

11 Australia had been suggested as early as 1545 as a suitable name for a supposed southern polar continent that included Beach. Conversly, in 1670 John Sellar had published a map of 'Terra Antarctica' that similarly showed Australia, Tasmania and New Zealand as parts of a polar continent.

12 *Hobart Town Advertiser*, 17 April 1840.

13 House of Commons Accounts and Papers 1841, session 2, no. 7.

14 *The Times*, 12 August 1841.

15 C. Wilkes, *Narrative of the United States Exploring Expedition*, C. Sherman, Philadelphia, 1844, vol. II, pp. 297–8.

16 J. Murray, *The Cruise of the Challenger*, n.p., [1877], p. 123.

17 *ibid.*, pp. 138–9.

18 C. Wyville Thomson, On the Conditions of the Antarctic Regions, William Collins, London, 1877, p. 29.

19 J. Murray, The Exploration of the Antarctic Regions, *Scottish Geographical Magazine*, vol. II, 1886, p. 532, map between pp. 576–7.

20 Murray was also influenced by the dubious account of Benjamin Morrell's 1823 voyage, in which the sealer placed his ship south of the then undiscovered Enderby Land.

21 Which now included Enderby Land, extended south over Morrell's claimed position. Ironically, the more that Murray's outline was extended to embrace the dots of discovery, the closer it approached the reality. Bartholomew had already affixed the label ANTARCTICA to the 'supposed outline' in his *Royal Atlas and Gazetteer of Australasia*, T. Nelson and Sons, London, 1890, p. 28. It had earlier appeared in his *Pocket Atlas* of 1889.

22 In his survey *Antarctica* (Richards Press, London, 1928), J. Gordon Hayes described the name as 'not yet familiar', although it had been 'generally received by geographers'. With Australia unavailable, which he regretted, he suggested that Ultima would be the best alternative but conceded that it was an unattractive word and had long been associated with northern lands.

23 J. Murray, The Renewal of Antarctic Exploration, *Geographical Journal*, vol. III, no. 1, January 1894, map between pp. 80–1.

24 *Report of the Sixth International Geographical Congress*, John Murray, London, 1896, p. 175.

25 J(ohn) G(eorge) B(artholomew), Antarctica, *The Scotsman*, 10 December 1898.

26 In *The Lands of Silence* (Cambridge University Press, 1921, pp. 452–3), Markham complained that 'all mention of the south pole as an objective was carefully avoided'. Or was he crowing?

27 R. F. Scott, *The Voyage of the Discovery*, Scribner, New York, 1905, vol. II, p. 265.

28 *ibid.*, pp. 426–8.

29 E. H. Shackleton (ed.), *Aurora Australis*, British Antarctic Expedition, 77° 32′ S & 166° 12′ E, 1908, Butter 267 copy, final article.

Epilogue

1 It had turned out to be an ice tongue attached to an ice shelf that was subsequently named for Shackleton.

2 *Nature*, 17 January 2011.

3 R. Flem-Ath and C. Wilson, *The Atlantis Blueprint*, Little, Brown, London, 2000, pp. 317–8.

4 Barnes, *op. cit.*, *Metaphysics*, p. 1552.

Bibliography

Alfonse, J., Les Voyages avantureux du Capitaine Ian Alfonse Sainctongeois, Marnef, Poitiers, 1559
Amherst of Hackney & Thomson, B., The Discovery of the Solomon Islands, Hakluyt Society, London, 1901
Andrews, K. R., Drake's Voyages, Weidenfeld & Nicholson, London, [1967]
Augustine, St., The City of God (trans. J. Healey), Dent, London, 1945

Bacon, F., The Advancement of Learning and the New Atlantis, Henry Frowde, London, 1936
Bacon, R., Opus Majus (trans. R. B. Bourke), Russell & Russell, New York, 1962
Ballantyne, T. (ed.), Science, Empire, and the European Exploration of the Pacific, Ashgate, Aldershot, 2004
Barnes, J. (ed.), Complete Works of Aristotle, Princeton University Press, 1984
Barros, J. de, Ásia Primeira Decada, Imprensa da Universidade, Coimbra, 1932
Bartholomew, J. G., Royal Atlas and Gazetteer of Australasia, T. Nelson and Sons, London, 1890
Beaglehole, J. C., Exploration of the Pacific, A. & C. Black, London, 1934
_____________ The Journals of Captain James Cook on his Voyages of Discovery, Hakluyt Society, Cambridge, 1955-74
_____________ The Endeavour Journal of Joseph Banks, Angus & Robertson, Sydney, 1962
Berggren, J. L. & Jones, A., Ptolemy's Geography, Princeton University Press, 2000
Bertrand, K. J., Americans in Antarctica, American Geographical Society, New York, 1971
Blake, J., The Sea Chart, Conway, London, 2004
Bougainville, L. A. de, A Voyage Round the World, J. Exshaw et al., Dublin, 1772
Brerewood, E., Enquiries Touching the Diversity of Languages and Religions etc., John Bill, London, 1614
Brome, R., The Antipodes, Francis Constable, London, 1640
Brosses, C. de, Histoire des Navigations aux Terres Australes, Durand, Paris, 1756
Brown, L. A., The Story of Maps, Dover, New York, 1979
Bunbury, E. H., A History of Ancient Geography, Dover, New York, 1959
Burrell, A. C. (ed.), Voyage of John Huyghen van Linschoten to the East Indies, Hakluyt Society, London, 1895

Callander, J., Terra Australis Cognita, A. Donaldson, Edinburgh, 1766-8
Casas, B. de las, Historia de las Indias (ed. A. M. Carlo), Fondo de Cultura Economica, Mexico, 1951
Clancy, R., The Mapping of Terra Australis, Universal Press, Macquarie Park, 1995
Clarke, I. F., The Pattern of Expectation, Jonathon Cape, London, 1979
Clissold, S., Conquistador, Verschoyle, London, 1954
Collingridge, G., The Discovery of Australia, Hayes Bros, Sydney, 1895
Cooke, E., A Voyage to the South Sea and Round the World, B. Lintot et al, London, 1712
Cook, J., A Voyage to the Pacific Ocean, Nichol & Cadell, London, 1785
Cordier, H., Ser Marco Polo, Scribner's, New York, 1920

Cortesão, A., Portugaliae Monumenta Cartographica, Lisbon, 1960-2
__________ (ed.), Tomé Pires: Suma Oriental, Hakluyt Society, London, 1944
Cosgrove, D., Apollo's Eye, Johns Hopkins Press, Baltimore, 2001
Couat, A., La Poésie Alexandrine, Hachette, Paris, 1882
Crozet, J. M., Nouveau Voyage a la Mer du Sud, Barrois, Paris, 1783

[Dalrymple, A.], An Account of the Discoveries made in the South Pacifick Ocean previous to 1764, (the author), London, 1767
Dalrymple, A., Memoir of a Chart of the Southern Ocean, 1769
___________ Historical Collection of Voyages in the South Pacific Ocean (the author), London, 1769-71
___________[Scheme of a voyage to convey the conveniences of life, domestic animals, corn, iron etc., to New Zealand], (the author), London, 1771
___________ A Letter from Mr Dalrymple to Dr Hawkesworth, (the author), London, 1773
___________ A Collection of Voyages Chiefly in the Southern Atlantick Ocean, (the author), London, 1775
___________ Memoir concerning the Chagos and adjacent islands, (the author), London, 1786
___________ Consideration of M. Buache's Memoir concerning New Britain and the North Coast of New Guinea, (the author), London, 1790
Dampier, W., A New Voyage Round the World, James Knapton, London, 1697
Dahlgren, E. W., Voyages Francais a Destination de la Mer du Sud avant Bougainville, Imprimerie Nationale, Paris, 1907
Debenham, F. (ed.), The Voyage of Captain Bellingshausen to the Antarctic Seas, Hakluyt Society, London, 1945
[Defoe, D.], The Life and Strange Surprising Adventures of Robinson Crusoe, Macmillan, London, 1866
_________ Farther Adventures of Robinson Crusoe, W. Taylor, London, 1719
_________ Serious Reflections During the Life And Surprising Adventures of Robinson Crusoe, Constable, London, 1925
_________ An Historical Account of the Voyages and Adventures of Sir Walter Raleigh ... , W. Boreham, London, 1719
_________ The Case of Mr Law Truly Stated, A. Moore, London, 1721
_________ A New Voyage Round the World by a Course never sailed before, A. Bettesworth & W. Mears, London, 1725
Destombes, M., Cartes Hollandaises, [Ardin], Saigon, 1941
Dunmore, J. (ed.), The Expedition of the St. Jean-Baptiste to the Pacific, Hakluyt Society, London, 1981
_________ Utopias and Imaginary Voyages to Australasia, National Library of Australia, Canberra, 1988
_________ (ed.), The Journal of Jean-Francois de Galaup de la Perouse, Hakluyt Society, London, 1994
_________ (ed.), The Pacific Journal of Louis-Antoine de Bougainville, Hakluyt Society, London, 2002
Dunn, O. & Kelley, J. E. jnr (eds), The Diario of Christopher Columbus's First Voyage to America, University of Oklahoma Press, Norman, 1989
Duyker, E., Mirror of the Australian Navigation by Jacob Le Maire, Hordern House, Sydney, 1999

Eden, W., History of New Holland from first Discovery in 1616 to the Present Time, Stockdale, London, 1787

Ellis, F. H. (ed.), Twentieth Century Interpretations of Robinson Crusoe, Prentice-Hall, Englewood Cliffs, [1969]
Erskine, T., Armata, John Murray, London, 1817
Estensen, M., Discovery: The Quest for the Great South Land, Allen & Unwin, St Leonards, 1998

Fausett, D., Writing the New World, Syracuse University Press, 1993
________ Images of the Antipodes in the Eighteenth Century, Rodopi, Amsterdam, 1994
Fernandez-Armesto, F., Columbus, Oxford University Press, 1991
__________________ Columbus on Himself, Folio Society, London, 1992
__________________ Amerigo, Weidenfeld & Nicholson, London, 2006
Fischer, J & von Wieser, F. (trans.), Martin Waldseemüller: Cosmographiae Introductio, University Microfilms, Ann Arbor, 1966
Fitting, P. (ed.), Subterranean Worlds, Weslyan University Press, Middletown, 2004
Flem-Ath, R. & Wilson, C., The Atlantis Blueprint, Little, Brown, London, 2000
Fletcher, F., The World Encompassed by Sir Francis Drake, Nicholas Bourne, London, 1628
[Fleurieu, C. P. C. de], Discoveries of the French in 1768 and 1769 to the South-east of New Guinea, J. Stockdale, London, 1791
Flinders, M., A Voyage to Terra Australis, G. & W. Nicol, London, 1814
Foigny, G. de, The Southern Land, Known (trans. D. Fausett), Syracuse University Press, 1993
Forster, J. R. (trans.), A Voyage Round the World by Lewis de Bougainville, J. Nourse & T. Davies, London, 1772
Frampton, J. (trans.), The Travels of Marco Polo and Nicolo de Conti, Argonaut Press, London, 1929
Frost, A., The Global Reach of Empire, Miegunyah Press, Melbourne, 2003
Frost, A. & Samson, J. (eds), Pacific Empires, Melbourne University Press, 1999
Fry, H. T., Alexander Dalrymple and the Expansion of British Trade, Royal Commonwealth Society, London, 1970

Galvano, A., The Discoveries of the World … unto … 1555, Da Capo, Amsterdam, 1969
Gibb, H. A. R., The Travels of Ibn Battuta, Hakluyt Society, London, 1994
Golding, A., The Worke of Pomponius Mela, T. Hacket, London, 1585
Gregory, D., Geographical Imaginations, Blackwell, Oxford, 1994

Hakluyt, R., Principal Navigations of the English Nation, Dent, London, 1907
Hall, J., Another World and Yet the Same (trans. J. M. Wands), Yale University Press, New Haven, 1981
Hammond, L. D. (ed.), News from New Cythera, University of Minnesota Press, Minneapolis, 1970
Hampden, J. (ed.), Francis Drake, Privateer, Eyre Methuen, London, 1972
Harlow, V. T., The Founding of the Second British Empire, Longmans, Green, London, 1952-64
Harris, J., A Compleat Collection of Voyages and Travels, T. Osborne et al, London, 1744
Hawkesworth, J., An Account of the Voyages … for making Discoveries in the Southern Hemisphere, Strahan & Cadell, London, 1773

Hayes, J. G., Antarctica, Richards Press, London, 1928
Heath, T. L., A History of Greek Mathematics, Clarendon Press, Oxford, 1921
Healey, J., The Discovery of a New World by an English Mercury, Theatrum Orbis Terrarum, Amsterdam, 1969
Heeres, J. E., Abel Janszoon Tasman's Journal, Frederick Muller, Amsterdam, 1898
_________ The Part Borne by the Dutch in the Discovery of Australia, Luzac, London, 1899
Henderson, J., Sent Forth A Dove, University of Western Australia Press, Nedlands, 1999
Herdman, W. A., Founders of Oceanography and Their Work, Edward Arnold, London, 1923
Herrera y Tordesillas, A. de, Description des Indes Occidentales, Colijn, Amsterdam, 1622
Heylyn, P., Cosmographie, Henry Seile, London, 1657
Hilder, B., The Voyage of Torres, University of Queensland Press, St Lucia, 1980
Historical Records of Australia, Commonwealth Parliament, Series I, vol. IX, Sydney, 1917
Howell, J., The Life and Adventures of Alexander Selkirk, Oliver & Boyd, Edinburgh, 1829
Howgego, R. J., Encyclopedia of Exploration to 1800, Hordern House, Sydney, 2003
Humboldt, A. von, Examen Critique de L'Histoire de la Géographie du Nouveau Continent, Gide, Paris, 1836
______________ Cosmos (trans. E. C. Otté), Bohn, London, 1849

Jack-Hinton, C., The Search for the Islands of Solomon, Clarendon Press, Oxford, 1969
Jane, C. (ed.), Select Documents Illustrating the Four Voyages of Columbus, Hakluyt Society, London, 1930
Jode, C. de, Speculum Orbis Terrae, Gerard de Jode, Antwerp, 1593
Jones, H. E. (trans.), *The Geography of Strabo*, William Heinemann, London, 1917-32
Jones, J. W. (trans.), The Travels of Ludovico di Varthema, Hakluyt Society, London, 1863

Kadir, D., Columbus and the Ends of the Earth, University of California Press, Berkeley, 1992
Kelly, C., Calendar of Documents: Spanish Voyages in the South Pacific etc., Franciscan Historical Studies, Madrid, 1965
_______ La Austrialia del Espíritu Santo, Hakluyt Society, Cambridge, 1966
_______ Some Early Maps Relating to the Queirós-Torres Discoveries of 1606, Congresso Internacional de História dos Descobrimentos, Lisbon, 1961
Kenihan, G. H., The Journal of Abel Jansz Tasman, Australian Heritage Press, Adelaide, [n.d.]
Kerguélen de Trémarec, Y.-J. de, Relation de deux Voyages dans les mers Australes et de l'Inde, Knapen et Fils, Paris, 1782
Kidd, I. G., Posidonius: The Commentary, Cambridge University Press, 1988
Kimble, G. H. T., Geography in the Middle Ages, Methuen, London, 1938
Knapton, J. & J. (eds), A Collection of Voyages, James & John Knapton, London, 1729

Levathes, L., When China Ruled the Seas, Simon & Schuster, New York, c.1994
Linschoten, J. H. van, The Voyage of … Linschoten to the East Indies, Asian Educational Services, New Delhi, 1988

Macrobius, A. T., In Somnium Scipionis, Ioan Gryphius, Venice, c.1560
McIntyre, K. G., The Secret Discovery of Australia, Pan, Sydney, 1987
Ma Huan, The Overall Survey of the Ocean's Shores, Hakluyt Society, Cambridge, 1970
Major, R. H. (ed.), Early Voyages to Terra Australis, Hakluyt Society, London, 1859
__________ Further Facts Relating to the Early Discovery of Australia, J. B. Nichols, London, 1873
Markham, C. R., The Letters of Amerigo Vespucci, Hakluyt Society, London, 1894
______________ Narrative of the Voyages of Pedro Sarmiento de Gamboa to the Straits of Magellan, Hakluyt Society, London, 1895
______________ Antarctic Exploration: A Plea for a National Expedition, Royal Geographical Society, London, 1898
______________ The Voyages of Pedro Fernandez de Quiros, Hakluyt Society, London, 1904
______________ Early Spanish Voyages to the Straits of Magellan, Hakluyt Society, London, 1911
______________ The Lands of Silence, Cambridge University Press, 1921
______________ Antarctic Obsession, Bluntisham Books, Alburgh, 1986
Martin-Allanic, J. E., Bougainville Navigateur et les Decouvertures de son Temps, Presses Universitaires de France, Paris, 1964
Martyr, P., The Decades of the New World or West Indies (trans. R. Eden), London , 1555
Masefield, J. (ed.), Dampier's Voyages, E. Grant Richards, London, 1906
Medina, J. T., El Piloto Juan Fernandez y Juan Jufre, Gabriela Mistral, Santiago, 1974
Menzies, G., 1421:The Year China Discovered the World, Bantam, London, 2002
Mills, J. V. (trans.), Eredia's Description of Malaca, Meridional India and Cathay, Malaysian Branch, Royal Asiatic Society, Kuala Lumpur, 1997
Moore, J., A New Geography, Robert Scott, [London], 1681
More, T., Utopia (trans. R. Robynson), Dent, London, 1910
______ Utopia (trans. P. Turner), Penguin, London, 2003
Morison, S. E., Admiral of the Ocean Sea, Little, Brown, Boston, 1942
Morga, A. de, The Philippine Islands, Moluccas, Siam, Cambodia, Japan and China at the Close of the Sixteenth Century (trans H. E. J. Stanley), Hakluyt Society London, 1868
Murray, J., The Cruise of the Challenger, n.p., [1877]
Musset, G. (ed.), La Cosmographie … par Jean Fonteneau, E. Leroux, Paris, 1904

Newton, R.R., The Crime of Claudius Ptolemy, Johns Hopkins University Press, Baltimore, c.1977
Nicholson, I. H., Via Torres Strait, the author, Yaroomba, 1996
Nowell, C. E. (ed.), Magellan's Voyage Around the World, Northwestern University Press, Evanston, 1962

Pigafetta, A., The Voyage of Magellan (trans P. S. Paige), Prentice-Hall, Englewood Cliffs, 1969

__________ First Voyage Around the World, Filipiniana Book Guild, Manila, 1969
Pingré, M., Memoire sur le Choix et l'État des Lieux où le Passage de Vénus …, Cavelier, Paris, 1767
Plumtre, E. H. (trans.), Commedia and Canzoniere of Dante Alighieri, Wm. Ibister, London, 1886
Poe, E. A., The Narrative of Arthur Gordon Pym of Nantucket, Penguin, London, 2006
Pohl, F. J., Amerigo Vespucci, Pilot Major, Columbia University Press, New York, 1944
Pollard, A. W. (ed.), The Travels of Sir John Mandeville, Macmillan, London, 1900
Ptolemaeus, C., Cosmographia, N. Israel, Amsterdam, 1963
Purchas, S., Purchas His Pilgrimes, Henry Fetherstone, London, 1625
Purry, J. P., Memoire sur Le Pais des Cafres et La Terre de Nuyts, Humbert, Amsterdam, 1718

Quiros, P. F. de, Relacion de un Memorial, Luis Estupian, Seville, 1610
_____________ Terra Australis incognita, John Hodgetts, London, 1617

Rainaud, A., Le Continent Austral, A. Colin, Paris, 1893
Raleigh, W., History of the World, Walter Burre, London, 1614
Ramusio, G. B., Navigationi et Viaggi, Theatrum Orbis Terrarum, Amsterdam, 1970
Ravenstein, E. G., Martin Behaim: His Life and His Globe, George Philip & Son, London, 1908
Report of the Sixth International Geographical Congress, John Murray, London, 1896
Reynolds, J. N., Address on the Subject of a Surveying and Exploring Expedition to the Pacific Ocean and South Seas, Harper & Brothers, New York, 1836
Richardson, W. A. R., Was Australia Charted Before 1606?, National Library of Australia, Canberra, 2006
Rogers, W., A Cruising Voyage Round the World, A. Bell and B. Lintot, London, 1712
Roth, H. L. (trans.), Crozet's Voyage to Tasmania, New Zealand, the Ladrone Islands and the Philippines, Truslove & Shirley, London, 1891
Rotz, J., Boke of Idrography, Roxburghe Club, London, 1981
Rousseau, J.-J., Emile, or On Education, Basic Books, New York, 1979
_____________ A Discourse upon the Origin and Foundation of the Inequality among Mankind, R. and J. Dodsley, London, 1761
Ruelens, C., La Découverture de l'Australie, Van Merlen, Anvers, 1872

Sanderlin, G. (ed.), Bartolome de las Casas: A Selection of his Writings, Knopf, New York, 1971
Sarmiento de Gamboa, P., Historia de Los Incas, Emecé Editores, Buenos Aires, 1942
Satow, E. M., The Voyage of Captain John Saris to Japan, Hakluyt Society, London, 1900
Schilder, G., Australia Unveiled, Theatrum Orbis Terrarum, Amsterdam, 1976
_________ Monumenta Cartographia Neerlandica, Uitgevermaatschappij Canaletto, Alphen van den Rijn, 1986-96
Scott, R. F., The Voyage of the Discovery, Scribner, New York, 1905

Seaborn, A., Symzonia, J. Seymour, New York, 1820
Shackleton, E. H. (ed.), Aurora Australis, British Antarctic Expedition, 77° 32' S & 166° 12' E, 1908
_____________ The Heart of the Antarctic, W. Heinemann, London, 1910
Sharp, A., The Discovery of Australia, Clarendon Press, Oxford, 1963
________ The Voyages of Abel Janszoon Tasman, Clarendon Press, Oxford, 1968
________ (ed.), The Journal of Jacob Roggeveen, Clarendon Press, Oxford, 1970
Shiels, W., Daniel De Foes Voyage Round the World with Life of the Author, F. Noble, London, 1787
Shirley, R. W., The Mapping of the World, Early World Press, Riverside, 2001
Sigmond, J. P. & Zuiderbaan, L. H., Dutch Discoveries of Australia, Batavia Lion, Amsterdam, 1995
Skelton, R. A., Explorers' Maps, Routledge & Kegan Paul, London, 1958(ed.), Antonio Pigafetta: Navigation and Discovery of Upper India and the Isles of Molucca, where the cloves grow, Folio Society, London, 1975
Slot, B. J., Abel Tasman and the Discovery of New Zealand, Otto Cramwinckel, Amsterdam, 1992
Smith, S. & Walford, B. (eds), An Account of Several Late Voyages and Discoveries to the South and North, (the editors), London, 1694
Spate, O. K. H., Spanish Lake, Australian National University Press, Canberra, 1979
Spilbergen, J. van, The East and West Indian Mirror, Hakluyt Society, London, 1906
Stackpole, E. A., The Voyage of the Huron and the Huntress, Marine Historical Association, Mystic, 1955
Stahl, W. H. (trans.), Macrobius: Commentary on the Dream of Scipio, Columbia University Press, New York, 1952
Stanley of Alderley, The First Voyage Round the World by Magellan, Hakluyt Society, London, 1874
Stevens, H. N. (ed.), New Light on the Discovery of Australia, Henry Stevens, Son & Stiles, London, 1930
Stevenson, E. L. (ed.), Claudius Ptolemy: The Geography, Dover, New York, 1991
Suárez, T., Early Mapping of the Pacific, Periplus, Hong Kong, 2004

Taillemite, E., Dictionnaire des Marins Francais, Editions maritimes & d'outre-mer, Paris, c.1982
Taylor, A. E., Plato: Timaeus and Critias, Methuen, London, 1929
Taylor, E. G. R., The Haven Finding Art, Institute of Navigation, London, 1971
Thompson, J. O., History of Ancient Geography, Cambridge University Press, 1948
Thomson, C. W., On the Conditions of the Antarctic Regions, William Collins, London, 1877
Tomasch, S., & Gilles, S., Text and Territory, Penn, Philadelphia, 1998
Tooley, R. V., The Mapping of Australia and Antarctica, Holland Press, London, 1985
Toomer, G. T. (trans.), Ptolemy's Almagest, Duckworth, London, 1984
Tozer, H. F., A History of Ancient Geography, Ess Ess, Delhi, 1975

Vespucci, A., The First Four Voyages, Bernard Quaritch, London, 1885
Vignaud, H., Toscanelli and Columbus, Sands, London, 1902
Villiers, J. A. J. de (trans.), The East and West Indian Mirror, Hakluyt Society, London, 1906

Wafer, L., A New Voyage and Description of the Isthmus of America, James Knapton, London, 1699
Wallis, H. (ed.), Carteret's Voyage Round The World, Hakluyt Society, Cambridge, 1965
Wallis, H. M., & Robinson, A. H. (eds), Cartographical Innovations, Map Collector Publications, Great Britain, 1987
Warner, O. (ed.), An Account of the Discovery of Tahiti, Folio Society, London, 1955
Walter, R., Voyage Round the World by George Anson, C. & J. Rivington, London, 1828
West, D. C., & Kling, A. (trans), The Libro de las Profecias of Christopher Columbus, University of Florida Press, Gainsville, 1991
Wieder, F. C., Tasman's Kaart van zijn Australische Ontdekkinge 1644 …, Martinus Nijhoff, The Hague, 1942
Wieser, F., Magalhaes-Strasse und Austral-Continent, Meridian, Amsterdam, 1967
Wilkes, C., Narrative of the United States Exploring Expedition, C. Sherman, Philadelphia, 1844
Williams, G. & Frost, A. (eds), Terra Australis to Australia, Oxford University Press, Melbourne, 1988
Wiseman, R., The Spanish Discovery of New Zealand in 1576, Discovery Press, Auckland, 1996
Wood, G. A., The Discovery of Australia, Macmillan, Melbourne, 1969

Yule, H., Cathay and the Way Thither, Hakluyt Society, London, 1866
______ The Book of Ser Marco Polo, John Murray, London, 1921

INDEX LIST